Library of Congress Cataloging-in-Publication Data

Schwarzwäller, Wulf.
(Hitlers Geld. English)
The unknown Hitler: his private life & fortune/Wulf
Schwarzwäller.
240 p. 15 x 23 cm — (A Zenith edition)
Translation of: Hitlers Geld.
Includes index.
ISBN 0-915765-63-2 : $17.95
1. Hitler, Adolf, 1889-1945.
2. Heads of state—Germany—Biography.
I. Title.
DD247.H5S34813 1988
943.086'092'4—dc19
(B) 88-29992
CIP

Canadian Cataloging in Publication Data

Schwarzwäller, Wulf.
The unknown Hitler.
Translation of Hitlers Geld.
ISBN 0-7737-2176-2
1. Hitler, Adolf, 1889-1945.
2. Heads of state—Germany—Biography.
I. Title.
DD247.H5S34813 1988    943.086'092'4    C89-093117-8

PRINTED IN THE UNITED STATES OF AMERICA
First Edition

# THE UNKNOWN HITLER

*His Private Life & Fortune*

WULF SCHWARZWÄLLER

Stoddart

*For Maria de los Milagros*
*and*
*C.v.B.*

## Table of Contents

# Prologue

The year was 1906. The place was the upper Austrian provincial town of Linz. One balmy autumn evening in the Opera House, the applause for Richard Wagner's "Rienzi" had just faded away, and the audience was pouring into the street through the main doors. Among the crowd was a slim, pale, elegantly dressed young man. He wore a black silk-lined overcoat, black kidgloves, black patent-leather shoes, and a black silk tophat. In his right hand, he twirled a walking stick with an ivory handle. His serious expression gave him the appearance of being much older than his years, and his ascetic face with its high receding forehead, pointed nose, and long chin was further distinguished by forceful blue eyes.

On his way home to the Urfahr section of the city, which was located on the other side of the Danube, he stopped in front of an elegant baronial apartment house at 2 Kirchengasse. Leaning on his walking stick, he looked up at the darkened windows. The next day he would be renting a lavish six-room apartment on the second floor. He would live there with his friend Gustl, a high school student and son of a local upholsterer.

Soon these same windows with the magnificent view of the Danube would be brightly lit, and the cultural elite of Linz—painters, art experts and patrons, actors, theater critics, musicians and poets—would rendezvous in the drawing room which was decorated in the grand style of the decadent Rubens imitator Hans Makart. Gustl would be in charge of the musical entertainment, and the pale young man would be in charge of the intellectual entertainment, reciting poems or giving his rapt guests the benefit of his views on aesthetics, culture, and history. At

the foot of the gaily lit staircase, the visitors—as he enthusiastically told his friend Gustl—would be greeted "by
an older, already somewhat gray-haired but unusually
elegant hostess." Yes indeed, a "select, high-spirited circle
of friends" would soon gather here, at 2 Kirchenstrasse in
Linz.

The furnishings had already been selected, the materials had been coordinated and the decorative patterns
had been completed. There was no need to hire an architect; the young man was confident he could do the work
much better by himself. And before they moved in, he
and Gustl would cement their friendship by taking a
long trip to Germany, the high point of which would be
a pilgrimage to Richard Wagner's grave in Bayreuth.

Although these might seem like idle dreams to most
people of that time and place, the young man in the silk
tophat was convinced that they'd come true. His guarantee was sitting in the inside pocket of his dress suit: an
Austrian State lottery ticket. The drawing would be held
the next day. The young man was absolutely sure he
would win the grand prize!  After studying the second
floor windows a while longer, he headed home to his
mother and a nine year-old sister in unusually high
spirits.

The next afternoon, he sat in the Café Baumgartner on
Linzer Landstrasse—the city's equivalent of Fifth Ave-
nue—sipping a glass of white wine. The well-off sons of
burghers could be seen strolling up and down the boulevard ogling and flirting with the lyceum girls in their
long pleated skirts and sailor dresses. The evening papers
had just been delivered to the café, where they were
slipped into the tabletop holders. The young man in the
well-tailored Scottish tweed suit nonchalantly reached
over to one of the newspaper holders and turned to the
page with the lottery results. His face froze in an expression of incredulous despair. He couldn't find the number
of his ticket! Incredulousness turned to painful certainty.
He had lost! He threw the newspaper holder on the marble tabletop, reached for his broad-brimmed black hat
and his fancy walking stick, and charged out into the
street. His face distorted in furious anger, he ran to the

workshop where his friend Gustl helped his father after school.

Gustl watched in horror as the young man suffered an attack of raving madness. At first, his frothing fury was directed at the State Lottery Administration, "that organization of criminals who exploit gullible citizens and openly commit fraud." Then he shifted targets. Now it was directed at the State itself, the Danube Monarchy, "that patchwork of ten, twelve or God knows how many ethnic splinter groups; that monster, that offspring of Habsburg marriages." What else would you expect from that kind of State, he told Gustl, except that it would swindle its own citizens out of their last pennies?

The young man slowly calmed down. His shirt soaked in perspiration, his face red and bloated, he slumped onto a bench in the upholstery shop.

This raving maniac was born on April 22, 1889, in Braunau on the Inn, Austria, and was baptized the next afternoon with the name Adolf Hitler. He was the son of a Customs Official named Alois Hitler and his wife Klara (nee Poelzl). Now at the age of seventeen, his loss in the state lottery had deprived him of his dream of a comfortable bourgeois existence. He would neither forgive nor forget this.

# Chapter One

# The Myth About Hitler's Roots

For many years after his rise and fall, Hitler's biographers were kept busy trying to track down the Führer's alleged Jewish origins. These conjectures have not entirely faded away to this day.

For example, in the Jewish cemetery of Bucharest—at Grave No. 9, in the 7th row, Group 18—there is a tombstone with the inscription "Adolf Hittler." This Bucharest Jew was born in 1832 and died in 1892. According to the internment records, he was buried at the expense of a Jewish society called "Filantrofie." In October 1933, resourceful London journalists working for the *Daily Mirror* pronounced this Bucharester to be none other than Adolf Hitler's grandfather. In so doing, however, they overlooked the fact that Adolf Hittler, the Bucharest Jew, was only five years older than Hitler's own father Alois, which, barring any sexual miracles, made this contention impossible. Nevertheless, the story was picked up by a number of papers and spread far and wide. It was further aided by the fact that the name Hitler was not entirely uncommon among Jews from the East. As Simon Wiesenthal has reported, some Jews, an Abraham Hitler from Sosnowiec, Poland, for one, changed their names after the erroneous article appeared in the *Mirror*.

Briefly sketched, here is a somewhat more credible speculation about Hitler's Jewish roots, one that was taken seriously by Hitler's own legal advisor, Hans Frank. Hitler's grandmother on his father's side, Maria Anna Schicklgruber, from Strones in the Waldviertel section in

Lower Austria, worked as a cook in the Graz home of a Jewish businessman named Frankenberger. While working there, she reportedly became pregnant and, after returning to her hometown, gave birth in 1837 to a boy whom she baptized Alois. Frankenberger and his 19 year-old son were both suspected of being the boy's father. Whichever was the case, the senior Frankenberger reportedly paid Maria Anna alimony up to the time her son was 14 years old. There is even some evidence of a correspondence that lasted many years between the Frankenbergers and Hitler's grandmother, the general drift of which, according to Frank, "was the tacit common knowledge of the participants that the illegitimate child of the Schicklgruber woman was conceived under circumstances that made Frankenberger liable for the payment of alimony. "In other words, I must say," Frank continued, "that one cannot entirely rule out the possibility that Hitler's father was a half-Jew, the offspring of the extramarital relationship between the Schicklgruber woman and the Graz Jew. This, if true, would make Adolf Hitler a quarter-Jew."

Werner Maser has thoroughly researched this Frankenberger story and has found absolutely no evidence that a Jew by the name of Frankenberger lived in Graz in 1836; nor is there proof that any German Jews with the name Frankenberger lived in Austria during the entire 19th century. In the city of Graz itself, Maser was unable to find a single resident Jew who lived there from the end of the 15th century until a hundred years after Maria Anna Schicklgruber's death. Likewise, there is no evidence whatsoever that Maria Anna Schicklgruber was employed in any Graz household in 1836 or 1837. Her name isn't recorded in either the Graz Servant Register or in the Citizen Register. Last, but not least, Maser believes there is some significance to the fact that alimony obligations weren't customary in Austria at the time of Alois' birth. The fathers of illegitimate children paid the expenses for the delivery or they simply took them into their own homes. When it came to distributing the inheritance, they were given the same consideration as the legitimate children.

But on the other hand, the name "Hitler" in its various forms—"Hiedler," "Huettler," or "Huetler"—can be found in the impoverished Waldviertel area. It has, in fact, been traced back as far as the early 15th century and is obviously of Czech origin. The differences in spelling can be explained by the fact that very few of the local peasants were able to read and write; thus, the entries in church records were made by the pastor who merely wrote down what he was told, leaving plenty of room for misinterpretation.

In any case, Maria Anna Schicklgruber gave birth to the boy Alois Schicklgruber on June 7, 1837, in Strones near Doellersheim. When asked who the father was, she stubbornly remained silent, but today it is almost certain that he was Johann Nepomuk Huettler, who was born in the village of Spital in 1807. At the time of the birth, Maria Anna was 42 years old, an astonishing fact given that Alois was her first and only child.

Five years after Alois' birth, bizzarely enough, Maria Anna married Johann Nepomuk's brother Johann Georg. Johann Georg spelled his last name "Hiedler" and lived in Doellersheim, where he was a journeyman carpenter. Johann Georg couldn't abide having an illegitimate child in his house and Maria was forced to give the boy back to his real father, the well-to-do Johann Nepomuk. When Alois was ten years old, his mother died of dropsy.

At the age of fourteen, Alois became an apprentice for the master shoemaker Ledermueller, a distant uncle who lived in Spital. Two years later, he moved to Vienna, finished his apprenticeship there and worked as journeyman shoemaker.

Alois was smart and ambitious. He didn't want to be a shoemaker all his life. Although he was self-taught, he dreamed of a career as an Imperial and Royal civil servant. He continued his education intensively on his own with this goal in mind. In 1855, at the age of 18 he joined the Imperial and Royal Finance Guard, advancing up the ranks as quickly as his fellow civil servants who had high school diplomas. In 1871, he held the mid-level rank of inspector, Grade Step X.

Two years later, the 36-year-old Alois married Anna

Glassl, a custom official's daughter who was 14 years his senior. When his wife took sick, he hired a 13-year-old girl to help in the Schicklgruber household; her name was Klara Poelzl. The bizarre familial connections continued to interweave, for she was none other than the granddaughter of Johann Nepomuk Huettler, Alois' real father, which made her Alois' niece. The presence of this pretty teenager soon became a thorn in the side of the jealous and quarrelsome Anna and, to keep peace in his household, Alois sent Klara back to Spital.

In spite of his successful career as a civil servant, Alois constantly worried about the "blemish" of his illegitimate birth. He feared it would become an obstacle for him as he continued his climb up the bureacracy's ladder. With peasant cunning, however, Johann Nepomuk, his real father, managed to figure out a Solomonic solution to the problem. With two witnesses—Johann Breiteneder and Engelbert Paukh—he turned up in the office of Pastor Zahnschirm in Doellersheim and stated that it had always been the wish of his late brother Johann Georg Hiedler, Alois' stepfather, to make the son legitimate. Pastor Zahnschirm made an entry in the birth record to the effect that Johann Georg admitted being the father of the child Alois and requested that his name be entered in the local birth register. The witnesses—neither of whom knew how to write—signed their names with three crosses, unable to read what the pastor had entered in the register. The birth record, in fact, did not read "Hiedler" as it should have. Johann Nepomuk pronounced his own name—"Huettler"—very clearly, but the pastor didn't hear him correctly and put down "Hitler." This is how the name that would later terrorize the world came to be.

At the end of 1876, the Office of the Vienna Governor officially confirmed that the Imperial and Royal Customs Official Alois Schicklgruber was now "fully entitled to bear the last name of his father—Hitler."

In 1880 Alois Hitler began a relationship with 19-year-old Franziska Matzelsberger, who had moved in with him as a domestic employee. Because of his infidelity, his wife Anna won a "separation from bed and board," from him. On January 13, 1882, Franziska gave birth to their illegitimate son, Alois. When Anna passed away a year later, Alois was able to marry Franziska and legitimize his son's birth. Just four months after the wedding, a daughter by the name of Angela was born. Franziska Hitler (nee Matzelsberger) died less than a year later of pulmonary tuberculosis. In the meantime, Alois Sr.'s 24-year-old niece, Klara Poelzl—who had come from Spital to help during Franziska's illness—took care of the now orphaned children.

Alois petitioned for a dispensation from the Church so that he could marry his niece, Klara. The bishop in Linz refused to give his permission for the marriage because the kinship was too close, but when he forwarded the petition to Rome, dispensation was finally granted. It couldn't have come at a more fortuitous time, for Klara was already in her fifth month of pregnancy. The baby, Gustav Hitler, was born on May 17, 1885, but died two years later. Ida, born the next year, also died at the age of two and Otto, the third child, died shortly after birth.

Though the parents were to have more luck with the fourth child, the same can't be said for the rest of the world. On April 20, 1889, the Saturday before Easter at 6:30 p.m., a son named Adolf was born, his humble birthplace was the government-provided hotel apartment of the Imperial and Royal Customs Office in Braunau on the Inn. The first people to see the future dictator were the hunch-backed Johanna Poelzl, Klara's sister, and midwife Franziska Pointecker. Later, Franziska Pointecker recalled that the child was "rather weak, darkhaired, and strikingly blue-eyed." Alois Sr. was 52 years old and Klara—who still addressed her husband as "Uncle Alois"—was 28.

Though Adolf Hitler would later mythologize his humble origins, Imperial and Royal Customs Office Official Alois Hitler was not a poor man. In his book *Mein Kampf,* Hitler tried to spin a tale of "conditions of poverty, need and tight quarters at home." Reality, however, was quite different.

Until 1888, Alois Hitler had to live on his salary, which came to 216 crowns per month, a sum that included station allowances. At the time, this was a higher salary than a junior high school principal made, although the latter was considered a more solid member of the bourgeois middle class. By comparison, a skilled worker with a family made about 90 crowns per month. Alois paid between 16 and 20 crowns per month for rent and only 40 crowns per year in taxes. Thus, the family didn't suffer any great privations. Of course, Alois wasn't able to stash away any savings because the illnesses and deaths in his family had cost him a great deal of money.

A year before Adolf was born, his father's financial situation suddenly changed for the better. Johann Nepomuk Huettler died at the age of 81 on his farm in Spital. He left his legitimate daughters Johanna, Josefa and Walburga the farm and the inn he owned in town. Shortly before his death, he had given his cash to his "natural" son Alois, whose "brilliant career" he'd taken great pride in during the last years of his life. The amount of the old man's cash isn't known, although it was substantial enough that in March, 1889 Alois Hitler could purchase a respectable home with a stable, barn, farmyard, garden and farmland for the sum of 10,000 crowns. Alois hired his hunch-backed niece, Johanna, to run the farm. She did such a good job that he was able, just four years later, to sell the entire estate for 14,000 crowns to a farmer named Johann Hobiger.

Little Adolf thus grew up in a bourgeois, well-organized and financially secure home. He was the pampered center of attention for his mother and his half-sister Angela.

In August 1892, Alois Hitler was promoted to senior customs office official and, at the same time, transferred to Passau, on the German side of the border. Adolf's brother, Edmund, was born there but died of measles at the age of six. Two years later another transfer brought the family to Linz. Alois Hitler purchased a mansion and 38,000 square meters of land in the nearby village of Hafeld near Lambach. He retired there in 1895 after forty years of civil service. Comfortably ensconsed, he devoted himself to agriculture and to raising bees, which was his favorite hobby.

Young Adolf attended primary school in Fischlheim

near Lambach and a year later switched to the Lambach
monastery school of the Benedictine Seminary. He was
considered a very good pupil, making almost all A's on
his report card. He even became a choirboy in the monastery school's Choirboys Institute. Father Alois was
proud of his son and hoped that he'd become a civil servant and have an even more brilliant career than he had
had.

The local villagers treated the family with reverent
respect. Little Adolf soon learned that, as a member of
the "better bourgeoisie," property and prestige play a
decisive role in life. Later, when he was a struggling
artist, he was in constant fear of sinking into proletarian
poverty. Even during the years he lived the life of a
Bohemian, he sensed that he belonged body and soul to
the bourgeoisie. His most vehement attacks on "satiated
Babbitry" were always an expression of a desperate desire for acceptance and membership.

Adolf's sister Paula, the "straggler," was born in 1896.
During that same year, fourteen-year-old Alois Jr. ran
away from home due to the constant nagging of his
father, who considered him lazy and good for nothing.
He went to Vienna, where he worked as a waiter and, in
subsequent years, twice ended up in prison for theft.
Later we will look at Alois Jr.'s checkered career and his
relationship with his half brother Adolf.

Alois Hitler Sr. sold his Hafeld estate at a sizable profit
and purchased a new house in Leonding, five kilometers
from Linz. Later this house became the official home of
the Führer, and after 1938 it became a "pilgrimage place"
for thousands of visitors from all over the world.

When brother Edmund died of measles in February
1900, Adolf was the only son in the house and the sole
hope of his ambitious father. His father sent him to the
government science high school in Linz, but he didn't
adapt well. His performance in mathematics and natural
history was so poor that he had to repeat the first year.
His good grades in history, geography and drawing didn't
compensate for his shortcomings in the other subjects.
His father's disappointment and his harsh words of discipline only reinforced his son's aversion to compulsory

school attendance. In his biography of Hitler, Werner Maser writes: "All details and interrelationships clearly show that young Hitler already considered systematic work to be a kind of compulsion and control whenever he himself was supposed to do it. He received unsatisfactory grades in all subjects which, in addition to talent, required hard work."

On January 3, 1903, while drinking a glass of wine at a leading restaurant, Alois Sr. suddenly collapsed. Before the doctor and the pastor could arrive, the 66-year-old man died in a side room of the restaurant. The liberal Linz *Tagespost* printed a lengthy obituary. It praised Alois' "progressive outlook, his committed sense of citizenship, and his thrifty character." His authority in the field of bee-raising was also given special mention.

Financially, the father's death didn't result in any excessive cutbacks for the family. The widow received a death allowance of 605 crowns and a monthly widow's pension of 100 crowns. In addition, there were education allowances of 20 crowns each for Adolf and Paula so that Klara Hitler now had an income of 140 crowns per month and lived in an almost debt-free house. Stepdaughter Angela married a civil servant named Leo Raubal and left the parental home. Stepson Alois broke all contacts with the family. Klara's hunchbacked sister Johanna Poelzl, who also lived in the house, had her own income from her share of the inheritance and contributed to the expense of running the household.

Half a year after her husband's death, Klara Hitler sold the house in Leonding for 10,000 crowns (seven years earlier, Alois had bought it for 7,700 crowns) and moved with the children to Linz, where she rented a handsome apartment at 31 Humboldtstrasse in the Urfahr section.

After deducting the remaining mortgage payments and the investment of the inheritance shares for Adolf and Paula (so as to protect them against a potential guardianship situation), the mother was left with more than 5,000 crowns. In addition to her widow's pension, this amount of money enabled the family to lead a comfortable, worry-free life. Klara Hitler was an undemanding woman. She saved her money for her children, especially for her "gifted" darling Adolf, whose demands upon her purse became increasingly bold and insatiable.

# Chapter Two

# Adolf's Adolescence

Witnesses have reported that the 14-year-old Adolf "collapsed sobbing" on his father's casket, a lugubrious performance that didn't escape the eye of his coddling mother. She realized that the death of Alois had relieved her son of his burden. Immediately following the funeral, in fact, Adolf began beseeching her not to make him keep going to the dreaded science high school. In the end, she could only implore him with tears in her eyes to do part of his father's bidding and at least finish the fourth year of junior high school. (In Austria, completion of the fourth year was a prerequisite for the government-financed Cadet School which, in turn, opened the way for a career as a commissioned officer or a higher level civil servant.)

Adolf, however, didn't want to be a commissioned officer or a civil servant. He wanted to be an artist, more specifically, a painter. If he were to continue to attend junior high school, he explained to his mother, he would never achieve this goal. Somehow his mother convinced him that high school graduation was a prerequisite to enrollment at Academy of Arts, and so reluctantly, Adolf continued to attend the high school in Linz.

It was not smooth sailing for the impetuous lad. He got past the third year by the skin of his clenched teeth, but only after having to repeat the French examination. After he'd barely squeaked by in the repeat test, he was given a certificate of promotion but only on the condition that he'd finish the fourth year elsewhere. Later,

Professor Dr. Eduard Huemer, the teacher who administered the French repeat test to him, would say, "Hitler was definitely talented although he was rather one-sided, and he really didn't have that one side under control either. He was obstinate, high-handed, dogmatic and irascible, and he found it very difficult to fit into a school situation. He simply wasn't diligent. Otherwise, in view of his undeniable talents, he could have done much better."

For his fourth year, his mother sent him to the State Senior High School in Steyr. He lived as a boarder in the home of Court Official Conrad Edler von Cichini at 19 Gruenmarkt, an address that in 1938 would be renamed Adolf Hitler Square. The house itself, where the young student found room and board, was years later bedecked with a worshipful plaque by the Nazis.

He did rather well in German, his lessons taught by a Jew named Robert Siegfried Nagel. He also received outstanding grades in drawing, but his performance in physics and mathematics was less than spectacular.

Hitler's interim report card was so miserable that spring that he felt compelled to get drunk. In his drunken rampage he used the document for toilet paper. The next morning, massively hung over, he was forced to appear in the school principal's office to get a duplicate copy of the report card.

In the autumn of 1905 Hitler's final grades where adequate enough to get him into the fifth year. He half-heartedly promised his mother—who was encouraged by her son's improvement—that he'd continue to attend school until the final comprehensive graduation exam. Even before the start of the new academic year, however, he managed to get out of having to keep his promise. He was struck down by a mysterious illness, or, as he preferred to call it, "a serious lung ailment." Later, in his book *Mein Kampf*, he was to describe it as "a sickness that came just in the nick of time." It was in truth, a case of bronchitis, probably caused by too much smoking. Dr. Edward Bloch, the family physician, recommended that he recover in the fresh country air of Spital.

His health improved and he soon returned to Linz, although in order to prolong his carefree existence, he played the role of the suffering "consumptive." His mother fell for Adolf's lies. She agreed that under no circumstances would he be able to cope with school work, and while he rested and relaxed under her roof, he promised her that he'd apply for admission to the Academy of Arts in Vienna as soon as he was fully recovered.

Now began what Hitler later portrayed as "the most beautiful time" of his life. He'd been freed of all duties. He led the life of a well-off, privileged young idler. He convinced his mother that he, as the only son of a civil servant's widow and future academic artist, needed to be seen in clothes that befitted his station in life. Without complaining, she gave him the money for an elegant tailor-made wardrobe. His former school chums at the Linz junior high school watched with envy and astonishment as he transformed himself into a dandy Dangling his walking stick and rakishly perching his black tophat on the back of his head, he promenaded up and down Linz "Landstrasse" exuding the aura of an artist who had already arrived. He quickly became a regular at the Café Baumgarten, where the "creme-de-la-creme" of Linz rendezvoused and where he enjoyed slice after slice of cake with whipped cream.

He also became a paid member of the Museum Association and the People's Education Association, in the process making a name for himself as an "expert" on all manner of topics—art, music, history, architecture and psychology. His best friend, August ("Gustl") Kubizek, became a faithful chronicler of his utterances, much as Eckermann had been for Goethe. Gustl, the son of an upholsterer, admired the imaginative idler and his grandiose projects. In music, he discovered Richard Wagner, a composer he'd come to consider "the greatest genius the world has produced to this very moment," one who, in effect, matched his own grandiosity. He never missed a single Wagner performance at the Linz Opera.

Biographer Joachim Fest wrote, "In the fantasy world that Hitler built for himself, above and beyond reality, he projected the ambitiousness and self-confidence of a genius." The world, as he informed Gustl, would have to be "changed thoroughly and in all parts." He began designing urban building projects for the city of Linz; he drew designs of theaters, baronial mansions and museums. Often, the dividing lines between reality and his dreams became blurred. For example, for a birthday present that year, he gave his friend Gustl the design of a house in the Italian Renaissance style. "I will build this for you some day," he told him. He also designed a new and impressive bridge that he dreamed would one day span the Danube. Thirty-five years later, as the "Führer of the Greater German Reich," he did indeed order this bridge to be built, exactly as he'd drawn it up at age 17. In March 1945—with the Red Army already banging at the gates of Berlin—Hitler ordered all of his original blueprints for the rebuilding of Linz to be brought to him in his bunker under the Reich Chancellery. Hour after hour he languished over these blueprints, thinking back to the "most beautiful time of his life" 40 years earlier, correcting a sketch here or changing a design there, in the waning hours of his existence.

Hitler's mother was worried about his future. In the summer of 1906, she sent him to Vienna where she urged that he try hard to get into the Academy. Adolf traveled to the capital, well-supplied with cash. For two months he lived in a small hotel, sauntered through museums, inspected the architecture on the Ring Boulevard, and almost daily went to hear an opera by Wagner. As he wrote to his friend Gustl, "I really keep on the go all the time. Tomorrow I'm going to see 'Tristan' and the day after tomorrow the 'Flying Dutchman'." He didn't try very hard to get into the Academy. He put that off until the following year.

Back in Linz, he resumed his existence as an idler. His mother, in the meantime, had fallen ill. She no longer had the strength to battle with her son's raging egomania. He continued to make more grandiose new plans. He suddenly wanted to become a composer, so his mother bought him a piano; for four months she paid for his piano lessons with the former Army Band musician Prewatzky-Wendt. When Adolf discovered that music, like every other creative endeavor he'd abandoned, required discipline, hard work and practice, he gave it up. The expensive piano sat in their house, gathering dust. He did, in fact, begin composing an opera in the grand style of Richard Wagner but became embittered when Gustl, a music student himself, tried to criticize objectively his bombastic and amateurish musical sketches.

Hitler's mother became increasingly worried about her beloved son's future. She'd been told by the doctors that she didn't have long to live but kept this fact from Adolf. On January 18, 1907, she underwent a breast operation in the Linz Hospital of the Sisters of Mercy. The medical record called it "sarcoma musculi pectoralis minoris" (malignant tumor in the small chest muscle). Somewhat recovered after the operation, she bravely played the part of the convalescing patient for the benefit of her son. Immersed in his egomania, however, Adolf didn't catch on to the fact that his mother was dying. At last, in September 1907, at his mother's insistence, he returned to Vienna to take his entrance examination. Though Klara Hitler was only 47 years old, she looked like an old woman. When Gustl's father August Kubizek visited her, she sadly admitted that "Adolf will continue to go his ruthless way as if he were the only one in this world." In the meantime, 18-year-old Adolf reported to the examination commission of the General School of Painters in Vienna's Academy of Fine Arts. "Equipped with a fat portfolio of drawings," he wrote, he was convinced that "it would be child's play to pass the examination," despite the fact that the test had a fearsome reputation. The first session lasted six hours, during which time the candidates were required to choose two composition assignments from a long list of topics. Although 33 of the 112 applicants had already fallen by the wayside, Adolf made it through the first leg safely.

The candidates were then required to submit sample drawings of what they'd already done outside the Academy. Hitler handed in a stack of drawings he'd done in Linz, but they didn't meet the requirements. More than anything else, he was criticized for not having enough portrait sketches. "Adolf Hitler," the commission found, "born in Braunau on the Inn, Upper Austria, on April 20, 1889, German Catholic parents. Father Imperial and Royal Senior Official. Sample drawings inadequate. Few heads." Fifty-one other applicants also failed to make the cut. Werner Maser writes, "What might the world have been spared if Hitler, in 1907, had included a couple more 'heads' in his portfolio? Some of his portraits and portrait studies dating back to that time, which undoubtedly would have met the Academy's requirements, are still in existence today."

It would be completely wrong to conclude from his failure to pass the entrance examination that Hitler was less talented than the applicants who passed. Many biographers have endeavored to create the impression that he was a megalomaniacal amateur who tried to get into a prestigious Academy but was cut down by expert examiners for being "insufficiently talented." This opinion—which can be found in early books by Heiden, Bullock, and Shirer— has also made its way into more contemporary biographies. Books by Fest and Maser are the only exceptions. The decision to accept or reject an applicant was at times arbitrary and subjective. Many of the applicants who were originally accepted for being "highly talented" later sank into obscurity or became mediocre drawing instructors, while some of those who flunked went on to make a name for themselves as professional artists. Applicant Robin Christian Andersen, for example, failed the same examination as Hitler. He eventually became an art professor and director for the School of Masters in Painting at the Vienna Academy of Fine Arts. He even went on to become president of the same Academy that in 1907 rejected him as being "untalented for the study of painting."

Hitler's drawings at that time were rather emphatically derived from the work of Franz von Alt, an Austrian landscape painter who was considered by the critics to be a moderate, impressionistically inspired realist. Although Hitler's sketches contain outstandingly rendered details of streets and buildings, they make a rather oddly sterile impression because of the almost total absence of people or animals. Where he does depict living things, Hitler makes his subjects look like puppets that serve merely as decoration or accessories. One can only assume that the examiners were put off by this absence of life. Even the trees in these early drawings looked more like plaster-cast scenery than living organisms.

Rejection was a shock for the 18-year-old Adolf. He requested a conference with the Academy's president, Professor Siegmund l'Allemand. L'Allemand was a Jew. Later, Hitler was conveniently able to blame his failure on "Jewish conspiracy." The president, however, was by no means negatively inclined toward the young artist. He devoted a good deal of time in order to have a detailed conversation with the lad. He emphasized the rejected candidate's strong suits, which, as he put it, "are to be found more in the field of architecture." He strongly advised Hitler to apply for admission to the Academy's School of Architecture, because his drawings revealed a great deal of promise and would almost guarantee his being accepted there were he to apply.

Adolf Hitler left the conference with warm words of thanks for the liberal and unbiased adviser. Inspired, he suddenly wanted to become an architect. The next day in the office of the School of Architecture, he was told he lacked the one thing he needed for admission to the study of architecture: a diploma from an institution of higher education. "What I had missed out on in high school due to sheer spite was now to bear bitter fruit," Hitler wrote later. The acquaintances with whom he lived in Vienna urged him to return to Linz and get his high school diploma, especially since such a respected person as L'Allemand had told him he had the talent to become an architect. But Hitler's aversion toward school, actually against any kind of methodically, disciplined work, was stronger than his desire for a systematic "bread-and-butter course of study," even if it was in an artistic field. For the time being he remained in Vienna. He couldn't bring himself to tell his mother that his "dreams of becoming a freelance artist" had failed.

He returned home in November when Dr. Bloch wrote to tell him his mother was dying of incurable cancer. A month later, on December 21, 1907, Klara died at 2:00 a.m. To the very last moment, Dr. Bloch had kept her as free of pain as possible, using opium potions and morphine

injections. Two days later, Adolf arranged to have her
buried next to his father in the Leonding cemetery. Dr.
Bloch later remembered Hitler without any hatred:
"During my almost fourty years as a doctor, I have never
seen a young man so broken by pain and so filled with
sorrow as the young Hitler had been." (After Austria's
incorporation into Germany in 1938, Bloch, a Jew, was
allowed on special orders from the Führer to emigrate to
America with all his property.

Whether his pain was genuine or theatrical, it couldn't
cover up the fact that Adolf Hitler was now a fully
orphaned young man. Shortly after his mother's burial,
he asked his guardian, Leonding Mayor Josef Mayrhofer,
to give him an accurate inventory of the monies and
inheritance shares due him. His 12-year-old sister
Paula—who in the meantime had been attending the
Linz Girls' High School—was placed with the family of
halfsister Angela Raubal. When Josef Mayrhofer asked
young Adolf about his own plans—after he'd told him
how much money he'd been willed, he replied firmly,
"Mr. Guardian, I'm going to Vienna!"

# Chapter Three

# The Peacock Loses His Feathers

Adolf Hitler would later maintain that his father's inheritance had "been almost completely eaten up" by his
mother's illness and death. That seems highly unlikely. At
the time of Klara's death, the daily rate for the Linz hospital was 2 crowns, while the cancer operation itself cost
40 crowns. Dr. Bloch's bill came to an estimated 100
crowns. The funeral cost 370 crowns, which included 110
crowns for the coffin. Even if Klara Hitler had had to
dip into her savings to meet her son's increasingly demanding needs, at least 2,000 crowns—1,000 for him and
1,000 for Paula—should have been left over because his
mother was otherwise tighter than a drum with money.

From his father's inheritance—which had been invest-
ed for him in the Upper Austrian Mortgage Institute—Adolf received 800 crowns. Before he returned to
Vienna, he asked that 58 crowns per month be remitted
to him which means that the inheritance money should
have lasted until the middle of 1909. He also received an
estimated 50 crowns per month from his mother's inheritance over the course of the next year and a half. In addition, he was given a monthly orphan allowance of 25
crowns. Thus, when Hitler left for Vienna, in the beginning of 1908, he had a monthly income of around 125-130
crowns, a sizable amount of money he got without having to do a thing. By way of comparison, Leo Raubal, a
civil servant and husband of Hitler's half sister Angelika,
earned a monthly salary of 90 crowns. Out of that he had
to feed a wife and two children. Further comparison

shows that after a year of work, a judge could make 70 crowns per month, a young teacher could get 66 crowns during his first five years of service, and a senior instructor at a high school in Vienna could only earn 82 crowns. When Benito Mussolini was chief editor of the newspaper *L'Avvenire del Lavoratore (The Worker's Future)* in Triest, as well as the secretary of the Socialist Party, he collected a total of 120 crowns for both jobs. So Adolf was sitting pretty with his 125 crowns.

He took off for Vienna to try his luck again. A family friend from Linz was able through family connections in Vienna to get Adolf access to Alfred Roller, an internationally renowned stage scenery painter. Roller was the co-founder of the Vienna Secession Art Movement, as well as being an instructor at the School of Applied Arts. Gustav Mahler had picked him as the stage designer for the Imperial Opera, and he created the scenery for Mahler's productions of all of Wagner's operas and, later, the premieres of Richard Strauss' operas.

Roller gladly received Hitler and gave him some friendly advice but was unable to take him on as a private student due to time constraints. He recommended the budding young artist to Panholzer, a seasoned educator, sculptor and drawing teacher. Panholzer accepted Hitler as his pupil. Later, when he was Führer, Hitler loved to brag that he'd been a pupil of Professor Alfred Roller, which wasn't the truth, although during his first year in Vienna, he attended every opera performance for which Roller had designed the scenery. Hitler's blind reverence for Roller went so far that in 1935 he suggested the now 74-year-old man be called to Bayreuth to become a stage designer. Roller died that same year.

Hitler—the young man who traveled from Linz to Vienna in January 1908—was 5'7" tall and weighed 150 pounds. His coarse, bony face—typical of the farmers in the Waldviertel section of Lower Austria—was dominated by a big nose with huge blackened nostrils. Beneath this schnozz grew a rather sparse little mustache which had not yet been trimmed in the celebrated manner of Charles Chaplin. Hitler's big, bright blue eyes gave his homely face a rather odd appearance. To complete this gawky portrait, his feet were very big while his hands were small, delicate, and narrow-boned, like the hands of a surgeon or pianist. His clothing was, of course, elegant, and next to his suitcase, as an added affectation, he carried his walking stick with the ivory handle.

He rented a large room in Vienna's 6th District, at 29 Stumpergasse, near the Western Railroad Station. His landlady was a Polish widow named Maria Zakreys. He would soon share the room with his friend August Kubizek, who arrived in Vienna in February to attend the State Conservatory. They split the monthly rent of 20 crowns.

It was only now that Hitler was able to confess to his friend that he'd flunked the entrance examination at the Academy. Kubizek recalled later: "He worked himself into a fit of anger similar to the one in Linz after that lottery ticket incident. The entire Academy should be blown sky-high, he shouted. Nothing but old, hide-bound civil servants, uncomprehending bureaucrats and stupid pencil pushers." Hitler said he'd make his way even without that "riff-raff."

While Kubizek maintained a precise schedule, regularly attending the music Conservatory and increasing his rather meager funds by giving piano lessons, Hitler fell back on the disorderly life of his days in Linz. Kubizek's pragmatic realism made him nauseous. Once, as he entered their apartment, he watched as Kubizek said goodbye to a young high school coed at the end of their piano lesson. Hitler displayed the bare minimum of courtesy to the young lady, not bothering to disguise his antipathy. After she'd left, he threw the windows open and chewed his friend out. He told him that, by giving lessons to make a living, he would only attract "well-perfumed, hysterical womenfolk in pursuit of the arts." Hitler didn't seem to grasp the fact that Kubizek was financially strapped and desperately needed the extra money.

From time to time Hitler turned up in the Panholzer studio but eventually stopped going altogether when the instructor told him that art was only 10 percent inspiration and 90 percent perspiration. Hour after hour, Hitler strolled along the Ring Boulevard, admiring the pomp of the new Imperial Palace, the Imperial Theater, the Imperial Hotel, the Imperial Opera and the Stock Exchange.

The Ring Boulevard had been built between 1858 and 1888 on what were previously the city's fortifications. From a purely functional point of view, most of the buildings along here were a gigantic collection of pompous trash. All of the eclectic, pseudo-historical styles were represented, from the Neo-Gothic and Neo-Renaissance all the way to the Neo-Baroque—and most were simply hybrids of several historical stylistic components. In his book *Hitler's Journey Began in Vienna*, Jones J. Sydney describes this type of architecture as a "part of a stage design intended to conceal the inherent emptiness of the dying monarchy." In 1900 a British visitor to Vienna named Henry Wickham Steed described the fluffy atmosphere of the metropolis as "an empire that appears to be dying of diabetes."

Hitler, however, was fascinated by this architectural interpretation of history. Semper, Hasenauer, van der Nuell and Theophil Hansen became his architectural heroes. He particularly liked Hasenauer for his decorative style that reflected the tastes of the Makart Age. Other, more progressive and original architects, like Adolf Loos, were dismissed as being an "un-German horror."

In painting, young Hitler's tastes came to a similar, grinding halt with Makart and Franz von Alt. He didn't know—or he didn't want to know—that Gustav Klimt was also living in Vienna at the time. Or that another young painter named Egon Sciele, born the same year as Hitler, had just given his first showing, and had already made quite a name for himself.

When it came to music, Hitler was completely captivated by Wagner. He, of course, knew that the director of the Imperial Opera and the producer of the Wagner operas, was Gustav Mahler—but he'd never heard this equally celebrated man's music. For Hitler, music began and ended with Wagner. Even Mozart paled in comparison. When Richard Strauss gave the first performance of his classic "Elektra" in 1909, Hitler attended only because Roller had designed the stage setting—the music itself was alien to him. Likewise, the music of Arnold Schoenberg—who also lived and worked in Vienna at that time—completely baffled Hitlɛ Franz Lehar was the only other composer who Hitlɛɪ found acceptable. He saw Lehar's "The Merry Widow" at least a dozen times and was able to sing many of the lightweight melodies by heart.

Hitler hardly ever went to see plays. To him, Arthur Schnitzler was "swinish" and Hugo von Hofmannsthal was "decadent," though he didn't derive these opinions on his own; instead, he merely repeated what he read in the *German- Nationalist* and the anti-Semitic newspaper *Tagblatt*. Once, he told his roomate: "All books published after 1900 are decadent, obscene and unclean."

During his first year in Vienna, he went to the opera almost every evening, spending a bundle of money in the process. A ticket for the standing-room-only section, located directly under the Imperial Box, cost 2 crowns. Hitler often went there. He appreciated the fact that women were not allowed in this section. "They only come to flirt," he told Kubizek.

Women, in general, evoked a rather strange ambivalence in Hitler. He avoided female companionship and was rather awkward and inhibited in dealing with women. He seemed to have developed a purely platonic relationship with a girl named Marie, a waitress who worked in a café near the Western Railroad Station. "If I met a decent girl, I'd get tied down," he informed Gustl. "But those fast and easy girls will only give you syphilis." Indeed, syphilis in Vienna, as in all big cities of the time, was a disease to be feared. Considered incurable, the only known treatment for it was a long, drawn-out, unreliable rubdown with mercury that caused the patient to lose all his teeth. The syphilis rate in Vienna was very high, estimated at 10 percent of the entire population. It attacked all strata of society. Hugo Wolf and Makart had died of it. Otto, the brother of Crown Prince Franz Ferdinand, had to wear a "leather nose" in order to hide the devastation caused by the disease.

Hitler talked for hours on end about the dark and perverted aspects of sex. The sexual climate in the Vienna at the turn of the century was uptight, characterized by a double standard of morality. It's not surprising that Sigmund Freud found the city to have almost ideal "laboratory conditions" for his studies.

Young Hitler would have nothing to do with Freud. In the library, he was more fascinated with books like *Psychopathia Sexualis,* a collection of case histories of perversion that was published years earlier by Richard Krafft-Ebing, a noted neurologist. He also enjoyed studying the notorious works *Venus im Pelz (Venus in Furs)* by Leopold von Sacher-Masoch and *Memoiren der Josefine Mutzenbacher (Memoirs of Josefine Mutzenbacher)* by Felix Salten. Kubizek was forced to listen to his roommate's long-winded lectures on sexual perversion. Hitler seemed thoroughly familiar with this field in theory. But he shied away from the natural pursuit of his own sexual needs.

In the spring of 1908, the unemployed idler plunged headlong into a literary project. He wanted to write a play inspired by the nationalistic Germanic sagas. When the weather was nice, he'd go to the park at the Schoenbrunn Summer Palace and work there. He'd settle down on a stone bench directly below the Gloriette Summer House and work at the adjoining stone table. He, however, never finished the play, only managing to grind out a few fragments.

It was around this time that Hitler suddenly became interested in social issues. For days on end, he'd stroll through Meidling, Vienna's working class section, and study the crowded tenements. He began designing low-cost housing construction projects using an architectural model that called for small homes—holding between four and eight families—and surrounded by greenery. These complexes would include business establishments, but they would only be allowed to dispense nonalcoholic beverages. When Kubizek argued that Vienna's workers wouldn't be able to function without their daily portion of wine, Hitler shouted, "Nobody is going to give them a choice!" This project, like all his others, was put aside one day, unfinished.

August Kubizek left Vienna in September 1908 to meet a military obligation. Hitler went back to the Academy

to take his second entrance exam. This time he didn't
even get past the first round. When Kubizek said he'd be
returning soon—having been released from the service
after basic training—Hitler moved out of the apartment
without leaving a forwarding address. He was too embarrassed after his failure to face his friend. On November
18, 1908, Hitler moved into room No. 6 at 22 Felber
Street, which was in the same district near the Western
Railroad Station. When registering with the police, he
gave his occupation as "student"—when he'd first come
to Vienna he'd described himself as a "painter."

To lend credence to his new occupation, he also selected a "field of studies," steeping himself in the radically
anti-Semitic writings of a former monk who now went
by the falsely aristocratic name of Joerg Lanz von Liebenfels. A neighborhood tobacco shop carried Liebenfels'
ethnological magazine *Ostara,* which had a hefty circulation of 100,000. It was read mostly by students and the
academic middle-class. Liebenfels had developed a rather
kinky theory about the struggle of the "Asings" (or heroes) against the "Aefflings" (or miscreants). His "Aryan-
Heroic" Order of Men—in which esoteric and Free
Mason elements also played a role—was to be the van-
guard of the blond, blue-eyed Germanic Master Race in
the struggle against the "inferior" dark races. He wanted
to replace the class struggle with the racial struggle,
which would go "all the way to the castration knife." He
propagated breeding and extermination practices "for the
extermination of human animals and the development of
a 'new man'." Liebenfels wrote goofy proclamations like,
"Bring sacrifices to Frauja, you sons of Gods. Up, up!
And make him an offering of the offspring of
miscreants!" To popularize his theory, he even suggested
racial beauty contests. In his biography, Joachim Fest
thought that Liebenfels didn't exert any noteworthy influence on Hitler. His real significance, he argued, was as
spokesman for the neurotic mood of the times. Nevertheless, given what occurred years later, one gets an eerie
feeling reading these writings—especially when Liebenfels speaks of planned selective breeding and racial
hygiene, of deportations to the "forest of apes," of liqui-

dations through forced labor or murder. It's not surprising that these same theories were eagerly being read by the likes of Heinrich Himmler. Fest, of course, admits that Liebenfels decisively helped fashion, if not the ideology, then at least the pathology of young Hitler.

Hitler plunged into his "study" of anti-Semitic literature with the same initial mania he'd displayed with his other projects. He no longer had time for painting or drawing.

In the summer of 1909, Hitler noticed to his great consternation that the money from his inheritance was slowly running out. Only his 25-crown orphan allowance now arrived with any regularity. He had to cut back. He stopped going to the opera and he sold some of his expensive and elegant clothing. He also had to look for a cheaper room. On August 20, he moved in at 58 Sechshauser Street in the 14th District, which was a working class section. The fact that he'd received a notice to report for a military induction examination—the "preliminary exam"—made it seem advisable to change addresses.

Today, the house on Sechshauser Street is a shelter for alien workers. Even in 1909 it looked shabby. It appeared that Hitler's carefree dandy days were over, and his social standing began its relentless decline. Still, the burgher's son refused to look for paid manual labor. Instead, he sold off the remnants of his wardrobe, including his winter overcoat, keeping only a threadbare dark blue suit. He sold his paints, brushes and other assorted tools to a junkman. Even with these drastic measures, by September 16 he was no longer able to hold on to his cheap room on Sechshauser Street. The money was gone. The 25 crowns also stopped coming.

For the three months from September until December 1909, there are no police records of Hitler's whereabouts in Vienna and no reports from acquaintances. All we have to go on is what he later told his fellow inmates at the Men's Shelter. With some proper caution, that interval of time can be partially reconstructed as follows:

He spent some evenings in a cheap coffee-house on Kaiser Street near the Western Railroad Station, where the compassionate waitress Marie would occasionally slip him a few pennies. While the weather was still reasonably warm, Hitler slept in doorways or on benches in the Prater Park. When it rained, he crawled into the Park's Rotunda building. But at the end of October, winter hit Vienna with heavy snow and rain.

Luckily, the orphan allowance arrived via General Delivery at the end of the month, and Hitler managed to get a roof over his head at a so-called "bed warmer." In Vienna, the "bed warmer" was as well-known an institution as the "sleep boy" was in Berlin—it was a bed, located in a group worker's shelter, and he had to leave it first thing in the morning. He reported that he had as many as 16 different quarters of this kind. On one such occasion his bag, containing all of his remaining belongings, was stolen.

Hitler was just one among thousands of Viennese inhabitants who lived this kind of life. In 1909, the city was bursting at the seams with more than two million residents. Between 1860 and 1900, the housing shortage was almost beyond comprehension. The population of Vienna had grown by 250 percent, most of the increase being rural folk who migrated from all parts of the Danube Monarchy—Bohemia, Poland, Galicia, Croatia, Ruthenia and Upper Austria. They poured into the capital in hopes of finding work. The already precarious housing situation turned into a disaster. Public hygiene and local water supplies were in terrible shape, and the differences between the vulgarly displayed wealth and the dire poverty were unimaginable. "Cozy" Vienna on the "Beautiful Blue Danube" existed only in the imagination of the operetta wordsmiths. Behind the myth of the idle, hedonistic Viennese—who sits in his café every night or dances to the tune of a Strauss waltz—lay the reality of the housing shortage which drove people out of their overcrowded, foul-smelling quarters and into the open or into the bars and dives.

In 1910, 4.4 people, on average, were living in one room in the Viennese working quarter. The apartments in these districts—Brigittenau or Favoriten—were dark, primitive holes without running water, and the rooms were small and stuffy. Although living space for the families was severely restricted, many people were still compelled to accept "bed warmers" in order to pay the rent. In 1910, these "bed warmers," who had no room of their own and no place to cook, accounted for about 5 percent of the city's population.

There was even greater misery. Many of the homeless poor had to spend the night in "warming rooms," which were financed by private, mostly Jewish charities. These rooms—where the poor could get free soup and a thin slice of bread—were located all over the city but were hopelessly overcrowded. New arrivals had to elbow their way through the tightly packed bodies.

Many of the homeless didn't dare avail themselves of these legitimate institutions because they had police records and were afraid they'd be picked up for having no papers. For these people, the "sewer" was the last refuge. Near the Stephanie-und-Ferdinand Bridge, for example, the iron doors leading to the sewers were easily opened. The warm and moist steam stank horribly but kept out some of the wintry chill.

For weeks, Hitler struggled against the disgrace of having to go to a public shelter. He still believed that he was a proper citizen—the son of a civil servant—and he felt helpless in the face of his distress. He lacked the nerve to be a professional city bum. As long as he still had a few pennies in his pocket, he staggered from one "bed warmer" to the next, from one "warming room" to the next. He never sought refuge in the sewers. Only the initiated, the true professionals among the tramps, knew where to find those places.

Shortly before Christmas 1909, Hitler was finally reduced to standing in the long line in front of the gates of Miedling's homeless shelter, near the Southern Railroad Station. This shelter was operated by a philanthropic society, the main money source being the Jewish Epstein family.

People were allowed to stay at the shelter for five days, and everybody was required to take a shower, sharing the stall with someone else. For Hitler, this was horribly humiliating. All his life he was mortally afraid of appearing naked in front of other people. After the shower, soup and bread were served in the dining hall. Then everybody filed into the huge dormitories, where cots were neatly lined up beneath iron clothing hooks.

Most of the people who stayed at the Meidling shelter were young men around Hitler's age. They were looking for jobs. Many came from Germany—from the Rhineland, Bavaria or Saxony region. Crushed, looking demoralized, Hitler sat on his cot and listened in silence as the others joked with each other and told of the adventures they'd had during their travels. A few tried to cheer him up. In the spirit of solidarity that seems endemic to the poor, they took the shy newcomer under their wings and shared bread and sausage with him. One fellow, although he came from the Sudetenland and spoke with a definite Berlin accent, became his special friend. He was a trained graphic artist named Reinhold Hanisch. For the first time since he left Gustl Kubizek, Hitler had a buddy.

The shelter was closed in the morning, requiring the residents to leave until the next evening. Hitler and Hanisch spent their days in various warming rooms or earning a few pennies carrying luggage at the Western Railroad Station. If snow fell during the night, they were able to earn some money shoveling snow the next morning. Without his winter overcoat, Hitler was miserably cold.

After their five days at the Miedling shelter had run out, the resourceful Hanisch managed to get an extension on their stay by purchasing the certificates from departing residents. In this manner, the two of them stayed until early February. During that time, they found work as construction laborers. In *Mein Kampf* Hitler described how he worked on a lenghty construction project as a helper and how in that time he constantly clashed with the social-democratic workers. This was pure fabrication. After two days on the job, the gang boss sent Hitler home for being physically too weak.

Hanisch and Hitler became closer friends. Theirs was a miserable life but it was better than the life Hitler had just left behind. As far as the future was concerned, Hitler was deeply depressed. When Hanisch asked why he didn't try to better himself, given his education and social background, Hitler replied despondently: "I really don't know!"

Hanisch finally came up with an idea that looked as if it might help both of them. Hitler, after all, was an academic painter, or so he'd told him, and he had a few small postcard-size pictures to prove it. Hanisch suggested a partnership: Hitler would paint postcards and Hanisch would sell them. They would split the take. First, however, Hitler needed paints and brushes. Hanisch dragged him to the Café Arthaber near the Meidling Cemetery, where, if they ordered a small cup of coffee, they could get pen and paper. Hitler wrote to his hunchbacked Aunt Johanna in Spital and asked for a loan in order to continue his studies. He didn't tell her about his real predicament.

A few days later, 100 crowns arrived via General Delivery. Not only was Hitler able to buy paints, brushes, and an illustration board but in the Dorotheum, (the municipal pawn institution), he was able to purchase a warm, dark winter overcoat for 12 crowns. He had more than 50 crowns left over.

He next had to find a place where he could work. Someone had caught on to their gig at the Meidling Shelter and was threatening to evict them, so because Hitler once again had money, they went to the Men's Home on Meldemann Street in the Brigittenau Section that had recently been erected by the city in order to reduce the housing shortage. Compared to the Meidling Shelter, it was the "Ritz." It was not so much a homeless shelter as a spartan boarding house for single men. Only people who earned under 1,500 crowns per year were admitted to it. The weekly rent came to 3 crowns. Poor members of the nobility and former officers lived there along with artists, traveling salesmen, craftsmen, and low-level clerical employees.

On the outside, the Men's Home looked inviting and on the inside everything was neat and clean. Everyone had their own small cubicle, furnished with an iron bed, a three-part mattress, and a horsehair pillow. There was a narrow cabinet for storing personal belongings, and the bedding was changed every week. There were enough toilets, washing facilities, and shower stalls on each floor, and there was a kitchen for those who wanted to cook and a canteen where low-priced meals were sold at cost. There were several writing rooms, a game room for chess, cards and dominoes, as well as a library. Hitler moved in on February 9, 1910, and paid his four weeks in advance. Hanisch had earned some money as a temporary servant, and he joined his friend a couple of days later.

In the following days, you could find Hanisch prowling through the smoke-filled dives and cafés of Vienna, telling a tearjerker tale of woe. It had to do with a poor, consumptive artist who lived in a cold garret and painted little original postcards of scenic Vienna. These cards were small watercolors of Vienna's buildings, churches and squares, strangely devoid of people but architecturally correct. Hanisch collected pennies and crowns for the postcards. In the lower left-hand corner was the almost illegible signature: "A. Hitler."

This commercial venture got off to a successful start. Hitler would sit in a corner of the Men's Home writing room with his paints, photos, and brushes spread out before him. He sketched likenesses of the photographs and then painted over them with water-colors. Sometimes he would hold the cards over the stove to give them an artificial gloss. He worked slowly at first but with the untiring Hanisch urging him on, he soon produced a respectable stock for sale. Hanisch was compelled to urge Hitler on simply because he was all too fond of putting his work aside in order to debate with the other residents or to conduct lengthy monologues about politics and the Jewish question. Whenever anybody expressed a dissenting opinion, Hitler would become grotesquely animated, swinging his T-square around like a conductor's baton. "But the misery was over," Hanisch recalled 30 years later. "We had new hopes."

Life was comfortable in the Men's Home. An order of roast pork with vegetables sold for 19 pennies. In the basement, there was a barber, a tailor, and a shoemaker. Hitler did his own cooking—but most of the time he preferred desserts. According to Hanisch: "Whenever our business went particularly well, Hitler would boil some rice in milk and sprinkle cocoa on top of it later that same evening."

Hanisch soon found new and more profitable sales outlets. In Vienna, the frame dealers preferred to sell their frames together with cheap paintings so that the customer would be able to see right away how a picture would look in the frame. They were more interested in selling a frame than a picture. Similarly, upholsterers were looking for reasonably priced original paintings that could be hung above their chairs or sofas. Some customers liked to put such a piece of furniture in a decorative position in the middle of a room.

Thus, Hanisch successfully built up a circle of customers for his artist. Hitler now painted most of his pictures in a larger 30 by 40 centimeter format, and sometimes even bigger. Once he received an order for a water-color of a church on Gumppendorf Street, a job that presented him with a major problem: He had never really learned how to paint from nature. He had always preferred copying photographs. There, however, was no available photograph of the church. Early the next morning, Hanisch dragged the reluctant Hitler to Gumppendorf Street but he couldn't get a thing done. He blamed it on the cold, saying his hands were too stiff. From then on, Hanisch no longer believed his fairy tale about the "academically" trained painter.

Their best customers were Jakob Altenburg, a Polish immigrant from Galicia who owned four frame shops, Herr Morgenstern on Liechtenstein Street and Joseph Landsberger on Favoriten Street, all three of them Jews. Hitler and Hanisch preferred selling to Jews, in spite of what Lanz von Liebenfels and "Tagblatt" were propounding at the time. Said Hanisch: "The Christian dealers would only buy after they'd depleted their inventory, but the Jews bought regardless of whether they'd sold their stock or not."

Hanisch could have sold much more than he did, but the ever lazy Hitler loved to find excuses to put his work aside. Hanisch was constantly haranguing him to meet their delivery deadlines and even began demanding that he turn out one picture per day, which would fetch 5 to 10 crowns between them. By the spring of 1910, both men had achieved a modest measure of economic security.

In the meantime, Hitler still didn't pay much attention to his appearance. His days as a dandy were over. He wore his threadbare blue suit and an incredibly greasy derby. His hair was long and he had a stubbly beard sprouting on his face. Sometimes Hanisch needled him, telling him that he presented an appearance "found only rarely among Christians," teasing him further by hinting that he was of Jewish origin because he could hardly be distinguished from a resident of the Leopoldstadt, Vienna's Jewish ghetto. Besides, Hanisch joked, all Jews had big feet from running through the desert all those years. Hitler responded to this ridicule with nothing but laughter.

Once again he lived a comfortable life. He was able to resume collecting his orphan's allowance and he earned 50-60 crowns each month from the sale of the pictures. Soon he was able to pursue his passion for eating cake in the coffeehouses. He became friends with a Hungarian Jew named Josef Neumann, who gave him a Prince Albert coat as a present. With this garment he allowed himself the luxury of going to the Opera.

Hanisch wasn't pleased with Hitler's continually growing interest in politics. The moment he left the building in the morning to negotiate with customers, Hitler would put his paints and utensils aside to read the newspaper, to debate, or to read books about history and politics. When Hanisch returned, Hitler would not have done a thing. Hanisch reproached Hitler, initiating ugly quarrels and their friendship began to cool off.

On June 21, 1910, Hitler suddenly disappeared from the Home for a week, leaving a desperate Hanisch behind. He rented a hotel room, once again patrolled the museums and engaged in full-fledged dessert orgies, sometimes consuming five pieces of cake with whipped cream, one after the other. Hanisch tracked him down one day and implored him to go back to work. After all, Hitler was his meal ticket. Hitler would have none of it.

"He told me that the work over the past several weeks had overtaxed him," Hanisch said, "He still had some money. All he needed now was rest and recovery. He implied that he wasn't a coolie who could be ordered around."

After one week, Hitler was broke. He reluctantly resumed his work back at the Men's Home, although he was constantly being interrupted by political debates about socialism, the Jewish question, the achievements of Wagner and Gottfried Semper. Hitler's radical anti-Semitism didn't spare the feelings of his friend Joseph Neumann or the other Jewish residents of the Home. They smiled rather than become angry at his tactless remarks.

The more his friendship with Hanisch cooled, the better he got along with a new resident of the home: Josef Greiner, a poster painter who—with Neumann acting as his agent—earned money in the advertising field. Greiner fascinated Hitler with his wild dreams and get-rich-quick schemes, suggesting to him that the advertising field was the quickest way to get there. He persuaded Hitler to try his luck in the field, arguing that it was much easier to make money in advertising than by doing water colors or oil paintings. Hitler was finally convinced when he learned that Neumann took only 20 percent as his agent's commission whereas Hanisch got half of the proceeds. The first thing Neumann lined up for his new client was a poster for a shoe store called Ha-ha, a job that would pay 50 crowns. Hitler, Greiner, and Neumann celebrated the order in the Marhold Restaurant on Fleischmarkt in the 1st District, where Hitler ate heartily, devouring a double portion of egg pancakes for dessert.

By the time the poster was finished, Hitler was convinced that he could earn easy money in advertising in the future. Hanisch could look out for himself. Neumann brought him an order from a pharmacy for an odor-inhibiting foot concoction called Teddy Sweat Powder. Hitler's design sketch depicted two postmen, one of whom had taken his shoes off and was looking in disgust at his sweat-soaked socks. The other postman, quite amused, advised his co-worker to give Teddy Sweat Powder a try. Hitler "composed" the following text: "Ten thousand steps, day after day, is a big pain. But, dear brother, ten thousand steps is a joy with Teddy Powder!" The pharmacist wasn't very happy with Hitler's work and didn't accept the poster. The main criticism was that the letter carrier wasn't smiling convincingly but in fact was "grinning maliciously."

Hitler returned to Hanisch, but their close friendship was coming to an end. He worked on an oil painting of the Vienna City Hall for Hanisch but was already days behind schedule. He finally finished it but, spoiled by the advertising posters, demanded 50 crowns for his work. Hanisch was shocked but still tried to sell the picture. Nobody wanted it, not even at a lower price. The regular dealers considered it to be of poor quality. At last, a frame dealer named Wenzel Reiner took it for 12 crowns. Hanisch also sold him a Hitler water-color of the Dominican Cloister for 10 crowns. When Hanisch gave Hitler his share, he went into a blind rage over the paltry amount. Hanisch told him flat out why the regular dealers had turned it down and that he should be happy to have been able to sell it at all. Hanisch also admonished him to finish another painting that was long overdue. Furious, Hitler replied that he was not in a mood for work. He was an artist, not a coolie. Hanisch told him that he shouldn't have any illusions about his paintings being high art. "Without me," he said, "you would be nothing but a starving artist!" Hitler, alluding to Hanisch's having been a servant, retorted: "And you are nothing but an uneducated handyman!" Hurt, Hanisch packed his suitcase and left the Men's Home.

Hanisch's departure was a disaster for Hitler. He was too gauche, too inhibited, too poorly dressed to be able to negotiate with dealers by himself. Suddenly, he realized how much work the efficient and smooth-talking Hanisch had relieved him of. He was in a panic, afraid that he'd sink into misery once more.

He worked himself into such a frenzy over this "betrayal" that he went to the police station in Brigittenau and filed charges against Hanisch for "embezzlement of 50 crowns in the form of a picture that was to be sold."

He made the following deposition on August 5, 1910: "Because he (Hanisch) had no funds of his own, I gave him the pictures I had painted so that he could sell them. He regularly got 50 percent of the sales price from me. He has not been back to the Men's Home for about two weeks and has cheated me out of a painting entitled 'City Hall' worth 50 crowns and a water-color worth nine crowns."

Hitler used any means, even lies, to get even with Hanisch. A week later, the judge sentenced Hanisch to six days in jail, although the latter protested that he had properly split the amount collected with Hitler. As Hanisch was being led away, he called out to Hitler: "When and where are we going to see each other again, so we can even this score?"

Hanisch never saw Hitler again. After 1933, however, Konrad Heiden, Rudolf Olden and many other reporters found him to be a very talkative witness, able to tell more about Hitler's time in Vienna than the new Reich Chancellor would have liked. Once again, Hitler extracted his own form of revenge, having Hanisch arrested by the Gestapo immediately after the Germans marched into Vienna. Hanisch died in jail, allegedly of pneumonia, although Martin Bormann disputed this with a statement from Führer's Headquarters on February 17, 1944: "Hanisch hanged himself after Austria was taken over."

In the meantime, Hitler faced a big void. His agent and benefactor Neumann had moved to Germany. He wanted to take Hitler along but the latter refused. Greiner also disappeared. Hitler's charges against Hanisch—who was very popular—didn't exactly make him welcome back at the Men's Home. The people staying there didn't appreciate such treachery. Nobody wanted to sell Hitler's pictures on a commission basis. Winter was approaching. Hitler landed a temporary job as gold-plater in the painting shop of the Office of the Senior Lord Steward of His Imperial and Royal Apostolic Majesty. This workshop had been commissioned to restore some of the big rooms in the Museum of Art History.

The money he earned there didn't last long. He had to pay rent and buy his meals. He still had a stock of pictures but he didn't have anybody who'd peddle them for him. He had to handle this for himself. Donning his Prince Albert coat, he visited Altenburg, Morgenstern, and Landsberger. Surprisingly, he was able to sell his entire stock, and he returned to the Men's Home with his pocket full of money. Morgenstern had even introduced him to an attorney named Dr. Josef Feingold. This wealthy patron had already helped many young artists. He ordered a whole series of paintings from Hitler.

But Hitler was no longer able to paint. Without somebody to spur him on, as Hanisch had always done, he was unable to work. Again, he spent his days reading newspapers and debating, and he was soon seized with his fear of slipping into misery.

Suddenly he got an idea that would mean his salvation. His hunchbacked Aunt Johanna, his mother's sister, had always had a warm spot in her heart for him. The winter before, she'd helped him out of a dire situation by sending him money. So he decided to write her a letter and in highly emotional language he described how hard he'd been trying to earn a decent living. All he needed, he told her, was some capital to get a good start.

On December 1, 1910, Aunt Johanna went to her savings bank in Spital and withdrew her entire savings, an amount of 3,800 crowns. Hitler paid her a visit a few days later. She gave him the share of her inheritance that he would have gotten after her death—more than 2,000 crowns. Because she gave it to him in cash, he was able to avoid paying inheritance tax. Hitler then lived like a millionaire. He was free to move around again. If he lived economically, he'd be able to get along rather well for the next two years. He could also earn more money by painting. All this time in Spital, he never gave one thought to his half sister Angela. He didn't even visit her on his way back to Vienna, despite the fact that her husband, Leo Raubal, had died on August 10. Angela was now living on a small widow's pension with two children and Adolf's sister Paula.

Hitler continued to live in the Men's Home. For him, it was more comfortable than a furnished room. He hid the money—and told nobody about his windfall. Painting was suddenly easy once again. In 1911, Josef Greiner turned up and got him some new contracts for advertising work. He painted a poster for the Fernolendt shoe polish firm in black, white, and red. Another poster advertised a detergent called Neubozon. And on a poster for another detergent, the dome of St. Stephen rose majestically from amid a gigantic mountain of foam.

Hitler vowed that he would never be poor again. Greiner became his agent—with considerably more humor than Hanisch. He got Hitler a job as design artist in the studio of architect Florian Mueller at 115 Penzinger Street—although this was only a temporary arrangement. Later, Hitler was to expand on this experience by telling people he worked "as a full-time employed architect" during his days in Vienna.

In the spring of 1911, Hitler, on Greiner's advice, turned up at the Theater an der Wien and applied for a job as a singer in the choir. The director, Mr. Karezag, asked him to audition. Hitler selected Danilo's entrance song "Tonight I go to Maxim's!" from the light opera "The Merry Widow" by Franz Lehar. Hitler warbled in his juicy tenor, "I know all the ladies and I can call them by their nicknames . . ." Karezag was so impressed that he asked Hitler to report immediately to the choir director. Hitler, however, failed to get the job because he didn't have a pair of tails to wear. The choir members had to purchase their own clothing for the performance.

Hitler now realized that his unkempt appearance and sloppy clothing were an obstacle to his progress. He got a haircut, shaved his beard and bought a new suit.

His Aunt Johanna died on March 29. Going through the estate, his half sister Angela discovered that Adolf had already gotten a sizable donation. Because she wasn't in good shape financially she asked Mr. Mayrhofer, Paula's guardian, to transfer Adolf's orphan pension to Paula since he was obviously not in dire straits. Hitler had been receiving the orphan's pension all this time, under false pretense, having stated in court that he was a student at the Art Academy.

Hitler was summoned to appear in court in Leopoldstadt to provide information on his financial situation.

He was in a compromising mood, not wanting to stir up any trouble with the authorities. He was afraid they'd dredge up the matter of his military service. The judge put the following in the record:

"Adolf Hitler, residing as artist at 27 Meldemann Street, 20th District, made the following statement before the court in Leopoldstadt: He can provide for himself and is therefore ready to transfer the entire amount of his orphan's pension to his sister and, moreover, investigations revealed that Adolf Hitler has a considerable amount of money which was given to him by his aunt Johanna Poelzl to promote his career as an artist."

On May 4, 1911, the Linz court officially transferred his orphan's pension to 15-year-old Paula.

From then on, Hitler took his painting very seriously. Apart from the money given to him by his aunt—which he handled very economically—he now had to earn everything with his own work. And he did it. He even made good money. He spent his mornings drawing sketches copied from postcards and early in the afternoon, after a light lunch, he'd complete the painting. Then he'd immediately take it down to the art dealer. Gone were the times of shabby clothing, unkempt hair, and bristly beard. Except for his neatly trimmed mustache, he was smooth-shaven and well dressed. He bought new suits and visited his customers Altenburg, Morgenstern, Landsberger or Dr. Feingold in proper attire. Sometimes Altenburg invited Hitler to tea in the high-class Bristol Hotel. The smart Polish Jewish businessman never heard a single anti-Semitic word from the lips of his opinionated painter. When it came to business, Hitler was learning what was productive and what was counterproductive.

In his magazine, *Fackel (Torch)*, Karl Kraus once published the following aphorism: "Vienna remains Vienna. That is the most fearful of all threats." In the year 1913, Adolf Hitler no longer wanted to change Vienna; he wanted to leave. He wanted to go to Munich to study painting or architecture seriously. Things were too hot for him in Austria. It would only be a matter of time before he'd be drafted into the army—a horrible thought for him. While still living on Meldemann Street, he received his order to report for the initial screening. On May 24, 1913, Hitler filed his departure notice with the police and took the train to Munich where, two days later, he booked a room in the house of master tailor Popp, at 34 Schleissheimer Street. The room had a separate entrance. Hitler once again looked elegant. Even the worldly-wise, Paris-trained gentleman's tailor Popp could find nothing to criticize in his new roomer's smart wardrobe.

On his arrival in Munich, Hitler learned from the newspapers that the chief of staff of VIII Corps—the homosexual Colonel Alfred Redl, blackmailed by the Russian intelligence service—had shot and killed himself the night before in Vienna. Hitler reacted with joy. He'd found a confirmation for his opinion that it was not worth the trouble to play soldier in the Austrian Army. He was happy to be in Munich.

# Chapter Four

# Munich Interlude

In 1913, 31-year-old Franklin D. Roosevelt was under-secretary of the Navy. The House of Commons in Great Britain turned down a bill to give women the right to vote. English suffragettes blew up the country home of Britain's Chancellor of the Exchequer Lloyd George.

Willy Brandt was born. Emperor William II ordered German officers not to dance the Tango in uniform. In Hanover, 66-year-old Paul von Hindenburg lived on his general's pension. Prince Regent Ludwig ascended the Bavarian throne as Ludwig III, although the legitimate King Otto—mentally disturbed for many decades—was still alive.

In Vienna, Yosif Vissarionovich Dzhugashvili, 34, for the first time signed a leaflet with his revolutionary pseudonym, "Stalin."

Charles (Charlie) Spencer Chaplin, 24, made his first movie for $150 per week. Richard Nixon was born.

Benito Mussolini, 30, published the Socialist Party newspaper *Avanti (Forward)* in Milan. Winston Churchill, 39, was the First Lord of the British Admiralty.

Albert Schweitzer, 38, founded a jungle hospital in Lambarene, French Equatorial Africa.

Francisco Franco y Bahamonde, a 20-year-old 2nd lieutenant, fought in the Spanish Army in Morocco against the Rif-Kabyles.

That same year artist and painter Adolf Hitler moved into a furnished room in Munich. Hitler was living not far from Schwabing, the Munich suburb that, at the time, was a magnet for artists, writers, strange characters of all kinds, people bent on improving the world, anarchists and health nuts. Schwabing is where the poet Stefan George had gathered a circle of highly-talented young men who were trying to outdo each other in the glorification of youth and contempt for bourgeois morality. This was the Schwabing of Franziska von Reventlow, of "Simplicissimus" and also of the wild Mardi Gras orgies. This is the Schwabing where radical endeavors from the Right and from the Left ran into each other, mitigated somewhat by "cozy" Munich and not infrequently coexisting peacefully in the same cafe or beer hall. Vladimir Ulyanov (alias Lenin) lived on Siegfried Street, not far from Hitler's domicile.

Hitler didn't join any of these groups, referring to them as "hot-air clubs." He was a loner, he made no friends, he had no contacts. His only social relationships were with the family, friends, and neighbors of the honest and upright master tailor Popp. The folks there appreciated and listened to the somewhat odd, intense Austrian who treated the lady of the house with old fashioned courtesy and bought candy for the kids. He had a few casual beer-drinking acquaintances whom he met in the local restaurants. Over a stein of beer, he loved to hold court about politics, to discuss the decay of the Danube Monarchy and the rise of the "Jewish Menace." He was one among hundreds of very loud, well-spoken yarn spinners. People would listen to him and then move on to the next person.

Although ostensibly a painter, Hitler never noticed that Wassily Kandinsky, Franz Marc or Paul Klee were living in his neighborhood. Their names meant nothing to him. Day after day, he'd sit at the window of his room on the third floor and paint his postcards depicting local Munich scenes—places like the Hofbrauhaus, the Sendlinger Gate, the big food market and the National Theater. He copied each brick and each tile, just as it looked in the original—but his were completely devoid of people.

He would also sit for hours on end in the coffee houses, reading newspapers and devouring mountains of cakes

and pastries. He was able to sell his watercolors to frame
dealers and decorators and live a modest lifestyle on the
income. Shortly before his departure from Vienna, he
had received a letter announcing the "transmittal of the
assets in the community orphan account." This came to
819 crowns and 98 pennies, a modest but sufficient base
on which to build his new life in Munich. No longer
paranoid, he even registered with the Munich Finance
Office, reporting his annual income as 1,200 marks,
derived from self-employed work as an artist. In 1913, by
comparison, a bank clerk his age could earn no more
than 70 marks per month. Hitler paid 20 marks per
month for rent. Lunch in an average restaurant cost him
about 20 marks per month and dinner about the same.

When he painted at home, he wore his oldest suit, but
when he left the house, he was always well dressed. He
liked to wear his Prince Albert suit, which his host always ironed expertly for him. The frame dealers—to
whom he brought his pictures—were located on Brienner
Street and around Odeon Square. To get there, he often
would stroll through the Royal Gardens to Maximilian
Street and then to the nearby Hofbrauhaus where he
loved to sit in the tap room with his sketch pad, but none
of these hastily outlined "heads" ever turned into a finished product. As in Vienna, all of his watercolors were
meticulously copied from photos or postcards.

He didn't try to take regular courses at the Academy
or the School of Architecture. He only painted to sustain
his modest life-style. He had discarded his big dreams
about a brilliant career as a painter or an architect. In
spite of his rather irregular schedule, he lived quietly,
comfortably, almost like a petty-bourgeois. Later on,
looking back, the days he spent in Munich before the
war appeared to him to have been "the happiest and by
far the most satisfying" days of his life.

In *Mein Kampf*, Hitler wrote that he left Vienna primarily "for political reasons." "I did not want to fight for
the Habsburg State." He employed this rather diplomatic
language to get around a fact that would turn out to be
quite embarrassing for him—he had in truth left Austria
as a draft dodger.

Back in his home country, the authorities were already looking for him. On August 22, 1913, Police Officer Zauner in Linz made the following entry in his notebook: "Adolf Hietler (sic) appears to be registered with the police neither here nor in Urfahr and his whereabouts could not be ascertained in any other direction." His former guardian, as well as his sisters Angela and Paula were questioned but knew nothing. No further details were dug up until the investigation went back to Vienna.

On December 29, the Austrian police contacted the Munich Police Headquarters through the following letter: "The artist Adolf Hietler (sic), who was born in Braunau on the Inn in the year 1889, moved from Vienna to Munich on May 24, 1913. By way of official assistance, we request that you inform us as to whether the individual named is registered there." On January 10, the Munich police reported to its counterparts in Linz: "The wanted individual has been registered since May 26, 1913, at the home of a person by the name of Popp, 34 Schleissheimer Street, 3rd floor."

Just eight days later, a Munich criminal police officer turned up in Hitler's private room, arrested the painter, took him to the police headquarters on Ett Street and put him in jail. The next day, he was presented to the Austrian consul for his extradition.

Hitler was a pitiful sight. Because the criminal police officer wouldn't allow him to change, he wore his old, paint-splattered suit. The night spent in the Ett Street jail didn't help his outward appearance either. He asked for pen and paper at the consulate and drafted the following statement of justification:

"The summons described me as artist-painter. Although I am within my rights to use this title, it is nevertheless not completely correct. I do earn my living as self-employed painter-artist, but only to pursue my further education because I have no funds whatsoever (my father was a civil servant). I can only spend a fraction of my time to earn a living because I am still learning to be an architectural painter. My income is very modest, just enough for me to get along.

"As evidence, I am enclosing my tax declaration and I

hereby request that it be returned to me. My income is estimated at 1,200 marks, which is rather high, and this should not be construed to mean that I make exactly 100 marks each month. Not at all. My monthly income fluctuates greatly but is currently certainly very low because this is the slack season in the Munich art world.

"Regarding my sin of omission in the autumn of 1909, that was an indescribably tough time for me. I was a young, inexperienced person, without any money to fall back on, and I was too proud to accept money from anybody nor to ask for it. Entirely on my own, without any help whatsoever, the few crowns and sometimes only pennies that I could get for my work were hardly enough to get me a place to sleep. For two years, my only girlfriends were worry and poverty, my only companion was a constant, unstillable hunger. I never got to know the beautiful meaning of the word 'youth.' Today, five years later, I still have the souvenirs of that time in the form of frostbite on my fingers, hands, and feet. Still, I am able to recall that time with a certain measure of joy because, after all, I survived the worst. In spite of the most dire poverty, in the midst of an often dubious environment, I always preserved my decent name, and I stand blameless before the law and pure before my conscience. Very respectfully, Adolf Hitler, artist-painter."

His pathetic confession, his subservient appearance, and the additional reference to his past "serious lung ailment" did not fail to impress the consul. Here is what the latter wrote to Linz:

"According to the impression gained here officially, his statements, made in the attached letter of justification, would appear to be entirely truthful. He also reportedly has an affliction which would render him unfit for military service. Because Hietler seems to be very much worthy of special consideration, I temporarily refrained from carrying out the extradition order and the above-named individual was instructed absolutely to report for the follow-up induction examination in Linz on February 4. Hitler, in other words, will start out on his journey to Linz if the magistrate, as a result of the above situation, and the poverty of the individual concerned, does not believe that he must allow him to report for the make-up induction examination in Salzburg."

He was allowed to report for the induction examination in Salzburg on February 5. And here is the result: "Unfit for general and limited service; too weak."

The Austrian Crown Prince Franz Ferdinand and his wife died on June 28, 1914, in Sarajevo, Bosnia, as a result of the pistol shots fired by the Serbian student Gavrilo Princip. Europe was granted only one hot summer month of shaky peace. English tourists left the Continent, Germans returned from the Cote d'Azur, Russians pulled out of Bad Homburg and Baden-Baden. Emperor William II (Willy) exchanged hectic telegrams with his "dear cousin Nicky" (Tsar Nicholas of Russia) and his other cousin, George V of England. But kinship among the crowned heads was unable to save the day. The alliances had been fashioned mercilessly. Austria-Hungary marches against Serbia, Russia against Austria-Hungary. Germany had to do its alliance duty by Austria and declared war on Russia. France, allied with Russia, had to declare war on Germany. England, a member of the Entente Cordiale, stood by France. A war broke out which, a few years later, became the "World War."

On August 1, an officer, standing on a platform in front of the Royal Palace on Odeon Square, announced the general mobilization of the Bavarian Army. Thousands lined the square, including Adolf Hitler. He had taken his hat off. His eyes shone with a strange brilliance. Later on he wrote: "Those moments were a big relief for me. I am not ashamed to say that, overwhelmed by impetuous enthusiasm, I had gone down on my knees and thanked Heaven with all my heart that I was lucky enough to live in this age."

On that same day, the "4-F" submitted an urgent petition to King Ludwig III, asking to be allowed to join a Bavarian regiment even though he was an Austrian. Days later, he received permission from the Palace Office. On August 16, in the Elizabeth School in Munich, he joined the 6th Recruit Replacement Battalion of the 2nd Bavarian Infantry Regiment No. 16. On October 8, he took the oath of loyalty to King Ludwig and then to his own sovereign, Franz Joseph, Emperor of Austria, King of Bohemia, and King of Hungary. In the middle of October, after inadequate training, the regiment was shipped to the Western Front.

Four years later, on November 11, 1918, in the Military Reserve Hospital, in Pasewalk, Pomerania, artist-painter Adolf Hitler decided "to become a politician" because of his experience in the Great War.

# Chapter Five

# Education of a Medicine Man

On September 10, 1919, Private First Class Adolf Hitler, who was assigned to Section Ib/P 4th Bavarian Reichswehr "Armed Forces" Group HQ, received a letter from his commanding officer, General Staff Captain Karl Mayr. Section Ib/P was alternately called the Information Section or Intelligence Section. It was involved in counterintelligence and intelligence activities. In his letter, the captain gave PFC Hitler the assignment of attending the meeting of a small new party and reporting to him about its leanings and participants. The party called itself the German Worker Party and wanted to hold a meeting in the back room of the Sterneckerbrau beer joint near the Isar Gate.

This was by no means an unusual assignment for a member of the military counterintelligence service, but the style in which the letter was couched was quite unusual. The General Staff officer addressed the simple PFC as "Highly Esteemed Mr. Hitler."

The very recent revolution had by no means eliminated the crass class differences in the Army. Although there was a somewhat more relaxed atmosphere in contacts between officers and enlisted men, the social barriers were crossed only rarely. What caused the captain to address his PFC with such a respectful tone of voice? What had happened to Hitler during those turbulent months since his return to Munich?

PFC Hitler was discharged from the Pasewalk Military Reserve Hospital near Stettin on November 21, 1918, after recovering from being gassed at the front. A few days later, he was back in Munich, reporting to his regiment in the Max II Barracks at Oberwiesen Field.

Since his last visit, Bavaria had become a republic. The monarchy was overthrown on November 7. The head of government was Kurt Eisner, a 53-year-old journalist and theater critic and leader of the Independent Socialists— the left wing of the SPD Social Democratic Party of Germany. The deposed King Ludwig III released all officers, enlisted men and civil servants from their loyalty oaths to him. The Regular Army had "unreservedly and sincerely placed itself in the service of the people's state, while preserving its convictions."

PFC Hitler worked in the clothing room of the barracks and stood guard for a short time in the Traunstein Prisoner-of-War Camp. He visited master tailor Popp on Schleissheimer Street and was able to see for himself that his civilian clothing, his books and painting utensils were still there. Over the next few months, Hitler kept his nose clean, not reading much, not arousing much attention and avoiding close contact with his old buddies.

Meanwhile, the situation in Munich was reaching the critical stage. Shortly before 10:00 o'clock on the morning of February 21, 1919, Kurt Eisner left his Ministry on Promenade Square to attend the opening of the State Diet on Pranner Street. In his pocket he had his resignation papers. The recent elections had been disastrous for the Left. Normally, he would take the shortcut along a corridor through the lobby of the Bayerischer Hof Hotel. But that day, of all days, he did not do so and turned into what today is Kardinal Faulhaber Street. Several shots were fired at the corner. Eisner collapsed dead in a pool of blood. The assassin was arrested and barely escaped a lynching. His name was Count Anton Arco auf Valley. He was 22 years old, a university student, former 2nd lieutenant and a member of the Rhaetia Catholic Student Association. His justification: Eisner was a Bolshevik and a Jew. Count Arco was a half-Jew.

The State legislature opened amid roaring tumult. Butcher and bartender Alois Lindner fired several shots from a Browning. Two deputies were killed and SPD

Minister Erich Auer was seriously wounded. The first
Bavarian Revolution was over as a result of the shots
fired by a noble-born lieutenant and a proletarian butcher. The second Revolution was now to begin. A "Central Council of the Bavarian Revolution" was established
in Munich and proclaimed a state of emergency. A strict
curfew was ordered, effective 7:00 p.m.

The legislative deputies left the city and went to
Nuernberg and finally to Bamberg; they formed a minor-
ity government under the moderate Social Democrat
Hoffmann. Hoffmann was given full dictatorial powers
but had no say whatsoever in Munich.

On April 6, 1919, in what used to be the bedroom of
the Queen of Bavaria in Wittelsbach Palace, left-wing Socialists and anarchists proclaimed the soviet republic. The
Communists refused to go along. For them, the soviets
were "petty-bourgeois and undisciplined people playing
at revolution."

The brains of the revolution were writers from
Schwabing, among them Gustav Landauer, Erich
Muehsam, and Ernst Toller. They had a good reputation
in literary circles, but when it came to politics, their
concepts were very fuzzy and utopian.  Forerunners of
the hippies, they wanted to turn the world into a
"meadow full of flowers." Their endless committee
meetings became magnets for "life reformers" and
plotters of all hues and shades. They were honest people
who sincerely believed in a world of anarchism that
would be free of violence and hierarchy. But they did not
have the faintest idea of administration.

Life in Munich grew chaotic. The farmers no longer
delivered food to the city which they believed "had gone
crazy." The trains ran only intermittently. Long lines
queued up in front of the local bakeries. Milk and meat
were no longer available. The citizens felt helpless and
insecure.

On April 13, 1919, with the approval of the government
in Bamberg, the Republican Guard Force staged a coup
against the anarchic soviet republic.  It was equipped and
financed by the counter-revolutionary Thule Society
which would later come to play a much larger role in

Hitler's rise. Bavarian government forces from outside Munich also came to help. But they were beaten back near Dachau by the advance troops of the Red Guards led by the passionate pacifist Ernst Toller. Inspired by the Red Army, the Communists joined the fray and fired on the main railroad station. The Republican Guard Force was eventually driven out of Munich.

The anarchist soviet republic came to an end. The Communists proclaimed a "second" communist soviet republic. Lenin dispatched Eugen Levine and Tobias Axelrod from Russia as "advisers", and they quickly took over. Rudolf Egelhofer, a 23-year-old sailor, became Munich's city commander.

The regular army units in the Munich barracks "circled the wagons" and remained on the alert. The supply situation was catastrophic. By decree, milk was given out only to "seriously ill infants."

To add to the mayhem, Prime Minister Hoffmann asked the central government in Berlin to send military assistance. The Wuerttemberg Government also offered troops. In Ohrdruf, in Thuringia, General von Epp had already assembled a well-armed Free Corps. The combined effort of the government units and the free corps captured Munich after heavy fighting on May 1 and May 2.

What was PFC Adolf Hitler doing during those turbulent days? He sat in the barracks wearing a red armband, looking out for his personal safety. He heeded the warning in the posters which read: "Anybody who acts against the representatives of the soviet republic will be shot!"

Later, in *Mein Kampf,* Hitler explained his inactivity: "I had a thousand and one plans in my head at that time. For days on end, I was trying to figure out what could be done but, in the end, it all boiled down to the rather sober realization that I, not having name recognition at all, lacked even the very least prerequisite for any kind of effective action."

During the first few days of May, Hitler was arrested by members of the Epp Free Corps and kept under investigative detention. He was shown an application for

membership in the left-wing-socialist USPD which he
had allegedly signed. But Hitler was not under arrest for
long. He had influential patrons.

Not only was he released, he became a valued member
of the investigating commission. Viktor von Koerber, one
of his early followers who later broke with him,
remarked: "Assigned to the investigating commission,
Hitler's indictments injected ruthless clarity into the
military betrayals made by the Jewish dictatorship during
Munich's soviet interlude." In his capacity as officially
appointed stool pigeon, Hitler fingered the noncommis-
sioned officers and enlisted men who had sympathized
with the communist soviets. Hundreds of his former
"buddies" died before the execution squads of the
"Whites" after a brief kangaroo court in the English Garden.

His superiors were very satisfied with his activities.
They sent him to attend special anticommunist training
courses and seminars at the University which were financed by the Reichswehr administration and by private
donors from the Thule Society. Here is where he made
the acquaintance of prominent politicians and scholars,
including government law expert Alexander von Mueller.
After that, he was detached for duty at the Lechfeld
returnee camp where soldiers returning home were
indoctrinated with anti-Semitic and anti-Marxist ideas.
Professor von Mueller was one of the first to discover
Hitler's rhetorical talent: "After the end of my lecture
and the subsequent lively discussion, I came across a
small group in the auditorium who stayed behind. The
members of that group seemed to be fascinated by a man
in the center who talked at them ceaselessly and with
growing passion in a rather odd guttural voice. I had the
strange feeling that their excitement was caused by his
oration and, at the same time, Hitler was fueled by their
excitement. I saw a pale, thin face under strands of hair
hanging down in an unmilitary fashion, with a short and
well-trimmed mustache and strikingly big, fanatically
cold, bright blue flashing eyes."

Hitler told his superiors that he was toying with the
idea of becoming a professional orator. He inquired

about the possible fees he could charge and was disappointed to learn that he could not get rich solely by making speeches. He tried his luck as a journalist, but his writings, in contrast to his spoken words, turned out to be rather stilted and boring and were rejected by several editors.

For the time being, however, he integrated himself into the intelligence division of the Reichswehr, the post-war German armed forces, becoming contact man. Hitler later maintained that he had been an "education officer," but records show no such job description. Although he continued to be a PFC, he was allowed to wear civilian clothing and was given an expense account. The very highly esteemed Mr. Hitler was on good terms with his superior officers and he was almost on the same social level as well. He became very good friends with Captain Ernst Röhm, another officer who was assigned to Reichswehr Headquarters and who was primarily concerned with the financing and supervision of militant right-wing fighting associations. Captain Ernst Röhm would prove to be a valuable ally.

On the evening of September 12, 1919, Adolf Hitler, in civilian clothes, turned up in the so-called Leiber Room in the Sternecker beer hall where a couple of dozen members and friends of the German Workers Party had gathered. He quietly listened to the presentation by Engineer Gottfried Feder, a Thule member, who talked about Jewish control over lending capital. When one of the other group members called for Bavaria to break away from the rest of Germany, Hitler could not stop from springing into action. The astonished audience let his highly subjective and aggressive remarks sweep them over. This cozy, petty-bourgeois club had never seen anything like it. After Hitler had finished his harangue, he wanted to leave the room abruptly. But the party chairman and founder, toolmaker Anton Drexler, blocked his way and thrust a pamphlet in this hand. The pamphlet was a rather plain little brochure which Drexler had written under the title *Mein Politisches Erwachen (My Political Awakening)*.

A few days later, Hitler was invited to attend a committee meeting of the DAP German Worker Party in the Altes Roemerbad Restaurant at 46 Herrn Street. At that time, the party had 54 members, six of whom were on the committee. Hitler joined the fledgling party with the knowledge and approval of Captain Mayr, his superior officer. His membership card bore the number 555 (to make more of an impression, the membership numbers began with 501) and he was immediately asked to join the committee as its seventh member, responsible for advertising and propaganda.

What persuaded Hitler to pick this obscure and insignificant group as his springboard to a political career? In *Mein Kampf,* Hitler mocked the "petty-bourgeois club" and justified his actions with these words: "This ridiculous little outfit, with its handful of members, seemed to me to offer the one and only advantage that it had not yet become rigidified into an 'organization,' rather it gave me the opportunity to engage in truly individual activity."

In his biography of Hitler, Joachim Fest described a further justification for Hitler's nascent foray into politics: "The desire to escape the oppressive demands of duty, performance and order prior to his feared discharge and reentry into civilian life very decisively guided all of the steps of this returning war veteran . . . He realized that politics was the occupation of the man who had no occupation and who does not want one either. His decision in the autumn of 1919 to join the DAP was a rejection of bourgeois society and its rigid and stringent social standards."

But Fest's argument only partially explained Hitler's true motivation. By virtue of his intelligence activities, Hitler had access to information that nobody else had. Using these connections, he discovered one very important fact. Behind this little splinter group that met regularly around its table at the beer hall, stood a mighty political, social and financial patron—the Thule Society. The Thule Society, organized in lodge-fashion, was one of Bavaria's most influential organizations.

Back in 1912, several German occultists with radical anti-Semitic inclinations decided to form a "magic" lodge, which they named the Order of Teutons. The main founders were Theodor Fritsch, a publisher of an anti-Semitic journal; Philipp Stauff, pupil of the racist Guido von List, and Hermann Pohl, the Order's chancellor. (Pohl would drop out three years later to found his own bizarre lodge, the Walvater Teutonic Order of the Holy Grail.) The Order of Teutons was organized along the lines of the Free Masons or the Rosicrucians, having differing degrees of initiation, although it was a sworn enemy to the Marxists and Jews. Only persons who could fully document that they were of pure "Aryan" ancestry were allowed to join.

In 1915, Pohl was joined by Rudolf Glauer, an adventurer of Silesian origin, who held a Turkish passport and practiced Sufi meditation. He also dabbled in astrology and was an admirer of Lanz von Liebenfels and Guido von List, both pathologically anti-Semitic. Glauer went by the name of Rudolf Freiherr von Sebottendorf, a variation on the name of the Austrian nobleman who adopted him. Sebottendorf was very wealthy, although the origin of his fortune is shrouded in darkness. He became the grand master of the Bavarian Order Province and he founded the Thule Society, with Pohl's approval, in 1918.

The Thule Society got its name from a legendary, prehistoric Nordic civilization. It chose as its symbol the rounded swastika with wreath and swords. The Thule Society is listed in the Munich Association Registry under the rather innocuous-sounding name Study Group for Teutonic Antiquity. Outwardly, the Society initially posed as a literary circle engaged in the study of ancient German history and customs.

The "inner circle" of the Thule Society was relatively small and was accessible only to the initiated masters of the esoteric. This is where occult and magic rituals were performed with great seriousness. There were secret recognition signs, symbols, and all of the paraphernalia of a mythical-esoteric brotherhood. There were crosslinks to the English Brotherhood of the Golden Dawn, to the theosophists of Madame Blavatsky, and to the notorious magician and adventurer Aleister Crowley.

The "outer circle" consisted of around 250 people in Munich and more than 1,000 altogether in Bavaria. It came to be of political interest to another 1,000 in the rest of Bavaria. Even though small in number, the members of the Thule Society were influential. The Thule Society included lawyers, judges, university professors, higher ranking police officers, industrialists, noblemen from the circle around the House of Wittelsbach, doctors and rich businessmen like the Walterspiel brothers, who owned the Vier Jahreszeiten (Four Seasons) Hotel, where the Thule Society also had its offices and meeting rooms.

During the final months of the war, the members of the Thule Society were still advocating the most extreme Pan-Germanic ideas. They subscribed to the idea of the racial superiority of the Germans and kept striving for a Greater German State of tremendous power and size.

After the Bavarian Revolution of 1918, the Thule Society became a center of the counterrevolutionary subculture. An espionage network and arms caches were organized. The Thule club rooms became a nest of resistance to the Revolution and the soviet republic. In their well-equipped workshop, they forged identity papers to enable counterrevolutionaries to get out of Munich and join the various Free Corps. Rudolf Hess, a former lieutenant and university student who had been introduced to Sebottendorf by a wartime buddy, became a particularly active organizer.

All of these conspiratorial activities were augmented by a more or less open propaganda campaign during which hundreds of thousands of anti-communist and anti-Semitic leaflets and pamphlets were distributed. One aspect which separated the Thule Society from other reactionary and nationalist associations was that it made energetic efforts in order also to win over the workers who were "poisoned by the Jewish ideas of Communism and Internationalism." The important thing was for the Thule Society to lead them back "into the nationalist camp."

Journalist Karl Harrer was given the job of founding a political "worker circle." He realized that the workers would reject any program that was presented to them by a member of the conservative "privileged" class.

Harrer knew that the mechanic Anton Drexler, who was working for the railroads, was a well-known anti-Semite, chauvinist and proletarian. With Drexler as nominal chairman, Harrer founded the German Workers Party in January 1919.

The German Workers Party was only one of many associations founded and controlled by the Thule Society. The Thule was the "mother" to the German Socialist Party, led by Julius Streicher, and the right-wing radical Oberland Free Corps. It published the *Muenchner Beobachter (Munich Observer)*, which later became the *Volkischer Beobachter (National Observer)*.

A few days before Munich was captured by the White Troops, the communists raided the offices of the Thule Society in the Vier Jahreszeiten Hotel and arrested seven members, including its secretary, Countess Heila von Westarp and Prince Gustav von Thurn und Taxis. On April 30, these prisoners were executed without court trial in the yard of the Luitpoldg High School in Schwabing. The death of these seven civilians would be used as an example of the "bestial soviet dictatorship." Eventually, hundreds were shot or beaten to death during the "White" retributive terror which followed.

Throughout the short reign of the Munich soviet republic, the Thule Society had been operating in the center of the enemy camp. With its outstanding intelligence machinery, it had decisively contributed to the Revolution's defeat. In fact, Colonel von Epp, the commander of the White Free Corps after Munich's capture, established his headquarters in the rooms of the Thule Society in the Vier Jahreszeiten Hotel.

The first few months of Hitler's political activity with the German Workers Party were marked by heated debates with the stubborn faction led by Harrer and Drexler. Hitler wanted to turn the German Workers Party into a mass-conscious fighting party, but Harrer and Drexler were hesitant, due in part to their woeful financial situation. The Thule Society was not yet supplying very much money and no one seemed to know how to build up a mass party. Hitler arranged two public meetings in obscure beer halls, and he drafted leaflets and posters, but there was no real breakthrough.

All of this changed dramatically at the end of 1919 when Hitler met his mentor, a man by the name of Dietrich Eckart. Most biographers have underestimated the influence that Eckart exerted on Hitler. Their meeting was probably more decisive than any other in Hitler's life. Eckart molded Hitler, completely changing his public persona.

When the 30-year-old Hitler met the writer Eckart, the latter was a medium-tall, fat, bald-headed man in his late fifties. He was a typical Bavarian Bohemian: hard-drinking, rough of speech, but extremely well-informed and highly educated. He was the wealthy publisher and editor-in-chief of an anti-Semitic journal which he called *Auf Gut Deutsch (In Plain German)*. He had written plays, had done a passable translation of *Peer-Gynt*, and written some mediocre poetry of a radical-nationalistic bent. More importantly, he was a well-known personality in Schwabing, with his own permanently reserved table in the Brennessel wine bar on Occam Street where he consumed several bottles of wine a day without ever appearing drunk.

Eckart not only was a heavy drinker, he also took drugs, including peyote, the South American hallucenogen, which Aleister Crowley introduced into Europe's artistic and occultist circles. In his younger years in Berlin, Eckart spent some time in a psychiatric clinic because of morphine addiction. While there, the charismatic Eckart got the other inmates to stage his plays.

But this description only scratches the surface of this remarkable man. Eckart was also a committed occultist and a master of magic. As an "initiate," he belonged to the inner circle of the Thule Society as well as other esoteric orders. He was once a Rosicrucian and Free Mason, but he had broken with them because, as a racist, he could not embrace the internationalism of Free Masonry. He had found his spiritual home in the Thule Society and the Order of Teutons.

Briefly, the creed of the Thule Society inner circle was as follows: Thule was a legendary island in the Far

North, similar to Atlantis, supposedly the center of a lost, high-level civilization. But not all secrets of that civilization had been completely wiped out. Those that remained were being guarded by ancient, highly intelligent beings (similar to the "masters" of theosophy or the White Brotherhood). The truly initiated could establish contact with these beings by means of magic-mystical rituals. The "masters" or "ancients" allegedly would be able to endow the initiated with supernatural strength and energy.

With the help of these energies of Thule, the goal of the initiated was to create a new race of supermen of "Aryan" stock who would exterminate all "inferior" races.

Nutty as this "Aryan doctrine" might sound, the rituals practiced by the Thulists were anything but harmless.

The common concept of "magic" is engrained in most people during childhood with exposure to fairytales, witches and magicians. In the area of the esoteric, magic has an entirely different significance. According to C. G. Jung, "Magic is just another term for psychic." Looked at this way, magic involves the psychic potential of the individual and its conscious use. In most cases, the average person is unable to control his psychic energies. He experiences things but is almost arbitrarily swept along by his subconscious drives, reactions and emotions. By means of certain techniques, magic can be used to establish contact with psychic energies that are not normally accessible to the individual's consciousness. That energy can be used deliberately and knowingly. Use of "ritual" is an effective means toward achieving that end.

Basically built on the same principles, all rituals are used to concentrate, as if in a convex lens, the individual's psychic energy with his senses of sight, sound, smell, taste and touch. The goal of the magic ritual is consciousness expansion. It is in this state that the master can grow beyond his natural limitations.

The moment an advanced master understands the principles of psychic energy, he can generate these forces within himself and use them according to his will.

Like other esoterics, the Thulists engaged in magic practices, such as the Hindu's control of the Kundalini energy and the creation of desirable situations through concentrated, intensive and systematic visualization. As in all magic practices lights, colors, circles, triangles, symbols, aromatic substances and so forth were used as aids for the concentration of the will.

According to C. G. Jung, there is nothing dark and mysterious about magic. It is nothing more than consciousness expansion, an enhancement of human energy potential by means of special phychological techniques. Whether the magic is "good" or "bad," "white" or "black," depends only on its purpose. A "white magician" strives for self-discovery and self-liberation with no intention of bringing harm to others. The "black magician" wants to exercise power, rule over others and gain material goods. The rituals of the Thulists definitely involved "black magic."

There can be no doubt that Eckart—who had been alerted to Hitler by other Thulists—trained Hitler in magic techniques. He saw that there was an untrained potential in him and wanted to shape it. With Eckart as his mentor, the gauche and inhibited Hitler—the unsuccessful painter, former PFC, who had not even been promoted to corporal because of "lack of leadership qualities," quite suddenly developed astonishing qualities and talents. He became an outstanding organizer and propagandist capable of leading people astray and sweeping them along with him. In a short period of time he was able to move the obscure little workers party from the club and beer hall atmosphere to a mass movement. The emotion-charged lay speaker became an expert orator, capable of mesmerizing a vast audience.

An excerpt from the police records regarding one of his first big meetings contains the following passage: "After that, Mr. Hitler spoke, but he talked himself into such a rage that one could not understand much." A short time later, with the help of Eckart, he had mastered the secrets of the art of oratory to such a degree that observers credited him with the force of an "African medicine man or an Asian shaman." Rational, highly educated people would go to his meetings as skeptics but would leave them as religious converts, as if in a trance. Psycho-historian Alan Bullock said Hitler had the "magnetism of a hypnotist." What Hitler said at these meetings was irrelevant; it was the way he said it that fascinated people—turned even his opponents into enthusiastic followers.

He became the most prominent personality in the party. He caused Harrer to drop out, and he pushed Drexler, the nominal chairman, to the sidelines. He filled key positions with his own friends from the Thule Society and the Reichswehr. During the summer of 1920, upon his suggestion, the party was renamed the National Socialist German Worker Party (NSDAP). The name German Workers Party had not been very attractive to conservative nationalists. The new name was intended to equally attract nationalists and proletarians.

To go along with the new name his mass movement also required a flag with a powerful symbol. Among many designs under consideration, Hitler picked the one suggested by Thule member, Dr. Krohn: A red cloth, symbolizing socialism, with a white circle in the middle standing for nationalism, with a black swastika in a white circle expressing the "victorious struggle of the Aryan." (Note: the swastika is certainly not an Indo-Germanic symbol. It is an esoteric symbol, found not only among Mongolian peoples, such as in Tibet, but also among the Indians of North and South America.)

Hitler made one very important alteration in Dr. Krohn's design: Krohn's swastika was right-handed and rotated clockwise. To the esoteric individual, this shape symbolized light, white magic, creative force. Hitler insisted on a left-handed swastika which turned counter-clockwise—a symbol of darkness, black magic and destruction.

In 1923, shortly before his death, Dietrich Eckart wrote to a friend: "Follow Hitler! He will dance, but it will be to my tune. We have given him the means to maintain contact with them (meaning the "masters"). Don't grieve for me. I have influenced history more than any other German."

One should not underestimate occultism's influence on Hitler. His subsequent rejection of Free Masons and esoteric movements, of theosophy and anthroposophy, of "ethnic fools"—a rejection that went all the way to physical persecution—does not necessarily mean otherwise. Hitler knew that the public exposure of his esoteric interests would hinder his political rise and expose him to ridicule. Once upon a time, Hermann Rauschning remarked: "Nazism's deepest roots lie in hidden places."

Thus, the ideology of Nazism did not rest on a cool analysis of economics and social science, as does Marxism. It was fashioned by mystical and occultistic writers like Madame Blavatsky, Houston Stewart Chamberlain, Guido von List, Lanz von Liebenfels and Theodor Fritsch. Although Hitler later ridiculed and denounced many of them, he did dedicate his book *Mein Kampf* to his teacher Dietrich Eckart, his magic mentor, whom he once, in boundless hubris, called his "John the Baptizer." Eckart once told his fellow brothers in the inner circle of the Thule Society: "He is the one for whom I was the mere prophet and forerunner."

# Chapter Six

# The Seeds of Wealth and Power

Hitler drew his back pay on April 1, 1920, and was officially discharged from the Army. At first, he had hesitated to take this step. His position in the Intelligence Division had given him freedom of movement, free room and board in the barracks, plus a regular income he hardly ever needed to touch. But Dietrich Eckart convinced him that the time had come to focus all of his efforts on the party's development.

Hitler rented a furnished room from Mrs. Reichert at 41 Thiersch Street in the Lehel section of Munich, a typical petty-bourgeois section in a convenient location.

His friend Ernest "Putzi" Hanfstaengl later described Hitler's place as "clean and orderly although relatively narrow and sparsely furnished. On the floor, there was cheap, worn linoleum along with some threadbare rugs. On the wall opposite the bed was a chair and a table, as well as rough-hewn shelves holding Hitler's treasured books."

Hanfstaengl also described the content of these bookshelves. On the top shelf stood the "show works," mostly historical tomes and biographies. "But then began an instant descent from Mars to Venus: As you poked in the next row of light novels and murder mysteries, to get somewhat closer to Hitler's literary inner sanctum, I found the works of the talented Jew Eduard Fuchs neatly lined up and well-worn, 'suitable' for poisoning the normal sensitivity of the Aryan individual. *Geschichte der erotischen Kunst (History of Erotic Art)* as well as the diverse, rich and rather daring *Illustrierte Sittengeschichten (Illustrat-ed Tales of Morals])*, both by Fuchs, were on Hitler's shelves."

Hitler seems to have been an ideal roomer for Mrs. Reichert. "A really fine man, that Mr. Hitler. And he always pays his rent exactly on time. That way, you don't mind that he is moody occasionally."

In those days Hitler usually wore a simple, dark blue suit (often covered with dandruff on the shoulders) a long, black overcoat and a broad-brimmed, black floppy hat. Sometimes he displayed rather bizarre tastes in his dress. An eyewitness reported that Hitler once wore a purple shirt, a brown vest and a fire-engine red necktie with his blue suit. When Pfeffer von Salomon (later his top SA Commander) met Hitler for the first time, Hitler was wearing an old cutaway, yellow leather shoes and a rucksack on his back. Pfeffer was so taken aback that he forgot to introduce himself.

Hitler spent most of his time during the day at the party's business office, which he had set up in a basement room of the Sternecker beer hall. In the evening, the inner circle of party members frequently met in the Café Neumaier on the Food Market.

In contrast to the other full-time party officials, Hitler saw to it that he was not carried on the books as a party employee with an official salary. He realized that if he were an employee he would have had to follow instructions from his superiors. But this was neither what Hitler, nor Dietrich Eckart had in mind.

So then, where did Hitler get money to live on? Other party members wanted to know. His official job title, by which he was registered with the police, was still "painter." But he neither painted nor sold pictures. However,as fellow party members from the early days noticed, he always had money in his pocket.

Hitler had various income sources. First of all, it is very likely that, even after his separation from the Army, he continued working for the Intelligence Division on a fee basis. There are indications that Captain Röhm—who was in charge of the press and propaganda activities of the Reichwehr—not infrequently gave him an unreported allowance, drawn from a secret fund of the Reichwehr Command. Hitler also collected fees for his speeches, depending on how much money came in from admission tickets and donations. Once, after addressing a gathering of the still independent German Socialist Party in Nuernberg, Hitler was very peeved when the envelope, discreetly given to him by Julius Steicher, contained only 600 marks. After a heated dispute, Steicher increased the fee to 1,000 marks, a fairly substantial amount of money.

Hitler's real nest egg was Dietrich Eckart, who freely spent money on his protégé. Eckart usually paid Hitler's coffeehouse tab, slipped him cash and frequently invited him to dinner in good restaurants, including the Walterspiel Restaurant in the Vier Jahreszeiten Hotel.

Eckart also saw to it that Hitler paid more attention to his outward appearance. Once he told him that his long black overcoat and floppy hat made him look like a Galician Jew. To correct Hitler's appearance Eckart bought Hitler a new trenchcoat (the status symbol of the "Aryan" British officer) and a grey velour hat. Hitler's ubiquitous riding crop, which during the Twenties became one of his signature pieces, sprang from a suggestion by Eckart. Young Rudolf Hess, also a Thule Society member with whom Hitler became close friends, also advised him to swap the starched, old-fashioned "choker collar" for a soft American-style shirt.

Those were the least of the services that Eckart rendered to his upwardly mobile pupil. Above and beyond all these other things, Eckart rescued him from the musty ambience of the Café Neumaier and introduced him to moneyed society.

Hitler's very first foray into the world of the wealthy took place while he was a PFC in the 41st Rifle Regiment and a staff member of Captain Mayr's Intelligence Division.

On March 13, 1920, reactionary circles had just staged a successful coup d'état in Berlin. The coup was headed by East Prussian General Karl Kapp, who was proclaimed Reich chancellor. Militarily, the coup was supported by the Ehrhardt Free Corp Navy Brigade. President Ebert and the German government fled to Dresden and then to

Stuttgart. The coup was not supported by the population, and the Social Democrats called a general strike. The coup collapsed after just a few days.

But in Munich, the conservative followers of the Wittelsbach monarchy exploited the confused situation in Berlin by launching a coup d'état of their own. The Social Democratic administration under Johannes Hoffman was forced to resign by means of an ultimatum. The new administration, supported by the military, was headed by Gustav von Kahr, a reactionary monarchist.

To establish contact with the insurrectionists in Berlin, the people in Munich sent two liaison men to Berlin. They picked Dietrich Eckart of the Thule Society and Adolf Hitler, who Captain Mayr and Captain Röhm had pursuaded the Kahr administration to take on board. A military plane was made ready for Eckart and Hitler. The aircraft lost its way during a thunderstorm and had to make an emergency landing 70 kilometers southwest of Berlin in Jueterbog.

The trains were not running and the streets leading to Berlin had been barricaded by striking workers. At the small airfield in Jeuterbog the two emissaries from Munich were questioned by officials of the ousted, but still legal, government. If they had stated the true purpose of their visit, they would have been executed. Dietrich Eckart passed himself off as a Munich businessman who had urgent affairs to take care of in Berlin, and introduced Hitler as his bookkeeper. After some discussion the travelers were able to continue their journey. Hitler and Eckart arrived in Berlin at precisely the same moment the Kapp government resigned.

Nonetheless, Eckart had excellent business connections in Berlin, and introduced Hitler to Borsig, a locomotive manufacturer, and to other industrialists. Eckart also introduced Hitler to General Erich von Ludendorff, the second-highest ranking general of World War I. Ludendorff was the leading officer of the right-wing patriotic camp. He shook hands with the PFC and chatted in a friendly manner; Hitler positively gushed with reverence. His behavior at the time was still awkward, bordering on servility. An eyewitness reported that Hitler hardly spoke at all, continually bowing. After every sentence that Ludendorff spoke Hitler stood up and stammered, "Yes, your Excellency. As your Excellency says."

His introduction into the salon of Mrs. Helene Bechstein, wife of the piano manufacturer Carl Bechstein, was a little more relaxed. The Bechsteins lived in a large home in the center of the city, built in the grand-bourgeois style of the 1870s. The interior decor was gawdy. Around Mrs. Bechstein's neck and her arms were cherry-sized diamonds. Hitler was welcomed with an amiable smile and performed his first, perfect hand-kissing act since his dancing lesson days in Linz. Helen Bechstein was captivated by the shyness of this 30-year-old man, but when the conversation turned to politics, Hitler opened up. Before the evening was over he had won his first, and most faithful, lady supporter from the high society. With Mrs. Bechstein as his patroness, he was able to gain access to the highest circles of society. The Bechsteins frequently visited Munich, where they stayed in a luxury suite at the Bayerischer Hof. While Carl Bechstein maintained a rather aloof relationship to Hitler, Helene gradually became a sort of motherly friend of the aspiring politician. She even toyed with the idea of officially adopting the parentless Hitler until her husband admonished her not to go too far in her enthusiasm. At any rate, she saw to it that he received large donations for the party as well as his own personal needs. Later, during his trial in April 1924 for his part in a failed Munich coup, Helene Bechstein testified as follows: "In addition to the regular financial support which my husband channeled to the NSDAP, I also gave Mr. Hitler a number of contributions—not in the form of money. Instead, I gave him art objects with the remark that he could do with them what he wanted. These were art objects of great value."

Whenever the Bechsteins came to Munich, Hitler was invited to dine with them in their luxury suite. "I was quite embarassed in my blue suit," Hitler later told Ernst "Putzi" Hanfstaengl. "All the servants wore livery and before the meal we drank nothing but champagne. All the faucets in the bathroom were gold plated and, just imagine, you could even regulate the water temperature to suit you." During one of those evenings, Mrs. Bechstein discreetly handed her protégé an envelope full of money and urged him to buy a tuxedo, some starched shirts, and patent-leather shoes. As a rising young politician, she believed, he was important enough to look sharp among the hoi polloi. After Hitler bought his patent-leather shoes with Mrs. Bechstein's money, he frequently wore them during the day, until Eckart pointed out that the shoes were meant for evening and were counterproductive at mass meetings and among the poor party members.

After Hitler and Eckart had returned to Munich, his mentor introduced him to the renowned publisher Hugo Bruckmann, who put out the works of the fascist writer Houston Stewart Chamberlain, Richard Wagner's son-in-law. His wife Elsa Bruckmann (nee Cantacuzene), a Romanian princess, also became a quick disciple of Hitler's. She had a big fortune of her own and frequently made donations to Hitler. She was also very possessive and jealous of him, as he soon found out. "One fine day," Hitler later reported, "I discovered an unexpected reaction from Mrs Bruckman. I'd invited a very pretty Munich society lady to join us for a chat. As we took our leave, Mrs. Bruckman detected that her lady visitor displayed a certain degree of interest in me. As a result, she never invited the two of us together again."

Hitler soon became a familiar figure among the more well-to-do of Munich, especially among the women of advanced age who seemed positively enchanted by him. Usually he'd give the hostess a big bouquet of roses and, as he kissed her hand, he'd bow in the exaggerated Viennese style. When he talked to women, he'd even change his voice. While often harsh and guttural, his voice became smooth and he affected a Viennese accent. During conversation, he gave each woman the impression that he was completely captivated by her and her alone. Though most women expected some kind of ruffian, they were swept away when they suddenly discovered themselves alone with a charmer. "I simply melted away in his presence," said Mrs. Bruckman. "I would have done anything for him."

In Munich society, it soon became chic to be able to show Hitler off to the other guests at soirees, despite the fact that he quite consciously cultivated the image of a social outsider. Historian Karl Alexander von Mueller described one of Hitler's appearances. "The rest of us were sitting in the drawing room, when the apartment bell rang. Through the open door we could see Hitler, in the narrow corridor, as he greeted the hostess with almost subservient courtesy, how he put down his riding crop, his velour hat, and his trenchcoat, after which he finally unbuckled a belt with a revolver and likewise hung it on a clothing hook, which seemed odd to us. None of us knew it yet, but each of these details in dress and behavior were already calculated to produce a desired effect."

Even his lapses into rage were staged quite consciously. Once, according to eyewitness reports, he was making light conversation when the hostess suddenly made a friendly remark about the Jews. "Hitler began to talk. And then he jumped up, still talking or, rather, screaming in a voice more penetrating than ever heard before. A child woke up in the next room and began to cry. Hitler suddenly broke off, walked toward the hostess, apologized, and took his leave with a kiss on the hand, walking quickly out of the house without so much as a glance at the other guests."

At the fund raiser for the party and for himself, Hitler developed skills that no one suspected he had. Whenever he got cash, receipts were never asked for or given. Once, when a money donor asked for a receipt, Hitler handed him a copy of the party program. Hitler was one of the few committee members who was not involved in any supervised activities. Chairman Anton Drexler continued to work during the day as mechanic with the railroad and the other officials also had their regular jobs. Whenever other party members asked him how he was making ends meet, Hitler would become extremely rude, telling them he was sacrificing his health for the party, that for weeks on end he was living exclusively on Tirolian apples and that a lady grocer on Thiersch Street, a certain Mrs. Schweyer, would occasionally give him a piece of bread or a jar of marmalade.

Hitler didn't just tap the rich. Other party members loved to help this inspirational boss who got along without a party salary. At least twice a week, Hitler visited Quirin Diestl, the owner of a stationery store near the Regina Hotel. Diestl always scraped a little money together for him.

In the summer of 1920, Hitler was obsessed with the idea of getting a car. He frequently showed up in the salesrooms of car dealers and looked at the models. One Monday evening in the Café Neumaier, he informed his speechless party members that they'd have to buy him a car so he could get to the meetings faster. A car would give him—and the party—a certain amount of dignity and put them a notch above the Marxists who walked or took the streetcar. Somehow Hitler managed to rebut all the counter-arguments and the party treasury scraped the money together for a vehicle that looked "like a horse-drawn coach without a roof." At first, Hitler, who'd learned how to drive while in the Army, drove the car himself, but it broke down so often he became disenchanted with it. He returned the pre-historic car to the party and, with his own money, he purchased a used "Selwe." The new car did not look much better than the old one, but it was in better shape. From then on, Hitler was never again seen getting into a streetcar or on a bus.

Next he argued that because he had bought the car with his own money, he deserved to have a driver. Again, this would make a more dignified impression on people. Drexler and the treasury gave in and appointed a party member and auto mechanic named Haug to drive the propaganda chairman around on a full-time basis. Ernst Haug had a sister named Jenny, a pleasant good-looking young lady, who became quite smitten with Hitler and frequently volunteered to drive him around without pay. On those occasions, Jenny would show up in a leather jacket with a pistol strapped to a shoulder holster, looking like a lady storm trooper. Rumors had it that Jenny dragged Hitler from the platonic drawing room atmosphere of his rich older ladies' homes into the country for love-making, Bavarian style. A jeweler named Fuess allegedly set up a love nest for them in a room behind his shop on Cornelius Street. Putzi Hanfstaengl, who claims that Hitler was impotent, denied this ever happened. Be that as it may, the pair was seen together on many an evening in the coffeehouses and bars but, according to eyewitnesses, dear Jenny had always fallen asleep in Morpheus' arms, worn out by Hitler's constant monologues.

In December 1920, Hitler made a move that would pave the way for his party to gain real political strength: He bought a newspaper. The *Muencherner Beobachter*, renamed in 1919 to *Volkischer Beobachter*, had been the official publication of the Thule Society since 1918 and was considered the leading right-wing, anti-Semitic newspaper of Bavaria. The major stockholder was Kaether Bierbaumer, the scurrilous Sebottendorf's lover. Other stockholders included Dora Kunze, Sebottendorf's sister, Nazi Gottfried Feder, Dr. Wilhelm Gutberlet and Theodor Heuss, a paper manufacturer.

The *Volksischer Beobachter* was on the brink of bankruptcy in December 1920. The stockholders were ready to sell the paper along with the Franz Eher Publishing Company for 120,000 marks. Through General von Epp, Dietrich Eckart was able to secure 60,000 marks from the secret German Army fund for which he made out his own personal IOU. That left 60,000 marks to be raised by the party treasury. Anton Drexler, however, felt that Hitler's desire to purchase a newspaper was an unsafe and megalomaniacal idea.

Hitler went to Augsberg to visit Gottfried Grandel, a local industrialist. Grandel, who had previously given money to the party, met Hitler at a soiree in Munich. After Hitler had worn him down with several hours of conversation, Grandel promised to help. He and Simon Eckart, a relative of Dietrich and a leading official at the Hansa Bank, provided the security that made it possible for the deal to go through. When Kaethe Bierbaumer and Dora Kunz suddenly demanded cash payment for the transaction, Grandel paid 55,000 marks out of his pocket. Hitler got the remaining 5,000 marks from Dr. Gutberlet.

The next order of business for Hitler was to extract his revenge on the party for refusing to relinquish its funds for the newspaper. During the following years, he rounded up enough money from his various patrons and patronesses to cover Eckart's IOU and repay Dr. Grandel. On November 16, 1921, Hitler appeared at the Registration Court in Munich to declare that he now held all shares of the *Volkischer Beobachter* and the Franz Eher Publishing Company.

At last, he had a respectable occupation: Hitler was a newspaper publisher. In the beginning his business venture yielded little or no return, but it offered him a valuable political platform. Although he placed the paper in the party's service, he maintained total control over the paper's content and the makeup of its editorial staff. He appointed Dietrich Eckart publisher and Hermann Esser, a 21 year old, editor-in-chief. Esser had once done volunteer work for a newspaper and had briefly worked as press officer under Röhm at the Army Group Headquarters. Esser knew how to write in a folksy and clear style. He was particularly untiring in inventing juicy bedroom secrets about Jews and rich profiteers. Esser rejected the more puritanical wing of the party because he had a more dubious lifestyle. He had a keen eye for the tales of scandals involving others, and he publicly boasted that his many mistresses always paid his expenses. On several occasions, young Rudolf Hess, who was considered a "goody two shoes", tried to get Hitler to fire Esser, but Hitler kept saying that he knew Esser was a scoundrel, but he is an excellent editor and he needed him.

Shortly after the acquisition of the paper, Hitler ran into his old company first sergeant from their days on the western front. This was Max Amann. Being a member of the Thule Society, he was already acquainted with Dietrich Eckart. At Hitler's urging, his wartime buddy soon joined the NSDAP. Amann was a short, powerfully built man with a big head and a short neck. His rugged appearance belied his intelligence. Amann was an able administrator who had studied law and had held a good job with the Bavarian Mortgage and Exchange Bank. At Hitler's urging he quit his job at the bank and became the NSDAP's business manager. Amann also managed the newspaper. Hitler made an excellent choice with Amann. He introduced efficient business methods to the party and the newspaper. He was absolutely loyal to Hitler. In later years, Amann made sure that both he and his Führer would become multimillionaires.

Because of his excellent connections with the Thule Society, Amann was able, during the early days of the party, to get short-term loans that would have been impossible for others to obtain. In more than one instance, Amann was able to secure payment postponements for the newspaper when its survival was at stake.

The first critical clash between the NSDAP and Hitler took place in the summer of 1921. For months the NSDAP had been negotiating withcompeting nationalist parties—most importantly with Julius Streicher's German Socialist Party—in hope of leading to closer cooperation. However, all communication efforts failed because of Hitler. He did not want to make the party bigger through merger; he demanded the complete subjugation and dissolution of other groups. Once dissolved, the group members would then be allowed to join the NSDAP individually.

It became increasingly difficult for the other committee members to deal with Hitler. They appreciated his propaganda efforts and his fund-raising ability, but his ever-increasing demand for power troubled them. Their goal was to put the movement on a broad base, to unite it in a cooperative form with like-thinking groups in the North and to confine Hitler to Munich as their propaganda mouth. Hitler, on the other hand, demanded absolute primacy for the NSDAP under the Munich party directorate. The gulf between the old, plain and simple charter members and the Hitler clique, as it was bitingly called, grew wider. The "old-timers" reproached Hitler for his authoritarian appetites, his wealthy bourgeois friends and above all for his extravagant lifestyle. In the early summer of 1921, Hitler received a warning letter from party member Heinrich Dolle. Dolle, a man with a penchant for Germanomania in the style of Jahn, the father of German calisthenics: "Thee spendeth too much time sitting in the Fledermaus Bar with Dietrich Eckart. That is not good for thee!"

The crisis came to a head shortly thereafter. Amann kept Hitler informed on the plots that were being hatched against him. With the intention of enticing his opponents into making an ill-advised move, Hitler left for Berlin in late June for a six week visit. Leaving Eckart, Esser and Amann behind to mind the store, they continued to keep Hitler informed about developments by phone. Exactly as Hitler had suspected, Drexler resumed merger negotiations with the socialist right-wing parties in his absence and without his official knowledge.

Meanwhile in Berlin, Hitler stayed at the Bechstein home and took speech lessons every afternoon to strengthen his voice and eradicate his Austrian provincial dialect. He met prominent reactionaries, including Count von Reventlow, a Nationalist leader, and Walter Stennes, leader of the Free Corps, who soon thereafter joined the Nazis. Count von Reventlow's wife, a French countess, called Hitler the coming Messiah. Hitler also enjoyed the night life in Berlin, which he later called in *Mein Kampf* a "breeding ground of vice and shamelessness."

When Hitler learned about Drexler's and the committee's high-handed actions, he immediately returned to Munich. He showed up at party headquarters while he was furiously angry. On July 11, the committee demanded that he justify his role and give the party straight answers about his financial situation. Hitler dramatically announced that he was leaving the NSDAP at once.

The committee members were aghast. Drexler tried to patch things up. Three days later, with Dietrich Eckart's help, Hitler drafted a letter in which he stated the conditions for his return to the party. It was an ultimatum: "The committee must resign immediately, Hitler must be given the position of "First Chairman" with dictatorial authority, the Munich NSDAP must be in control and, finally, there must be no mergers with other parties. "Compromise on our part is utterly out of the question," Hitler wrote.

He didn't expect his conditions to be accepted. He was

fully prepared to break with the party and to create his own organization from the ground up. He knew that without him and his effective propaganda work, the "old" NSDAP was doomed. On the next day, an astonishing letter arrived from party headquarters. The letter read: "In recognition of your tremendous knowledge, your services rendered to the movement's progress at great self-sacrifice and your rare talent as an orator, the committee is prepared to grant you dictatorial powers. The committee would be most happy if you, after re-joining the party, would take over the position of First Chairman which had repeatedly been offered to you long ago by Mr. Drexler. Drexler will remain on the commit-tee as an associate and, if you so desire, he would hold the same position in the action committee. If you were to consider his complete separation from the movement to be useful, we would bring this up at the next annual meeting."

The committee had effectively castrated itself. From then on, there was no more talk about Hitler's financial manipulations.

Triumphantly, Hitler called a special membership meet-ing. At the time he still was not an official party member. Drexler was never informed of the meeting. In fact, he read about the invitation in the *Volkischer Beo-bachter*.

Even for someone as compromising as Drexler, Hitler had gone too far. On July 25, he turned up at Section VI of the Munich Police, which handled political matters, and made the following statement: "The signers of the appeal, Hitler and Esser (during Hitler's absence, Drexler had kicked Esser out of the party because of the latter's 'dirty private life'), are not party members and are not authorized to summon the members to a meeting in the party's name." Drexler also wanted it on the record before the authorities that Mr. Hitler was bent on revol-ution and the use of violence, whereas he, Drexler, was trying to achieve the party's goals by legal, parliamentary methods. The police official said that he was not author-ized to get involved in internal party squabbles.

On the same day, Hitler's opponents in the NSDAP

distributed leaflets in the streets of Munich, attacking the propaganda chairman as a traitor: "His lust for power and personal ambition pushed him to the point where he is causing disunity in our ranks, and he is playing into the hands of Jewry and its helpers. He intends to use the party as springboard for unclean purposes. Undoubtedly, he is the tool of shady men behind the scenes, which explains why he anxiously hides his private life and his origins. Whenever party members asked him where his money was coming from, he became angry and excited. Thus his conscience cannot be clean, especially considering his excessive contacts with ladies—among whom he refers to himself as 'King of Munich'."

The leaflet further accused Hitler of "pathological power mania" and concludes with the demand: "The tyrant must be overthrown!"

At this point, Eckart assumed the role of middleman in an effort to avert a complete break. A special membership meeting was held on July 29 with 554 members attending. The head table was led by the expelled Hermann Esser. With just one opposing vote (probably Drexler's), Hitler was elected first chairman of the NSDAP "with dictatorial powers." Anton Drexler was effectively neutralized by being given the figurehead position of honorary chairman. Esser was reinstated and Hitler officially joined the party. He was given membership number 3680. The committee was abolished through an amendment in the by-laws. Now Hitler no longer had to answer to anyone. The "leader principle" had been introduced. The NSDAP was firmly in his control.

From that day on, the Byzantine ritual surrounding the Führer figure had begun. Hermann Esser was the first to use the phrase "our Führer"; in *Volkischer Beobachter,* Dietrich Eckart celebrated Hitler as a "selfless, self-sacrificing, dedicated and honorable man." In the same issue, Rudolf Hess allowed himself to be carried away in a fit of quasi-religious enthusiasm by glorifying Hitler's "purest will," his "admirable knowledge," and his "clear intellect," closing with the sentence: "Adolf Hitler is pure reason incarnate."

In spite of the religious glorification that Hitler

received as the new party chairman from the pens of Eckart and Hess, in spite of his growing feeling of security among grand bourgeois society, Hitler still felt most comfortable among party members with working class backgrounds. These were the ones who were devoted to him unquestioningly and totally. They listened in rapt silence to his monologues—which they only vaguely understood—and they offered him the rough and chummy atmosphere of warmth reminiscent of his days in the Vienna Men's Home.

Among these new intimates were Emil Maurice, an unemployed watchmaker, who, in spite of his puny stature, made a name for himself in barroom brawls as a brutal fighter; Christian Weber, a former hotel servant, a loud Bavarian "man-and-a-half" who worked as bouncer in a disreputable dive, who was at home at the Daglfing racetrack, and who occasionally dealt in horses; and the journeyman butcher Ulrich Graf who became Hitler's official bodyguard. While the virtuous Rudolf Hess was intent on keeping his distance, Esser and Amann were only too happy to join this boisterous group in the evenings when they invaded the Osteria Bavaria, the Schelling Salon or the Bratwurstgloeckle Restaurant near the Church of Our Lady.

The Schloessl Restaurant on Belgrad Street and the Eiserne Kreuz Restaurant on Reichenbach Street were also among the eating places preferred by the group around Weber and Graf. Soon, the deformed, equally talented and hard-drinking photographer Heinrich Hoffmann joined this clique. Hoffmann had a photo studio with a store opposite the editorial offices of the *Volkischer Beobachter* on Schelling Street. He also had a great store of jokes which he was always ready to tell. Later, he would be rewarded by being named "court photographer" of the Third Reich. He also became one of Hitler's most lucrative business partners.

Hitler spent hour after hour in the Café Heck near the Royal Garden, eating pastries and whipped-cream cakes. A table had been permanently reserved there for him and his companions. One of the party leader's favorite pursuits was the cinema. On some days he did no work

whatsoever for the party or the newspaper and instead
watched three or four movies, one after the other—
mostly American films starring Charlie Chaplin, Buster
Keaton, Mae West or Douglas Fairbanks. While watching
the films he would be gobbling down mountains of
pralines.

During these excursions to the movies, he was often
accompanied by Rudolf Hess. He had developed a special
fondness for the straight-laced Hess and enjoyed provok-
ing him and making fun of his strict code of morality.
Hess—who was always extremely formal, even among his
friends—was also disconcerted by the fact that Hitler, in
the living room of his landlady, Mrs. Reichert, in which
he was allowed to receive guests, liked to meet visitors
without a necktie, his trousers held up by suspenders and
felt slippers on his feet. He was successful in explaining
to Hitler that this was not in keeping with the dignity of
a party leader.

Dietrich Eckart also had to keep reminding Hitler not
to become involved in physical clashes with opponents.
At the end of 1921, Hitler, leading a goon squad that included Graf, Maurice, Weber and Hess, had broken up a
meeting of the League of Bavarian Separatists, and had
personally pulled their leader, Otto Ballerstedt, from the
podium and beaten him up. The Thule sympathizers in
the police headquarters were no longer able to settle such
matters out of court. On January 12, 1922, Hitler was sentenced to three months in prison. There were discussions
in the State legislature about expelling Hitler as a troublesome alien. Hitler served only one month of his sentence in the Stadelheim prison in the summer of 1922.

Before he named Max Amann business manager for
the party and the publishing house, Hitler had always
looked upon money as a means for creating a pleasant
but modest lifestyle for himself. He wanted enough
money to afford a car, to take occasional trips, to pay for
his frequent visits to the coffeehouses and restaurants or
to take his lady acquaintances to dinner in style. His
spartan living quarters were satisfactory to him. For the
time being, he wasn't interested in saving money or in
making safe investments.

One can therefore assume with certainty that he indeed channeled a large part of the donations from wealthy supporters—which he personally cashed in—into the party treasury. Financially, he considered the party to be his own private enterprise, an investment in his future. He intentionally saw to it that he wasn't put on the party payroll in order to propagate a myth that is still believed today: that Hitler never exploited his activities for the purpose of personal enrichment. His "part-time" activity, however, offered the advantage of being able to conceal his real income from nosy questioners within the party. After his takeover in the summer of 1921, he was no longer asked about his livelihood. Oddly enough, Hitler's name never showed up in the tax records between 1919 and 1925. Why the Finance Office didn't bother him during those initial years is something that can no longer be determined and is one of the secrets of the Bavarian treasury.

It was Max Amann, the former bank employee, who helped Hitler make his first long-term investment. As stated earlier, *Volkiskcher Beobachter* had been purchased at the end of 1920 with an interest-free loan of 120,000 marks. Eckart's IOU was held by the German Armed Forces while Hitler's was with Grandel, the manufacturer in Augsburg.

At the time the newspaper was purchased, the American dollar was worth around 20 marks. (The prewar exchange rate had been four gold marks per dollar). Six months later, the rate of inflation in Germany was 75 percent and rising rapidly. By November 1922, the dollar sold for 180 marks. The German paper mark was also losing value, but it was still possible to pay debts at their face amount, unless the contract expressly provided for repayment in foreign currency or in gold. Amann advised Hitler to become the sole owner of the shares in the newspaper and in the Franz Eher Publishing House. All he needed to redeem the IOUs from the Reichswehr and Grandel were a couple of donations from rich patrons. With just a small amount of foreign currency he could easily buy out his IOUs.

Although no one knows for sure who gave Hitler the

necessary foreign currency, 666 dollars—converted into
120,000 German marks—was enough to turn the *Volkis-cher Beobachter* over to him. With Amann's encourage-
ment, Hitler had become one of those inflation profiteers
whom he mercilessly castigated in speeches.

The inflation merry-go-round began to turn faster in
1922. In November, the dollar sold for 4,450 marks. The
main reason for the galloping inflation was the repara-
tions called for under the Treaty of Versailles. The
payments amounted to 132 million gold marks and had
to be paid in foreign currency or in gold. In order to
meet these payments, Germany's Reichbank was forced
to surrender its gold reserves and buy foreign currency
on the international market. More and more paper
money had to be printed for domestic use and that paper
became more and more worthless.   While big-time
German capitalists with foreign connections were able to
build empires by paying debts and redeeming loans with
worthless paper marks, the average German lost his shirt.
In just two months, from November 1922 until January
1923, the dollar's value increased ten-fold to 41,500 marks.
If Hitler and Amann had waited until early 1923, they
could have had *Volkischer Beobachter* for around three dollars.

In January 1923, the German currency collapsed completely when the French army occupied the Ruhr Region
in retaliation for the still outstanding reparation payments. The German government moved to help the hundreds of thousands in the Ruhr Region who had become
unemployed as a result of their passive resistance against
the French forces. More and more money was printed to
provide these vast sums.

On February 1, 1923, the U.S. dollar was worth 41,500
marks. Then seventy-five billion marks were printed
daily. Two thousand printing plants and more than 300
paper factories were kept busy turning out bank notes.
On May 22, the price of the dollar had risen to 57,000
marks and a month later it was 136,000 marks. On July 8,
the German consumer had to plunk down 4,000 marks
for 1 liter of milk. On July 25, the dollar shot up to
600,000 marks.  From that moment on, prices rose every

hour on the hour and employees were now paid daily. Wives were waiting at the factory gates for their husbands' daily pay, immediately rushing to the nearest shops to buy food for the evening meal.

On July 18, *Vossische Zeitung* reported about a physician who closed his clinic and took a job in a nightclub where he sang all the latest hit songs. Many of those songs expressed the mood of the nation. His former medical assistant accompanied him on the piano.

Anyone who had access to a stable foreign currency was able to live like a king. Ernest Hemingway, who was working as a journalist in Europe at that time, reported about a couple of days which he spent in a first-class German Hotel. The bill came to millions of marks—or 20 cents per day.

On August 1, the dollar exchange rate topped the million-mark level. On August 7, it was 3.3 million marks to the dollar, and in September it rose to 5.6 million. On October 19, it rose to 12 billion marks, and three days later it was 40 billion. On November 1, 1923, a pound of bread cost 260 billion marks, a pound of sugar 250 billion and a pound of meat was 3.2 trillion marks. A factory worker's daily wage was five billion marks. On November 9, the day of the Munich coup, a copy of *Volkischer Beobachter* cost eight billion marks.

This absurd situation is best illustrated by the following letter that a doctor, who had a savings account of 86,000 marks dating back to prewar times, received from his bank on September 5: "The bank deeply regrets that it can no longer handle your account of 86,000 marks because the related fees are way out of proportion to the capital. We therefore take the liberty of returning your capital to you. Since we do not have any bank notes small enough, we rounded the sum up to a figure of 1 million marks. Enclosure: One bank note worth 1 million marks." The stamp on the envelope was worth 5 million marks.

Paper money was usually printed only on one side. In offices employees used the blank side as scratch paper. It was cheaper than buying a note pad.

For Hitler and the party, it made no sense to accept

donations in paper marks. Only old debts were paid with that money. Gold, jewelry and foreign currency were the only items that had any value. It was a good thing that Hitler had hoarded jewelry given to him by Mrs. Bechstein and his other rich patronesses. A contract drawn up between him and the businessman Richard Frank of the firm of Korn-Frank in Berlin was typical. Here is how it read: "As security for a loan of 60,000 Swiss Francs, Mr. Adolf Hitler hereby transfers to Mr. Richard Frank ownership of the valuables deposited with the bank of Heinrich Eckert in Munich: One emerald pendant with platinum and diamonds on small platinum chains. One ruby ring mounted in platinum with diamonds. One sapphire ring mounted in platinum with diamonds. One diamond ring (solitaire), diamonds mounted in silver, on 14-karat gold ring. One Venetian raised lace piece, 6.5 meters long, 11.5 centimeters wide (17th century). One red silk Spanish piano cover with gold embroidery." Hitler remarked later that he could not have held on to *Volkischer Beobachter* in 1923 without Frank.

Switzerland turned out to be an excellent money source. Here, Dr. Emil Gansser, a prominent Berlin pro-Nazi, did valuable spade work. Hitler had met Gansser in 1921 in Berlin when he had invited him to the swank Berlin National Club, where right-wing officers and captains of industry met. Gansser was a member of the board of directors at Siemens & Halske and always wore a starched collar and a "Stresemann" (black jacket and striped trousers). He played a leading role in Prussia's Protestant Church and maintained good relations with prominent Lutherans and Calvinists.

In 1923, Gansser traveled to Switzerland and talked to rich Swiss Calvinists and Zwinglians. He painted them a frightening picture of the danger that would threaten the Protestant Swiss cantons if, as a result of separatist efforts in Southern Germany, an "enlarged Catholic Danube kingdom were to spring up along with separation from Protestant Prussia." France, in particular, would promote this kind of development. There was reliable information to the effect that the French would drop their demands for Bavarian reparation payments if it would break away from the German Reich. At the same time, he described for his Swiss conversation partners the "genial, simple worker and good republican Adolf Hitler who has made it his mission to make Germany once again a respected country under the leadership of Protestant Prussia."

After Gansser had done the ground work, Hitler went to Switzerland several times to appeal for donations. On one trip he was accompanied by Hanfstaengl; on another Prince zu Arenberg—who had joined the NSDAP via Göring—personally chauffered him in an antique Mercedes-Benz from Munich to Zurich via Lindau. Along with the Duke and the Duchess of Coburg, Arenberg was one of the few members of the high nobility who had joined the Nazis. His friend, the Duke of Coburg, was the son of Prince Alfred, Duke of Edinburgh and of Grand Duchess Marie of Russia. This made him a grandchild of Queen Victoria of England and Albert of Saxony-Coburg and Gotha.

In Zurich, Hitler and Prince Arenberg were entertained in the Baur au Lac Hotel with a twelve-course dinner. After the meal, a suitcase was brought in and the rich Swiss dropped different amounts of money into it. Over the next few days, Hitler—carrying the impressive letters of recommendation—paid visits to bankers and silk manufacturers along the "Gold Coast" on the Western shore of Lake Zurich and on Bahnhof Street.

Hitler and Arenberg returned to Germany with a suitcase that was stuffed with Swiss francs and dollar bills. Receipts had not been asked for nor were any given. Hitler did not even bother to count the money. He gave the suitcase to Amann who, in the meantime, had become Hitler's private financier and saw to it that the Führer had everything that he wanted.

One of the most important people who supported Hitler in his efforts to procure foreign exchange was Erwin von Scheubner-Richter. He was orginally from the Baltic area and was five years older than Hitler. During the Revolution of 1905, Scheubner-Richter had fought against the insurrectionists as a young cavalry officer in a Cossack regiment. After that, he studied engineering in

Munich, joined a fashionable Bavarian regiment and became a German citizen. During the Kapp Coup, he was Kapp's public relations officer in Berlin. After the coup had collapsed, he fled to Munich.

There he ran into Alfred Rosenberg, an old Baltic friend, with whom he had studied architecture in St. Petersburg and Moscow. Rosenberg was also a member of the Thule Society. He recently had begun to work with Hitler. Rosenberg, who played a leading role in Munich's Russian community, introduced Scheubner-Richter to Russian émigré circles and to Hitler. In his own words, Scheubner-Richter was so impressed by Hitler's "hypnotic force" that he called him the "prophet of the New Germany." He and his wife Mathilde joined the NSDAP by the end of 1920.

Scheubner-Richter had excellent contacts in all parts of society. He knew Bavarian aristocrats, businessmen, bankers and industry leaders like Reusch and Thyssen. He was also a very close friend of Ludendorff. According to the police report entitled "Hitler Coup File," housed in the archives of the Bavarian State Chancellery, he managed to drum up "enormous sums of money" for the NSDAP. Because of his wife's fortune and as a result of his own petroleum deals, he was a very rich man. Thus his fundraising technique was never hectic, always calm and nonchalant. After he was killed during the November coup, Hitler said of him: "He is the only one who is irreplaceable," not exactly a tactful statement in view of the other victims.

Scheubner-Richter spent a great deal of time with Russian émigrés and received donations from Russian industrialists, especially oil men from the Caucasus who had managed to move their fortunes and tangible assets to safety in Germany. The list of individuals who made contributions to Hitler via Scheubner-Richter is rather impressive. Names such as Nobel turn up in it, as do wealthy Russian noblemen, including Gukasov, Baron Koeppen and the Duke of Leuchtenberg.

It almost seemed as if Hitler's youthful dream about a life without a bothersome "bread-and-butter-job," an existence full of drama, glitter and applause, was coming true. He had cars, he was the center of attention during fashionable gatherings, he was quite at home among princes, captains of industry and local people of elevated standing. Frau Bechstein hinted rather discreetly that she would not be at all displeased if Hitler were to marry her daughter. Sometimes Hitler even thought about settling down to a quiet domesticated lifestyle. "All I really want is to make enough money as the boss of *Volkischer Beobachter*," Hitler is quoted as saying.

But he envied people like Mussolini, comparing himself unfavorably to them. With that in mind, he looked for an opportunity to stage his "March on Berlin." In the autumn of 1923, the situation looked so favorable to him that he bet everything on one roll of the dice.

Hitler realized that he could not pull off a coup d'état with his SA alone, no matter how well-armed and equipped it might have been. His friend Ernst Röhm managed to merge four radical right-wing armed organizations, including the Oberland Free Corps and Reichskriegsflagge (Battle Flag) with the SA to form the Fighting League of Patriotic Organizations. Röhm put this organization under Hitler's political leadership. Hitler in turn was able to persuade national hero General Ludendorff to join the "March on Berlin" as its figurehead.

Events followed in rapid succesion in the autumn of 1923. Between September and November, the price of a kilogram of butter jumped from 100 million to 6 billion marks while the cost of a shirt skyrocketed from 400 million to 8.5 billion. On September 26, the new Reich Chancellor Stresemann proclaimed the resumption of German reparation payments. There was reason to fear disturbances. This is why President Ebert proclaimed a state of emergency and gave Armed Forces Minister Gessler and General von Seeckt, the army chief of staff, executive powers for all Germany.

But Bavaria revolted against the central German government. Prime Minister von Knilling proclaimed a state of emergency and appointed Gustav Ritter von Kahr—the former pro-monarchist head of government—to the position of commissioner of state with dictatorial powers. Kahr put together a Junta with General Otto von Lossow, the Bavarian Reichswehr commander, and Colonel Hans Ritter von Seisser, the chief of the Bavarian State Police.

As his first official act, Kahr declared that the state of emergency proclaimed by Ebert did not apply in Bavaria. He refused to accept any orders from Berlin. Seeckt tried to prevail in Bavaria via his subordinate Lossow. He ordered him to outlaw *Volkischer Beobachter* and to arrest three Free Corps fighters who played a leading role in Röhm's Fighting League and against whom arrest warrants had been issued. When Lossow hesitated, he was relieved of his command. Kahr declared that Lossow would continue as commander in Bavaria. Officers and enlisted men would have to take an oath of loyalty to the Bavarian Constitution. The borders were closed. Troops moved into position along the border with Thuringia. They had received orders to repel any Prussian attacks. The border with Württemberg was also secured.

The rupture with Berlin was complete. It appeared to be only a matter of days before Bavaria would break away from the rest of Germany. Hitler believed that his hour had arrived. He implored Kahr and Lossow to march on Berlin before Berlin marched on Munich. But the two men firmly rejected his suggestion, warning him that they would smash any coup d'état he might stage.

To retain his credibility among his followers, Hitler could not turn back. The orders went out: "Fighting League units and SA are to march into Munich during the night of November 10 and proclaim the national revolution."

Hitler, however, received the news that Kahr was scheduled to speak on the evening of November 8 in the Bürgerbräu beer hall on Rosenheimer Street. Seisser, Lossow and other prominent leaders would be there as well.

Hitler was afraid that Kahr would proclaim Bavaria's independence and make Crown Prince Rupprecht king. He had to move before the junta did.

Around 8:00 p.m., Hitler and other Nazi leaders arrived

at the Bürgerbräu beer hall where Kahr was delivering a rather boring address. They pushed their way into the crowded room. Putzi Hanfstaengl ordered beer for himself and his friends at five billion marks per glass. In the meantime, 600 SA men surrounded the building. At 8:30 p.m., Hermann Göring and 25 SA men stormed into the large hall, positioning a machinegun at the entrance. Wearing a cutaway, Hitler jumped on a table and fired several pistol shots at the ceiling. "The national revolution has broken out!" he shouted. "The building is surrounded by heavily armed men. Nobody is allowed to leave the room!"

The people were confused but there was no panic. Here and there, were heard shouts of "Bravo!" or "South America!" or "cheap comedy!"

Pistol in hand, Hitler forced Kahr, Lossow and Seisser into the next room to "negotiate" with him. They refused and accused him of breaking his promise. Only General Ludendorff, who had just arrived, managed to persuade them to join Hitler's coup d'état against the Weimar Republic. Triumphantly, Hitler led the group back into the room where he delivered a speech that was received with enthusiasm.

When Hitler heard of clashes between the SA and the Reichswehr around the city, he left the Bürgerbräu beer hall and handed command over to Ludendorff. The general let Kahr, Lossow and Seisser go in return for a declaration of loyalty. But these three men did not have the slightest intention of behaving "loyally." They went to their offices and made preparations to smash the coup d'état.

During the early morning hours, Hitler ordered the SA to confiscate all paper money at the Parcus and Muehltaler printing plants and to bring it to the Bürgerbräu beer hall. Later, Hanfstaengl recalled: "The air was thick with cigar and cigarette smoke. In the anteroom there was a small platform with an approximately 1.5-meter-high pile containing thousands of billion mark notes in neat little bank bundles which had been requisitioned by the Brown Shirts.

In the meantime, Hitler had learned that Kahr, Lossow

and Seisser had double-crossed him. Desperately, Ludendorff tried to figure out how the coup d'état could be
salvaged. They decided on a march through Munich to
link up with Röhm's forces, which were ensconced in the
War Ministry Building on Ludwig Street.

The column moved from the Bürgerbräu beer hall
across the Isar River to Marien Square, continuing
through narrow Residenz Street and heading toward
Odeon Square. In the front ranks marched Ludendorff
and Hitler, who had linked arms with Scheubner-Richter.
Around 11:30 p.m., the coup d'état column ran into a
police cordon where Residenz Street meets Odeon
Square. A shot was fired from the column, followed by a
hail of bullets from the police. Sixteen Nazis, including
Scheubner-Richter, were killed. As he fell, Scheubner-Richter pulled Hitler down to the ground and Hitler
dislocated his shoulder. Göring was seriously wounded
but was able to find safety in the shop of a Jewish store-
keeper. Under an assumed name, he fled to Italy with his
wife. The young SA doctor Walter Schulz took Hitler to
a side street where they got into a car and raced out of
the city, heading south. Putzi Hanfstaengl took off for
Austria. Hitler fled to Hanfstaengl's house in Uffing
where Helen Hanfstaengl doctored him and kept him
hidden in an attic room. Two days later, after his failed
suicide attempt, Hitler was arrested there and was placed
under investigative detention. The first phase of his
political career was over.

Inflation was also somewhat under control at the end
of November. On November 20, the dollar exchange rate
was fixed at 4.2 trillion paper marks. At the same time,
the new rentenmark was introduced at an exchange rate
of one dollar to one trillion marks. The volume of money in circulation was not to exceed 24 billion renten-
marks. The new mark was slowly stabilized. The old
inflation slips, which for some time continued to be valid
along with the new currency, gradually disappeared from
the market. People became cautiously hopeful. Between
1924 and 1929 the Weimar Republic performed a minor
"economic miracle."

Hitler was held under investigative detention in Landsberg am Lech in preparation for his trial, which began in Munich in February 1924. He knew that he had moved too soon. From now on, he decided, he would play by the parliamental political rules of the game in order to come to power. Hitler established another goal: He wanted to be powerful, but he also wanted to be rich.

# Chapter Seven

# Close Friends?

In November 1922, Hitler became acquainted with Ernst Hanfstaengl, a giant of a man, who had just returned to Germany from the United States. Though six and half feet tall Hasfstaengl was known to his friends as "Putzi" (Cutie). He came from a cultured, prosperous family who owned one of the largest art publishing companies in Munich.

At the suggestion of his friend Truman Smith—the assistant United States military attaché—Putzi attended a Hitler meeting on the evening of November 22. He was captivated by Hitler's fiery rhetoric. Although his mother was an American, Hanfstaengl had very strong German nationalist feelings and feared Communism. After the meeting, he saw to it that he was introduced to Hitler. A few days later, he joined the NSDAP. Hitler, in turn, was fascinated by the witty, easy-going man, who although worldly-wise was not as grim and crabby as the "intellectuals" of the party like Eckart, Rosenberg or Hess. The two of them soon discovered a common interest in art and music (on the piano, Putzi did a passable job playing Wagner) and began spending time with each other.

One day, toward the end of 1922, Hitler confided in his new friend the grand plans which he had for his newspaper if he could only find the necessary money. "How can I possibly be successful with my miserable little four-age weekly rag? How can I trumpet my successes with such a small instrument?" he complained. "We could achieve much more if it were possible to publish *Volkisch-*

*er Beobachter* as a daily, coming off rotary printing presses." Hitler then dropped a hint about the two American rotary presses for sale in a bankrupt Munich printing plant. They,however, would take only foreign currency at constant value, not paper money. A thousand dollars would be sufficient, he said.

Hanfstaengl, coincidentally, had just received a $1,500 settlement for his share in his family's art gallery in New York. Although that wasn't much in the United States at the time, in Germany it amounted to a small fortune. Hanfstaengl recalled: "On the next day, I went to Amann and gave him $1,000 in U.S currency. He and Hitler were beside themselves with joy." Hitler exclaimed: "What magnanimity! Hanfstaengl, we will never forget what you did!"

Of course, Putzi's motives for giving this interest-free loan were not completely altruistic. He was hoping to be named editor-in-chief ahead of the increasingly sickly Dietrich Eckart. When Hitler then gave this job to Alfred Rosenberg, Putzi was hurt. Perhaps he might indeed have brought a breath of fresh air to the boring newspaper.

Nevertheless, soon Putzi became a kind of unpaid press secretary for Hitler and also got him interviews with foreign journalists. Privately, their relations became friendlier, in part because Hitler dated Putzi's sister, Erna.

Hitler also adored Helen Hanfstaengl, Putzi's American wife. Like a love-sick schoolboy, he fawned over her. Putzi once found Hitler kneeling before Helen in the drawing room of his house on Pienzenauer Street. After a serious man-to-man talk, Hitler, quite contrite, promised to control himself in the future. Mrs. Hanfstaengl had been amused by the whole thing. At any rate, several months later Helen saved Hitler's life. After the failure of his Munich coup, he was hiding out in her home on Lake Staffel when the police came to arrest him. In a dramatic gesture, Hitler wanted to shoot himself but Mrs. Hanfstaengl managed to wrest the pistol out of his hand with a well-practiced judo grip. Later, when she was back in America during World War II she occasionally regretted having done that. Putzi spent the war as an

advisor to his fellow Harvard alumnus, Franklin
Roosevelt.

Roughly at the same time as did Putzi Hanfstaengl,
another important man had joined Hitler; he was
Hermann Göring. He had been a fighter ace, winner of
the Pour le Merite Order, Imperial Germany's highest
decoration for valor. He was also the last commanding
officer of the Richthofen Fighter Wing. After the war,
Göring had gone to Sweden as test pilot where he
married the Swedish Baroness Carin von Kantzow. At
the end of 1922, the couple had moved to Munich and
rented a baronial- looking mansion in Obermenzing.
Göring had come from a rich family but his own fortune
had been considerably whittled down by inflation. At
that time, however, he was able to live very comfortably
on the foreign exchange held by his likewise prosperous
wife.

Göring heard one of Hitler's speeches for the first time
in November 1922. He sought him out afterwards and
offered him his services. Hitler was beside himself with
joy. Göring was a widely known war hero; that alone
brought prestige to the party. He also moved in aristocratic circles and was friends with high-ranking officers,
as well as with princes of the houses of Wittelsbach and
Hohenzollern. Hitler enthusistically told his party members: "Göring! Magnificent! What propaganda! Besides, he
has money and doesn't cost me a penny!"

Göring's mansion became a magnet for Hitler and the
top echelon of the Nazi Party. Hitler made sure that the
more loutish among his party comrades would not be
admitted there; only the "intellectuals" and the well-bred,
such as Eckart, Esser, Hanfstaengl, and Hess, were to be
allowed in. Even his close associate Hoffmann was dis-
couraged from attending—Hoffmann was frequently inclined toward getting drunk and telling dirty jokes. In
Göring's home, Hitler met Ludendorff, the son of Bavarian Crown Prince Rupprecht, and industrialists such as
Fritz Thyssen, who later became one of his important
contributors.

Again and again, his rich patrons helped Hitler with
foreign currency and jewelry during the turbulent

inflation year of 1923. Many of these patrons were women. One of them was Winifred Wagner, who was born in England but married Siegfried Wagner, the son of famed Viennese composer Richard Wagner. Dietrich Eckart introduced Hitler to her in Bayreuth in 1920. Winifred was one of the first members of the NSDAP. Soon she became one of Hitler's closest platonic girlfriends and one of his most resolute financial patronesses. Only Mesdames Bruckmann and Bechstein could compete with her.

Sometimes, Hitler would take Putzi Hafstaengl along as he made the rounds seeking contributions, in an effort to give himself greater "respectability." This was the case when he visited filthy-rich retired Consul General Scharrer, who resided on a huge estate in Bernried on Lake Starnberg. Peacocks strutted in the garden and swans swam in the pond. Hitler pointed out to Hanfstaengl that the radiator of the Rolls Royce parked in the front of the house was gold-plated. But for Putzi the place was the home of a nouveau-riche man. Scharrer's wife (nee Busch) came from the prominent beer brewing family in St. Louis. During World War II, Hanfstaengl reported to interviewers from the American OSS (Office of Strategic Services): "She was a big, fat woman whose hands were covered with such big rings that she was hardly able to move her fingers. Hitler rarely ever left the house without a considerable contribution in dollars or in Swiss francs."

One of the most important émigrés introduced to Hitler was General Vassiliy Biskupskiy. He later supported Hitler unreservedly and got him together with financial patrons. He even managed to put the touch on Sir Henri Deterding, the Shell Oil magnate. Biskupskiy, a fanatical Russian anticommunist, was deeply impressed by Hitler. To him, Hitler was the popular leader who could move masses away from communism. It was Biskupskiy's goal to destroy the Bolshevik regime in Russia with the help of a revived, strictly nationalist Germany, united with the counterrevolutionary Russian émigrés. Biskupskiy was also a radical anti-Semite, as were all of the other Russian émigrés.

Buskupskiy rendered his greatest service to the NSDAP when, in 1922, he supported the claim of Romanov Grand Duke Kyril Vladimirovich to the czarist throne and brought Kyril together with Hitler. As the cousin of Czar Nicholas II (who by this time had been shot to death), Kyril had legitimate claims to the deposed Russian throne, although many Russian monarchists supported Grand Duke Nikolai Nikolayevich, another cousin of the czar, who lived in Paris. But Biskupskiy passionately fought against Nikolai. The general, who advocated a return to absolute monarchy, accused Nikolai of democratism and constitutionalism and maintained that he was a puppet of the French.

Kyril spoke excellent German. His mother was Maria Pavlovna, born Grand Duchess of Mecklenberg. During his childhood he was surrounded by German maids, governesses and tutors. His aunt, Grand Duchess Alix, who was born into the house of Saxony-Alternberg, had also always spoken German with him. After the revolution, Kyril first fled to Southern France, but in 1922 he and his wife moved to Coburg where Grand Duchess Victoria, the sister of the Duke of Coburg, had a home. Not only was Victoria the driving force behind his claim to the czarist throne but she was also an enthusiastic National Socialist. Whenever she traveled abroad to collect donations for her husband's political activities, she also collected donations for the Nazis. Some said that she supported Hitler more than she did her husband. Privately she also slipped Hitler some of her jewels; Kyril and Victoria became close friends of Scheubner-Richter and the latter's wife.

The fact that pretenders to the Russian throne, grand dukes and generals had come out in support of Hitler's cause meant that he was becoming even more acceptable in the eyes of the German upper class.

During the early 1920's, the party and the paper were always short of cash. It took a lot of money to maintain the stormtroopers (SA), which consisted of several thousand men. They needed equipment and weapons that could be procured only through secret channels. Besides, to a great extent the SA was comprised of unemployed men and students, both groups needing pocket money to keep them under control. The conversion of the *Volkischer Beobachter* into a daily newspaper yielded great dividends in propaganda, but it was an expensive operation. The editorial offices had to be enlarged, while printing and paper costs multiplied. Always, there were debts that had to be paid. Adolf Mueller, a printer, hated to wait for his money and frequently threatened to stop the presses unless Amann would bring him cash.

In May 1923, when Putzi Hanfstaengl urgently needed hard foreign currency—his son Egon had just been born—he asked Hitler to repay his interest-free loan of 1,000 dollars. He felt that he was entitled to ask this because he had not gotten the editor-in-chief position which he had wanted. Amann and Hitler complained that the treasury was empty and persuaded him to accept an IOU. But Putzi desperately needed hard cash, so he sold the IOU at half its value to Christian Weber, who at the time was making lots of money trading horses and handling bets at the Daglfing Racetrack. Weber had no reservations about presenting the IOU to Amann in the editorial offices of *Volkischer Beobachter* a month later. When the publishing house manager failed to pay, Weber sent the bailiff over to intervene on his behalf. In the end, money had to be scraped together from the party treasury. Amann ranted and raved about the friend's "treachery," but Hitler did not really blame the "man-and-a-half." "That is typical of Weber," he said. "He is a rather brutal chap. But he is one of our oldest and most loyal party members and has done much for the party in the past."

Despite these sorts of setbacks, Hitler and his business manager hardly even suffered any personal privations. Exchanging a couple of dollar bills enabled Hitler to continue his lifestyle for weeks. Even comparatively small donations from sympathizers abroad turned into significant amounts when exchanged into German currency. Sudenten-German supporters donated Czech crowns, and even in Italy, Hitler's agent Kurt Luedecke was able to wheedle foreign currency out of sympathizing Fascists although the latter generally viewed their

Teutonic copycat from North of the Alps with derision and contempt. After the Nazis in 1922 had copied their "Roman salute" with the extended right arm from the Fascists, Mussolini called his German imitator "Caesar with the little Tirolian hat."

Hitler, on the other hand, admired Mussolini, and in the middle of 1923 already planned to copy the Italian's "March on Rome" of 1922 with a "March on Berlin." The March on Berlin in November turned into a miserable and bloody failure on Munich's Residenz Street.

In 1934, Hitler officially forbade party officials to have any kind of financial partnerships with party newspapers. This was a bitter loss to Goebbels who was publishing *Angriff* in Berlin and had also taken over the newspaper syndicate of the Strasser Brothers. One man didn't have to abide by this new rule; that was Max Amann. Amann represented Hitler's own interests in the party's central press and publishing syndicate.

Max Amann was born in Munich on November 24, 1891, making him two years younger than Hitler. He attended business school and did his apprenticeship in a Munich law office. He served in the Bavarian Army for five years and was Hitler's company first sergeant for awhile.

Outwardly a jovial Bavarian, Amann was by nature irascible, brutal and power-hungry; he was tyrannical and ruthless toward his subordinates. Although he was utterly unfamiliar with the publishing business, he quickly picked up the necessary knowledge on the job, put the *Volkischer Beobachter* on a sound financial basis and built up a successful book publishing house. Even after Hitler had come to power, Amann had the Führer's favor and confidence. Amann held the top slot in the Association of German Newspaper Publishers and was given even more power when the Nazi provincial party press was reorganized in 1934 and placed under his supervision. In 1935, the Eher Publishing House acquired about 100 larger newspaper publishing establishments, including Scherl and Ullstein, which gave Amann an absolutely dominant position in the German publishing industry. Amann knew how to defend his empire and managed to beat back every intruder. Whenever there was a turf conflict, Hitler always decided in his favor. Amann was always feuding with Robert Ley, the head of the one and only labor union, the Labor Front. "I do not tolerate any of Ley's plant cell chiefs in my print shops and publishing houses," he announced proudly, "Most of my workers and employees are not even members of the German Labor Front."

In 1936, Hitler gave Amann absolute general powers in the management of the publishing syndicate. Now he was responsible only to Hitler, no longer having to answer to the NSDAP treasurer or the chief of the Party Business Office. His newspaper sales agents went from door to door, increasing circulation by using methods that bordered on blackmail and duress. In 1939, the *Volkischer Beobachter* reached a circulation of 742,000. That figure rose to 1,192,000 in 1941. Rudolf Hess was peeved about no longer being under his supervision, and he sent a bristling letter to the Eher Publishing House. "No folk comrade must ever be bothered or put at a disadvantage if he refuses to subscribe to a party newpaper." He let Amann know that his advertising methods were severely frowned upon. As for the circulation agents who tried to intimidate people into subscribing to the newspaper, Hess threatened them with expulsion from the party and criminal prosecution. Disgruntled, Hess told Hitler, "As long as the *Volkischer Beobachter* is so abominably boring, you can't expect anybody, after a hard day's work, to read his way through this gooey stuff." Hitler again shielded his publisher. In 1944, the Eher Publishing House, with its affiliates "Herold," "Europa," and "Standarte," controlled 90 percent of the entire German press as well as a sizable part of the book market. In jest, Amann was called the "German Hearst." At any rate, he had become Europe's biggest publisher.

By war's end, the Eher Syndicate had assets worth 600 million marks. It is astonishing to note that the syndicate did not pay a single penny in taxes after 1940. This tax exemption came about through Hitler's personal intervention with the Finance Ministry. The famous party slogan "The Common Good Comes Before Self-interest" takes on a new meaning here.

Amann not only had tremendous power, but he also had a huge personal income. In 1936, he signed a new contract as general manager of the Eher Publishing House, entitling him to an annual salary of 120,000 marks and five percent of the company's net profits. By December 1933 he'd already secured for himself a one-third share in the Mueller & Son Party Print Shop. Mueller & Son printed the *Volkischer Beobachter* in Munich, Berlin and Vienna, along with the *Illustrierte Boebachter* and a dozen party periodicals and weeklies. The printing establishment also held a monopoly on all important books by party luminaries, most importantly Hitler's *Mein Kampf*. The profits of Mueller & Son exceeded that of any other printing outfit in Germany. In January 1940, Amann's real estate holdings and business partnership shares were assessed at 6,220,000 marks, and in January 1943 the figure was 10,306,000 marks. In 1941, Amann paid taxes on an annual income of 3,479,449 marks, and in 1942 the figure was 3.5 million marks. The diminutive bank employee, who had taken over a sick newspaper in 1922, had become a filthy rich businessman. The Führer allowed his publisher to become so powerfully rich simply because he, Adolf Hitler, was the chairman of the board of the Eher Syndicate. It is impossible to determine now how much the chairman of the board received in royalties from the net profits, but it was undoubtedly a substantial annual fee.

*Braunau-on-the-Inn, Austria, the birthplace of Adolf Hitler. This photograph was taken in 1939.*

*Hitler's family home in Waltershlag, watercolor, 1909 by Adolf Hitler.*

Corporal Hitler reporting for     Eva Braun, 1934, by Hitler.
duty as regiment writer-1916.

Caricature of public prosecutor in Hitler's trial
by A. Hitler, 1924.

Sketch of Volkswagen by Hitler for Jakob
Werlin, director of Mercedes Benz, 1932.

*Dietrich Eckart (1868-1923). The man who changed Hitler, the person who introduced him to black magic.*

*Hitler with Geli, 1930, Munich, in Hoffmann's garden.*

*Hitler with Geli. On the right—Paula Hitler. In front with camera is Max Amann.*

*Munich, 1930: Hitler with Max Amann, his publisher.*

*Hitler reviews building plans with Albert Speer.*

*At Opera in Berlin. From left: William Bruckner, Magda Goebbels, Sigrid von Laffort, Joseph Goebbels.*

*Heinrich Hoffmann.*

*Hitler congratulates Gustav Krupp on his 70th birthday.*

*Hitler at wedding of Marion Schonmann, friend of Eva Braun. Eva stands fourth from the left.*

*Hitler with Unity Mitford.*

*Hitler's chalet near Berchtesgaden.*

Hitler's teahouse near Berchtesgaden, with tunnel leading to elevator.

*A little girl visits Hitler and Eva Braun at their villa at Berghof.*

# Chapter Eight

# From Prisoner to Führer

On November 22, 1925, a conference of North German and West German Nazi province leaders took place in the apartment of Bernhard Rust, the Nazi Provincial Leader of Hanover. Joseph Goebbels, a 28-year-old Ph.D., took the floor. Goebbels was an unsuccessful dramatist, theater critic, and, until very recently, a messenger at the Duesseldorf Stock Exchange; at the time he spoke, he was secretary to Gregor Strasser and publisher of social-revolutionary *Nationalsozialistische Monatshefte (National Socialist Monthly)*. In a rather strangely bright, Rhenish voice, he announced, "I move that little bourgeois Adolf Hitler be expelled from the National Socialist German Workers Party!"

What had happened during the ensuing two years? What had reduced the "drummer of the national revolution," the arranger of coups and little revolutions to the status of a Bavarian bourgeois—in the eyes of his northern party friends?

When Hitler was arrested in Putzi Hanfstaengl's country home on Lake Starnberg on November 11, 1923, he seemed to have reached the end of his short and stormy political career. He was deeply depressed during his investigative detention in the Fortress of Landsberg am Lech. Charged with high treason, he had no idea what kind of punishment awaited him. In another wing of the fortress, the writer Ernst Toller had been sentenced to life imprisonment because of his participation in the Munich Soviet Republic—also for high treason—and had just barely escaped the firing squad. Would Hitler share the same fate? Physically, he felt miserable. His shoulder, which he'd dislocated when he fell on Residenz Street, hurt terribly even after it had been set. He was given morphine injections, though not nearly enough to eliminate the pain. He went on a hunger strike but terminated it after a few days when Anton Drexler implored him not to wreck his health in such a pointless dramatic fashion.

At the end of February 1924, the trial of Hitler and the others began in People's Court I in the former Infantry School on Munich's Blutenburg Street. The following people were included along with Hitler on the indictment: General Ludendorff, Ret.; Ernst Poehner, former chief of police of Munich; Dr. Wilhelm Frick, senior magistrate in the Munich Police Headquarters; veterinarian Dr. Friedrich Weber, leader of the Oberland League; Captain Ernst Röhm, Ret.; First Lieutenant Wilhelm Brueckner, Ret.; Second Lieutenant Robert Wagner, Ret.; Lieutenant Colonel Hermann Kriebel, Ret.; and Heinz Pernet, a retired first lieutenant and Ludendorff's stepson.

The trial was a fiasco. The defendants were treated with kid gloves. It was quite obvious from the start that judge, jury, and prosecutor sympathized with the men who had staged the coup. On April 1, the verdict proved that this was indeed the case: Ludendorff was acquitted. Brueckner, Röhm, Wagner, Frick and Pernet were given 15-month sentences and fined 100 marks apiece. Their sentences were immediately commuted and they were put on probation. Hitler, Weber, Kriebel and Poehner were given five-year sentences and fined 200 marks apiece. After six months, they were told, their sentences would probably be reduced to probation. The prosecutor's motion that Hitler be expelled as a troublesome alien after serving his sentence was rejected by the court in view of his "outstanding bravery in action." The court records indicate that "impetuous shouts of 'Hail!' came from the audience."

The other men who participated in the coup were sentenced to light terms in the secondary trials. Only Rudolf Hess and 40 members of the "Hitler Assault Squad" actually served a part of their sentences. Streicher, Amann, and Strasser were released immediately. Göring and Esser were abroad, waiting for a proclamation of amnesty.

Hitler recovered from his depression. He had no intention of giving up his party leadership just because he was behind the walls of the Fortress. The Bavarian law enforcement establishment didn't exactly make it difficult for him to continue his treasonous activities. He was allowed to receive delegations, hold conferences and issue proclamations. The only thing he wasn't allowed to do was travel.

An abundant stream of gifts now flowed into Landsberg Fortress—including flowers, chocolates, cakes, books and money. Once again, Hitler and his circle were able to afford the comforts and amenities of a hotel. The biographer Konrad Heiden described Hitler's "dungeon" in the following manner: "On the first floor, there was a big room with two windows that had a nice view of the surrounding countryside. In it was a bed, a chair, a cabinet and a big work table. This was the dungeon that Hitler had withdrawn into."

After a visit to the Landsberg prison, Putzi Hanfstaengl had this to say: "The place looked like a gourmet shop. You could have opened a flower, fruit, and wine concession with all the stuff that was stacked up in there. Presents were coming from all over Germany. Hitler had really put on some weight." Hitler also had a steady stream of female visitors, among whom were Mrs. Bechstein, Mrs. Bruckmann and Winifred Wagner. In order to visit Hitler more frequently, Mrs. Bechstein claimed to be his adoptive mother. But more importantly, she persuaded her husband to guarantee a personal loan of 45,000 marks with the German Hansa Bank in Munich so that Hitler would not be without money after his release from prison. Bechstein would later have to reluctantly convert the guarantee into a donation because Hitler never repaid the loan. He merely deducted the debt interest on his tax return.

For the other prisoners in Landsberg, reveille was at 6:00 a.m. and "lights out" was at 8:00 p.m. But Hitler and his inner circle—including Hess, Weber and Kriebel—

were able to sleep late in the morning and were allowed to read and work as long as they wanted at night. Hitler was even given another cell for his "work, conference and visitor room." Wearing short leather pants with knit green suspenders (a present from Mrs. Bruckmann) and a clashing city-style shirt and necktie, he would sit for hours in his rattan chair and read, his coffee cup and sugar bowl in front of him and a laurel wreath, donated by admirers, on the wall behind him. On his 35th birthday, the flowers and gifts that were sent to him filled several rooms.

On the outside, however, things weren't going well for Hitler politically. While in prison, he had named Alfred Rosenberg as his authorized agent. To replace the outlawed NSDAP, Rosenberg founded a "Greater German National Community" which made no headway whatsoever. Rosenberg had no real authority and his gruff manner alienated party members. Hitler replaced him with Poehner, who had successfully petitioned to delay his prison sentencing, but he was accused of inactivity. The movement fell apart. Several substitute organizations took shape, the North German Nationalist Freedom Party being the most successful. On May 4, 1924, this nascent party was even able to win 32 seats in the Reichstag, the German Parliament.

Meanwhile in Bavaria, the successor movements were whacking away at each other. Rosenberg vs. Streicher and Esser; Streicher vs. Strasser; Drexler vs. Esser. From Landsberg, Hitler vented his spleen against those who, according to him, "used their freedom to betray me and put me away in a corner like a useless piece of equipment." Finally, in a letter released to the newspapers, Hitler said he was resigning leadership of the National Socialist movement and that he would refrain from any political activity during his imprisonment. He requested that he be left alone.

Ludendorff, who despised Hitler for his "desertion" prior to the coup, seized leadership of the Freedom Party which in the meantime had been renamed the National Socialist Freedom Party. Hitler had been neutralized.

But he was not inactive. In July 1924, he began work

on the first volume of a book that would tell his own story and outline his political theory. At first, Hitler wrote by using the hunt-and-peck method on a typewriter loaned him by the prison warden. He gave that up and began dictating to his former fighting companion, Erich Maurice, who had in the meantime become Hitler's "valet" in Landsberg. Although he did an acceptable job as stenographer and typist, Hitler replaced him with Rudolf Hess, who not only became his secretary but was an enthusiastic collaborator as well.

The oft-told story about Hitler dictating the manuscript to Hess is not true. Certainly, Hess typed a number of the chapters, but he did much more than that. He provided an orderly arrangement for the flow of ideas. He advised, he edited, he revised and he injected his own ideas. It is no exaggeration to call Hess the co-author. Without him the endlessly stilted and indecipherable trains of thought might have been completely unreadable. Hess' son Wolf Rüdiger said: "My father kept a record of every one of his conversations with Hitler." These meticulous notes served as the foundation of the book. Hess never got a share out of the millions Hitler earned from the book, although he would really have been entitled to it as co-author.

A frequent visitor to Landsberg was Rudolf Hess' mentor General Karl Haushofer, a university professor and director of the Munich Institute of Geopolitics. Haushofer, Hitler, and Hess had long conversations together. Hess also kept records of these conversations. Hitler's insatiable demands for German "living space" in the East at the expense of the Slavic nations were given academic credibility by the geopolitical theories of the learned professor. Haushofer was not only a well-known geopolitician. He was also inclined toward the esoteric. As military attache in Japan, he had studied Zen-Buddhism. He had also gone through initiations at the hands of Tibetan lamas. He soon became Hitler's second "esoteric mentor," temporarily replacing Dietrich Eckart. In Berlin, Haushofer had founded a secret lodge, the Luminous Lodge or the Vril Society. The lodge's main objective was to explore the origins of the Aryan race and to perform exercises in concentration so as to awaken the forces of "Vril" which roughly corresponded to the Kundalini energy of the Hindus. Haushofer was a student of the Russian magician and esoteric Gregor Ivanovich Gurdyev. Both Gurdyev and Haushofer maintained that they had contacts with secret Tibetan lodges that possessed the secret of the "superman." They took the fantasied coming race of supermen quite literally.

It is not certain to what extent Hitler was exposed to Haushofer's esoteric influence. Hess, at any rate, was an enthusiastic follower of the professor and, at least until the outbreak of the war, exerted considerable influence on Hitler. Until he took power in 1933, Hitler seems to have concerned himself so extensively with occultist exercises that, according to the observations of Hermann Rauschning, Winifred Wagner once uttered a warning: "Beware of black magic. White and black magic are still accessible to you. But once you have given yourself over to black magic, it will determine your destiny." If we are to believe the words of Vril Society member Willi Ley, a rocket researcher who emigrated in 1933, the lodge included not only Alfred Rosenberg, Himmler, and Göring, but, along with Hitler's subsequent personal physician Dr. Morell, the Führer himself. It is also known that the infamous magicians Aleister Crowley and Gurdyev sought contact with Hitler. Gurdyev's "Hymn to Pan," which was quoted in his own funeral oration, would have also been suitable as epitaph for Hitler: "And I rage and ravish, I rip and rave, I storm eternally through the world in thrall to Pan."

Hitler's unusual powers of suggestion become more understandable if one keeps in mind that he had access to the "secret" psychological techniques of the esoteric lodges. Haushofer unquestionably taught him the techniques of Grudyev—which, in turn, were based on the teachings of the Sufis and the Tibetan lamas—and familiarized him with the Zen teachings of the Japanese Society of the Green Dragon. All of these teachings taken together are sufficient to awaken slumbering power centers in the individual known as Chakras. They do this by means of very strict exercises of concentration.

Seized with a new passion for writing, Hitler often worked on his book late into the night. When Max Amann, the director of the Eher Publishing House, visited him in prison, Hitler told him the working title: "Four-and-a-Half Years of Struggle Against Lies, Stupidity, and Cowardice." Amann explained that no publisher would be able to sell a book with such a title. Amann knew that Hitler would need to earn a living after his release from prison. He himself was in desparate straits. The *Volkischer Beobachter* was outlawed at the time and a bestselling book would keep the publishing house going. Why not shorten the title to "Mein Kampf" (My Struggle)? Hitler agreed. The manuscript for the first volume was almost ready when Hitler was released on December 20, 1924. Later, Hitler gave it to his long-standing patroness Mrs. Bechstein as a present.

Adolf Mueller, the printer of the *Volkischer Beobachter,* picked Hitler up at Landsberg in a Mercedes, accompanied by the photographer Heinrich Hoffmann. Hoffmann later made a fortune from the photograph he took of Hitler standing defiantly beside Mueller's car in front of the Landsberg city gate. About this interlude, Hitler wrote, "I left all my money, 234 marks, with my comrades in Landsberg. I returned to Munich in abject poverty." What he failed to mention was that a tidy sum of 45,000 marks was waiting for him at the Hansa Bank, courtesy of Mrs. Bechstein.

His return to Munich was undramatic. Esser and Streicher formed a welcoming committee at 41 Thiersch Street. His landlady had decorated the room with flowers. The group went to eat a lowkey meal at the Osteria on Schelling Street. The unemployed party leader spent the ensuing Christmas holiday comfortably at Putzi Hanfstaengl's mansion on Pienzenauer Street. He asked Hanfstaengl to play "Liebestod" from "Tristan and Isolde" on the piano. He became quite mournful thinking of his still imprisoned comrade, Rudolf Hess. "My dear little Hess, my dear little Hess," he wailed. "He is the most loyal. Why have they not let him go yet?"

Then he visited Poehner, who would shortly have to begin serving his five-year Fortress sentence in Landsberg. Poehner urgently advised Hitler to see Prime Minister Held of the Bavarian People's Party and to make his peace with the government.

Hitler did as Poehner advised. He went and kowtowed. Actually, he only went to ask that his comrades be released, but while there he assured Held that he'd be loyal and law-abiding. The coup, he said, had been a mistake. He was now ready for political cooperation. Held asked him how he envisioned such cooperation would come about since Ludendorff and his gang of German Nationalists had adopted a radical anti-Catholic position. Hitler said that was Ludendorff's business, washing his hands of the general. He violently disapproved of the general's "fight against Rome." He proclaimed himself to still be a loyal son of the Catholic Church. His struggle was only against Marxism. If the Bavarian prime minister would fight Marxism, then he, Hitler, would be loyally at his disposal. He had no desire to fight against the bourgeois Bavarian People's Party. Hitler and Held's leave- taking was friendly but not cordial. Held promised to consider lifting the ban on the *Volkischer Beobachter* and the NSDAP. He said, however, that he would not tolerate conditions like those that prevailed before November 9, 1923.

On the very next day, Hitler gave the administration "proof" of his change of heart. Armed with a bullwhip big enough to beat a rhino, he turned up at the State Diet delegation of the National Bloc, physically threatened the baffled deputies and reproached them for not having joined the administration but instead fighting against the Catholic People's Party and other bourgeois organizations. Hitler knew that he had to build his second political career up with the favor of the ruling establishment.

In Berlin, Ludendorff's National Socialist Freedom Movement reacted with scorn. Following his visit with Held, Hitler was referred to in the newspaper as a "prisoner of clericalism." Hitler, in turn, referred to the leaders of the Freedom Movement—Ludenforff, Graefe, and Count Reventlow—as "political busboys, National Party members who have been seized with megalomania, a society of Illuminati in the North whose members worshipped the god Odin, a coterie dripping with East Elbian snobism and East Elbian stupidosis."

Prime Minister Held's gratitude was not long in coming. The ban on the NSDAP and the *Volkischer Beobachter* was lifted. Only the speech-making ban on Hitler remained in effect but didn't apply to party meetings where the public was excluded.

The *Volkischer Boebachter* began publishing again on February 26, 1925. It announced the re-founding of the NSDAP on the following day. The setting was the Bürgerbräu beer hall, the scene of the failed coup d'état. Admission was 1 mark. Max Amann was named chairman. Drexler declined the position of honorary chairman "so long as mudslingers like Julius Streicher and Hermann Esser" were in the room. Rosenberg, Strasser, and Röhm were absent. The atmosphere was tense. Four thousand supporters gathered together but most of them were bitter enemies embroiled in mutual intrigues. The first unanimous ovation came when Hitler entered the room. After his speech—in which he emotionally implored them to create a common cause—there was no longer any feeling of hostility. The audience climbed on the tables, cheered, waved earthenware beer mugs and embraced each other. Amann exploited the rare moment of enthusiasm. His thundering voice drowned out the jubilation. "This fighting must now come to an end. Everybody fall in with Hitler!" Suddenly, old adversaries faced each other on the platform and solemnly shook hands. State Diet Deputy Buttmann, who shortly before then had threatened Hitler with a riding crop, confessed: "All my objections melted away as the Führer spoke."

From that day on, Hitler was "Der Führer." Soon thereafter, Rosenberg and Strasser re-joined the party and so did Röhm, for a short time, until a renewed squabble with Hitler persuaded him to move to South America as a military instructor and colonel in the Bolivian Army.

Gregor Strasser, the macho, well-educated pharmacist from Landshut, was commanded to build the party organization in the North. Strasser, however, was one of the very few Nazis who didn't go along with the Byzantine Führer cult. For him, Hitler was never "Der Führer" but always "Herr Hitler, to whom I have made myself available for cooperation." He also didn't go along with the new practice of greeting each other with "Heil Hitler"; instead, he stuck with a simple "Good Day." More importantly, Gregor and his brother Otto, a talented journalist, took the "socialist" part of the party name very seriously. If necessary, Otto would work with the Communists against reactionary forces. In North Germany, Gregor Strasser was much more popular than Hitler who was considered more of a Munich bigshot. The North German movement took on a definite "leftward spin." Strasser's secretary was Joseph Goebbels, a radical Social Revolutionary, whose articles, apart from their anti-Semitism, might just as well appear in the Communist Party press.

# Chapter Nine

# Financing the Führer's Lifestyle

Hitler wasn't overly concerned with developments in the North. It was more important for him to establish himself in Munich by using a good middle-class style. The donations began coming in again, adding to the 45,000 mark loan. Hitler retained his modest apartment on Thiersch Street for the time being, but he hired three private employees: Rudolf Hess, as his private secretary at a monthly salary of 300 marks; Julius Schaub, a former shipping clerk at the Eher Publishing House, as his bodyguard with a salary of 200 marks; and Julius Schreck, as his driver for a more modest salary of 100 marks per month. He had become friends with Jakob Werlin, the Munich representative of the Daimler Works in Stuttgart-Untertuerckheim. Print shop owner Adolf Mueller had taught Hitler how to drive the more recent car models. Hitler passed his driving test but drove rarely. Still, he became a car buff and learned everything he could about the mechanical aspects of automobiles. In the spring of 1925, Werlin sold him a Mercedes Compressor car at the steep price of 20,000 marks. When the Finance Office asked him where he got the money for such an expensive purchase, he said he'd taken out a bank loan.

Hitler spent a lot of time on Obersalzberg near Bershtesgaden, a spot Dietrich Eckart had introduced him to back in 1921. At the Moritz Boardinghouse and in the Platterhof Restaurant, Eckart, Esser, Amann, and Hanfstaengl spent many a happy booze-filled weekend.

This is where Hitler, assisted by his private secretary Hess, finished the first volume of his book, which was published in the summer of 1925 by the Eher Publishing House with the subtitle *Settling Accounts.* The book was 400 pages long and sold for 12 marks. At first, it was a flop. The readers, who had expected some big revelations, were disappointed by its boring tone. By the end of the year, Amann had sold 10,000 copies. Tough negotiations had gotten Hitler the unusually high royalty of 15 percent of sales so that by the end of 1925 he had made 18,000 marks.

Hitler immediately began to work on the second volume. Near the Platterhof Restaurant on Obersalzberg stood Wachenfeld House, the country home of a manufacturer from Buxtehude that was available for rent at 1,000 marks per year. Hitler moved in. Later converted into the Berghof, his own private fortress, Wachenfeld House in 1925 was still a cozy little log building with modest furnishings. Albert Speer described the interior as follows: "The furniture came from the Vertiko Period and gave the place a cozy and comfortable petty-bourgeois air. There was a gold-plated cage with a canary, a cactus, and a rubber tree, all of which only enhanced this impression."

Mrs. Bechstein helped Hitler furnish the place. Winifred Wagner stocked the house with linens and china. Later she sent a page from the original score of *Lohengrin.* Hitler asked his widowed half-sister Angela to come to Berchtesgaden from Linz and keep house for him. She brought her 17-year-old daughter Angelika ("Geli") with her. Geli immediately fell for her famous uncle with typical teenage enthusiasm and fondness. Hitler responded in a paternal-avuncular fashion. His relationship with a well-endowed Bavarian girl named Maria "Mitzi" Reiter, the daughter of the co-founder of the SPD in Berchtesgaden, was much more down-to-earth. Later, when Hitler's love for his niece took on more specific forms, Mitzi tried to hang herself out of jealousy. She was not the only woman who attempted suicide because of Hitler—successfully or unsuccessfully.

For most of 1925, Hitler let the party reins slip. He

seemed uninterested in the job. Now and then he rode to
Munich, mostly to take Geli to the opera, the Osteria, the
Café Heck or the Carlton Tea Room on Brienner Street.
During his visits to Munich, he turned up in Amann's
Publishing House office on Thiersch Street more
frequently than he did at the party business office on
Schelling Street. To handle the party's finances, he hired
a treasurer, the 50-year-old Franz Xavier Schwarz, who
managed the treasury reliably. Schwarz, however, had no
influence whatsoever on Amann and the business of the
Eher Publishing House. He and his auditors weren't even
allowed to go in the offices of the publishing house. Hitler made it clear that Amann's business was not the
party's business and that Amann was responsible only to
him personally.

While talking to Schwarz one time, Otto Wagener,
later the party's economic expert, unobtrusively asked
about Hitler's living expenses. At first, Schwarz refused
to talk about the issue but finally admitted that Hitler
never talked to him about it, either. Schwarz had
suggested to Hitler that he ask the party treasury to pay
him a certain amount of money each month or that he at
least take a salary as party chairman. But Hitler rejected
the idea emphatically. As the party's leader, he didn't
want to take a single penny out of the membership dues
that the poor and unemployed party members had been
scrimping to save. Hitler's only source of money, or so he
indicated, was the royalties from his book *Mein Kampf*.
Only the Eher Publishing Company, and Max Amann,
knew that.

Wagener persisted, however, explaining to Schwarz
that Hitler could not have possibly made enough from
the modest sales of *Mein Kampf* to support his expensive
lifestyle. Schwarz replied that, to his knowledge, Hitler
also collected fees for his articles in the *Volkischer Beobachter*. But the paper now belonged to the party so, in a
sense, he was taking money from his constituency.
Nevertheless, he, Schwarz, had no influence whatsoever
on the business management. Only Amann was responsible. Hitler was the chairman of the board. Decisions
were made between the two of them. "The Finance

Office is really after our books," said Schwarz. "Which is why the boss never wants to show up in the books."

Although Hitler was unable to prevent the Finance Office from investigating his royalties from *Mein Kampf,* he didn't want to show up in any other bookkeeping records. Something that Schwarz didn't mention was that to finance his elegant lifestyle, Hitler freely dipped into the party treasury. Quite often, Schwarz would help him out with amounts up to several thousand marks, entering these withdrawals in the books as "special expenditures for advertising activities." Hitler impressed upon him the need for not mentioning his name. The money of the "poor, unemployed party members" was never paid back.

At the end of 1925, Hitler's frequent absence from Munich, his luxurious lifestyle, his appearances at the opera and at parties in the country with elegant ladies in tow were noted by the more virtuous party members with increasing displeasure. The North German "left-wing" friends of the party were especially irked, referring to Hitler as the "Pope of Munich." These shady money transactions were what caused doubts about Hitler's ability to lead a party that had the word "Socialist" in its name.

These pointed criticisms continued coming from North Germany. Goebbels spoke about the "sclerotic bigshots in Munich," about the "big mess and womanizing at Headquarters," and about "Esser's and Streischer's braggadoccio." Gregor Strasser openly deplored the "horribly low level" of the *Volkischer Beobachter.*

The inevitable explosion came when the Reichstag began its debate on whether the German princely houses were to be expropriated or whether they could recover the assets that were confiscated back in 1918. Strasser, who had a seat in the German Parliament, was in favor of noncompensatory expropriation, as were the Social Democrats and the Communists. In a speech to the Parliament, he spoke about the "anticapitalist yearning in the German people." Hitler read Strasser's speech in a foul temper. For him, the word "Socialist" in the party's name was pure window-dressing.

Hitler was also greatly irritated by the foreign policy

views of Strasser and his group. He considered Soviet
Russia the target of his plans of conquest and agreed
with Rosenberg, who described the country as a "colony
of Jewish hangmen." Goebbels, on the other hand, in *Nationalsozialistische Monatshefte,* was full of respect for the
Russian "determination to achieve utopia." Strasser also
pleaded for an alliance with Moscow "against France's
militarism, England's imperialism, and Wall Street's capitalism." To Hitler, that was like a slap in the face. He'd advocated the exact opposite idea in *Mein Kampf.* Still, re-
laxing up on Obersalzberg, he remained silent.

The Strasser group interpreted Hitler's silence as
weakness and thus grew bolder. "Nobody believes in Munich any more," Goebbels rejoiced in his diary. Strasser
demanded that Hitler's "timid policy of legality" be replaced by a crisis policy complete with "coup d'état,
bombs, strikes, and street battles." Yet, Hitler was still silent. His messianic aura seemed to have paled.

A further affront came from Strasser when he and his
brother, without approval from Munich Headquarters, established their own newspaper publishing house which,
in competition with the Eher Publishing House, soon
grew into a large corporation. Strasser's newspaper, *Der
Nationale Sozialist (The National Socialist),* had a much larger
circulation than the *Volkischer Beobachter* and, thanks to
Otto Strasser, a seasoned newspaperman, it also offered a
higher level of journalism.

Hitler's star seemed to be waning. He was quite content
to sit in his mountain home, enjoying the speech-making
ban that freed him from the need to attend bothersome
public events. In Munich, he became involved in a slan-
der trial against Anton Drexler, the original party founder who had dropped out of the NSDAP and founded
his own splinter group. One of Hitler's early supporters
called out to him in the courtroom, "You will meet a
very sad end!" At the same time in Hanover, Goebbels
demanded that "little bourgeois Adolf Hitler" be expelled
from the party.

Hitler now employed the same tactics he'd used after
his release from Landsberg. And, again, he won. On February 14, 1926, he called the entire party together in Bam-

berg for a leadership meeting. Bamberg was one of the
strongholds of Julius Streicher, who was loyally devoted
to him. All of the "leftists" of the Strasser bunch had
come, including Goebbels and the party province leaders:
Hinrich Lohse from Schleswig-Holstein, Theodor Vahlen
from Pomerania, and Bernhard Rust from Hanover. Hitler spoke for five hours. He charged the advocates of expropriation of princely houses with lying because they
were sparing the property of the Jewish bank and stock
exchange princes. He declared England and Italy, not
Russia, to be Germany's natural allies. Point by point, he
picked the program of the Strasser group apart. All of
the leftists succumbed to his powers of suggestion. The
Working Group of North and West German Party Province Chiefs was dissolved and the expropriation of the
princely houses was rejected. Josef Goebbels was the only
one who had not yet fallen under Hitler's spell. On February 14, he made the following entry in his diary: "I feel
beat! What is Hitler! A reactionary? . . . Feder nods, Esser
nods, Streicher nods and Ley nods. It hurts me deep
down in my soul as I see them in such company!!!! Brief
discussion. Strasser speaks, hesitating, trembling, awkward. Good, honest Strasser, oh God, how little are we
able to stand up to those pigs down there! I cannot speak
a single word! I feel as if I had been run over!"

A few weeks later, however, Goebbels also fell under
Hitler's spell. Hitler invited him to be the main speaker
at a gathering in Munich's Bürgerbräu beer hall. "He
simply kills us with kindness," Goebbels noted. By July,
his about-face was complete. "He is a genius! . . . a real
man! . . . He pampers me like a child. That kindly friend
and master!" He also wrote the following about Strasser:
"In the final analysis, he is not smart enough. His heart is
in the right place, though! Sometimes I love him very
much!"

Goebbels became Hitler's most loyal vassal—to the
bitter end. In 1926, Hitler named him chief of the Berlin
party province. There, he not only fought against the
Communists but also against his old buddies, the Strasser
brothers. Thanks to Goebbels, the power of the left-wing
Nazis in North Germany crumbled. He now published

his own scandal sheet, called *Angriff (Attack),* competing with the newspaper of the Strasser brothers. In *Angriff* he spread the rumor that the Strasser brothers were descended from Jews and had been bought by big capital. So vindictive did Goebbels become that Hitler had to interfere personally to put the brakes on his radical new vassal. Hitler, however, did achieve his objective: He managed to swing the most talented propagandist of the Nazis over to his side. He had transformed a radical opponent into a radical follower. Looking at Goebbels, Strasser could only say, "I've been a stupid fool." In spite of all the humiliations, Gregor Strasser remained loyal to Hitler and was placated with the title of Reich Organization Leader.

Hitler also finally cemented his power in legal terms. At another "general membership meeting" on May 22, 1926, in Munich, he oversaw the adoption of new by-laws that were completely tailored for him personally. According to the Association Law, the National Socialist German Worker Party, Registered Association, in Munich, was the party's official operating body. To comply with the law, the first chairman had to be elected. Hitler made sure that only his own personal power group, the local Munich group, would function as a body of electors. Only this Munich group, which was totally loyal to him, would be allowed to demand an accounting from the chairman. Hitler's unrestricted control over the party had now been secured in a de jure fashion. No longer were there any majority resolutions that would be binding on him. In the future, the party province chiefs were no longer to be elected by the local party meetings but were instead to be appointed by the First Chairman, the "Führer." Also, membership dues from all over Germany were to be sent directly to Munich. The individual party provinces would then receive their disbursements.

Hitler's self-confidence received a tremendous boost from these victories. Until this time, his political development was still being determined by models like Dietrich Eckart or Ludendorff. Now, however, he began breaking away from such intellectual dependence. The fact that his superiors during the war had refused to promote him to corporal—with the justification that he lacked leadership qualities—had made big trouble for him. Now he had proven his leadership quality. He began comparing himself to Napoleon. He drew parallels between himself and the Frenchman who, in his youth, was ridiculed for his small stature and his Corsican accent. Napoleon began to fascinate him. He read everything he could get his hands on about the Great Corsican. After the Germans marched into Paris in 1940, he quickly toured the city on the Seine early one morning. Only two places seemed to interest him: the Opera and the Domes des Invalides, where he spent almost an hour in silent devotion before the emperor's sarcophagus. He ordered that the mortal remains of Napoleon's son, the Duke of Reichstadt, also be transferred to Paris and that they likewise be placed in the Dome des Invalides.

He picked a pseudonym for himself—Wolf. In private, he liked to have his immediate entourage and his intimate friends call him by that name. Mrs. Bruckmann, Mrs. Bechstein and Winifred Wagner were also given this privilege. He interpreted the name as the ancient Germanic form of Adolf, a symbol of strength, aggressiveness and solitude. He signed quite a few articles in the *Volkischer Beobachter* with "Wolf." His half-sister Angela, who was keeping house for him on Obersalzberg, dropped the name of her late husband Raubal and at Hitler's persuasive insistence called herself "Mrs. Wolf." Niece Geli addressed him as "Uncle Wolf." During World War II, the names "Wolf's Lair" and "Wolf's Gorge" became typical code names for his headquarters. In Germany today, there is still a place named after Adolf Hitler, the Volkswagen city of Wolfsburg. "After you, my Führer, the city is to bear the name Wolfsburg," Robert Ley, the dipsomaniac leader of the German Labor Front, had said as the plant was being built.

Another symbol of Hitler's drive for power was his passion for fast cars. During the night leading up to February 4, he said, in one of his many monologues in Führer Headquarters, which Bormann's aide Heinrich Heims had recorded: "In 1925, my Mercedes compressor was a joy for everyone. We went on trips to Luisenburg and then again to Bamberg and often to the Eremitage. Mrs. Bechstein had said: "Wolf, you simply must have the most beautiful car there is. You deserve it." She was thinking of a Maybach.

Hitler even claimed credit for having influenced the model program and the esthetic lines of the cars that bore the Mercedes star. During that same night-time monologue in the Führer Headquarters, he said: "I can claim credit for the things that make the Mercedes cars so beautiful today. In drawings and designs, I tried hard year after year to perfect that shape to the utmost." Today, the Stuttgart automakers refuse to discuss the issue. No matter what the real story is, Hitler was not only the company's best customer but he was also its best advertiser. Hitler's Munich friend, Mercedes representative Jakob Werlin, later climbed to the very top position in the corporation.

In their book *Hitlers Wegbereiter zur Macht (The People Who Cleared Hitler's Way to Power)*, James and Suzanne Pool maintain that Hitler, between 1925 and 1928, received a monthly amount of 1,500 marks—a considerable part of his personal income—from the divorced Duchess of Saxony-Anhalt. This statement cannot be verified because the authors do not name their source. However, if it is true—something which is entirely probable in view of the situation such as it was—then Hitler never mentioned this "monthly annuity" to the Finance Office.

Ever since his release from Landsberg, Hitler had been feuding with the Finance Office in Munich. On May 1, 1925, he received a notice warning him that he had to file his tax declaration for 1924 and the first quarter of 1925. On May 19, he replied: "I had no income in 1924, nor during the first quarter of 1925. I maintained my livelihood with the help of a bank loan."

After the purchase of his expensive car, the Finance Office asked Hitler "as soon as possible to inform the Office as to the funds with which you acquired the car." Hitler replied briefly to the effect that he took out another bank loan to buy the car.

Hitler failed to file the required quarterly statements. He was fined 10 marks. Eventually, he filed a statement for the last quarter of 1925, showing an income of 11,231 marks, deductible business expenses amounting to 6,540 marks, interest on debts to the tune of 2,245 marks, leaving a taxable net income of 2,446 marks.

He explained his deductions in a cover letter. The bank loan, he argued, was necessary because his trial had cost him a lot of money. He also had to borrow money in order to write his book. And he justified his travel expenses and the salaries of a private secretary, bodyguard, and driver as part of his business expenses incurred as a political writer. "Without my political activity, my name would be unknown. My political activity supplies me with the material that enables me to work as political author."

In the last paragraph of the letter, he wrote, "I can at any time provide a sworn statement about my income and my expenditures. I own neither property nor capital. I restrict my personal needs by doing without alcohol and tobacco, by eating my meals in the most modest restaurants and—apart from my low room rent—I have no expenses that would not be covered by the deductible business expenses of a political author. The information I am supplying does not constitute an attempt on my part to avoid my tax obligations; instead, it is a sober description of factual circumstances. The car is also only a means to an end for me. The automobile merely allows me to do my daily work."

The Finance Office would allow him only half of the deductible expenditures. Over the years, a stubborn correspondence developed between Hitler and the tax authorities.

In 1926, he reported a gross income of 15,903 marks and deductible expenditures of 31,209 marks—in other words, almost twice his income. Again, he said that the difference had been covered by a bank loan. Suddenly, in 1929, when he reported a gross income of 15,448 marks, he stopped deducting bank interest. What had happened? Had Hitler been able to repay his bank debts? We will pursue this question further.

According to Hitler's tax records, his income was derived exclusively from the royalties on *Mein Kampf*.

The volume was published in 1927. At first, the book sold very poorly. In 1925, 9,437 copies of the first volume were sold; in 1928, sales dropped to 3,015 copies but climbed back up to 7,664 in 1929.

The breakthrough didn't occur until 1930 with 54,000 copies; 50,808 copies were sold in 1931, while in 1932 the number of sales grew to 90,351, a figure that was increased ten-fold in 1933 with almost 854,127 copies.

In 1928, Hitler's income (as reported to the Finance Office) was still a modest 11,818 marks.

It must be assumed that Hitler's reported income was only a fraction of his actual income. How did he repay his bank debts? With what money did he buy the house on Obersalzberg in 1928 and how was he able to rent a luxury apartment on Prinzregenten Square in 1929? Hitler reported his royalties—and to some extent his fees from the *Volkischer Beobachter*—to the tax authorities because the Finance Office was able to audit the books of the publishing house. All other income was never mentioned and there was no documentation for it, either.

In 1928, Hitler bought Wachenfeld House for the sum of 30,000 marks. Because he wanted to avoid awkward questions from the Finance Office—as had happened when he bought his car—his sister Angela was listed as the "owner" in the Berchtesgaden real estate register. He informed the Finance Office that he spent only a few days each year there as his sister's guest.

On October 1, 1929, he moved into a swank nine-room apartment on the second floor of the building at 16 Prinzregenten Square, in the fashionable Bogenhausen section of Munich opposite the Prinzregenten Theater, where Wagner's operas were being staged. To do the housekeeping, he hired Mrs. Reichert, his former landlady on Thiersch Street, and later he added a domestic named Mrs. Anni Winter. Hitler's days as a roomer were over. He was 40 years old, a well-off gentleman in his prime, complete with household personnel, secretary, and his own driver. But he still refused to accept a salary from the party, maintaining that he was a free-lancer and referring to himself as a "painter and author"—precisely how he was recorded in the Munich address directory.

He would keep the apartment to the very end.

The lease contract was concluded with Hugo Schuehle, the owner of the ritzy building. The rent was set at 4,176 marks per year. (Compared to present-day purchasing power, the 1929 figure would be the equivalent today of 4,000 marks per month rent.)

Hitler's financial situation had improved quite definitely since the beginning of 1929. He suddenly seemed to have a lot of money. He bought expensive furniture, began collecting paintings and laid the foundation of his Spitzweg collection, which would one day be the world's biggest. His "official" income in 1929, however, was only 15,448 marks, which means that his funds were coming from an inexhaustible source. That source was one of Germany's richest men: Fritz Thyssen.

Fritz Thyssen slipped more money to the Nazi Party and to Hitler personally than any other individual. His father, August, had been a self-made man who grew up on a farm and built an industrial empire. When he died at 84 in 1926, his son Fritz was 53 years old. The son had always lived in his father's shadow and the father never gave the "crown prince" any accurate insight into the inner workings of his industrial empire. Just before he died, August founded the United Steel Works. After his father's death, Fritz was elected chairman of the board of this gigantic syndicate.

In contrast to his father, Fritz Thyssen was an introverted person. He was interested in religion and ideology. He worked diligently and showed up punctually in his office every morning, but his heart was really not in the company. He was considered an unusually intelligent and witty conversationalist. He loved good food and choice wines, and often spent many hours at fancy dinner parties.

During the French occupation of the Ruhr Region, Thyssen organized passive resistance in the Muelheim area. Although he was one of Germany's biggest capitalists, he had the support of the entire population, including the union leaders. Thyssen believed that Germany would have a bright future if the class hatred between workers and industry could be eliminated under

the aegis of National Socialism. It wasn't surprising that
he soon became interested in the work of the NSDAP. In
October 1923, Thyssen decided to visit Ludendorff in
Munich and gave him the sum of 100,000 gold marks on
the condition that the money be distributed between the
NSDAP and the Oberland Free Corps as required. At the
time, Hitler hadn't yet met the man. As far as Thyssen
was concerned, Hitler was an insignificant member compared to Ludendorff.

Five years later, in the autumn of 1928, the Nazis came
into contact with Thyssen. The party urgently needed
money to purchase the Barlow Palace on Brienner Street,
which they planned to remodel as their new headquarters
and call the Brown House.

Rudolf Hess contacted Emil Kirdorf, another Ruhr
magnate Hitler had met in Mrs. Bruckmann's drawing
room. But Kirdorf was unable to help out with such a
large amount of money. He sympathized with the Nazis
but was known to be extremely stingy. Kirdorf suggested
that Hess try his luck with Thyssen and arranged the
meeting himself. Thyssen was quite taken with the social
polish of the businessman's son from Alexandria. Hess
also displayed considerable negotiating skill on that
occasion. Thyssen arranged a loan, secured by him, from
the Bank Voor Handel en Scheepvaart N.V. in Rotter-
dam. Thyssen said the loan was for 250,000 marks but
1,250,000 marks seems to be the more likely figure. The
250,000 marks might have been enough to make the
down payment, because the remodeling and renovation
of the party palace alone cost more than 800,000 marks.
This time, Hitler was both architect and interior decorator along with Professor Paul Ludwig Troost. Money was
no object when it came to furnishing the building even
though an international economic crisis loomed on the
horizon. A party member, who visited the Brown House
for the first time after its opening, had this to say: "If the
swastika flag had not been waving on the roof, I would
have considered the building to be the palace of a curia
cardinal or the town home of a big Jewish banker."
"Everything exudes the kind of sterling quality that can
be achieved only with very expensive material," said

another visitor. Hitler, of course, magnanimously refused to accept the architect's fee that was offered to him by treasurer Schwarz, but it was generally known that suppliers, interior decorator firms and furniture makers slipped him tax-free "bonuses" for his private kitty.

After his break with Hitler in 1936, Thyssen said the Nazis had repaid only 150,000 marks of the original loan while he had to make good for the rest out of his own pocket.

Be that as it may, after Hess had sewn up the promise of a loan, he arranged a meeting between Hitler and Thyssen in Munich. Thyssen immediately fell under the spell of the hypnotic party leader. The highly educated, sensitive and artistically-inclined captain of industry became one of Hitler's passionate followers. For economic and social reasons, however, he at first did not join the party.

Hitler was invited several times to one of Thyssen's castles in the Rhineland. Whenever Thyssen came to Munich, he would invite Hitler to lunch or dinner at the Walterspiel Restaurant in the Vier Jahreszeiten Hotel which at that time had the reputation of offering Munich's finest cuisine. Thyssen loved to discuss not only the political situation with Hitler but also to talk about music, painting and architecture with him. Hitler admired the Canalettos, Rembrandts and El Grecos in Thyssen's castles and dreamed some day of owning such paintings.

Through Hitler, Thyssen also met Hermann Göring, for whom he immediately developed a very spontaneous liking. Göring had returned from his Italian and Swedish exile in 1927 and was now living in Berlin as a representative for a Swedish aircraft factory. Later, Thyssen wrote the following about Göring: "At that time, he lived in a very small apartment and very much wanted to enlarge it to make a better impression. I paid the bill."

Thyssen frequently visited Hermann Göring in Berlin. Both men shared their predilection for fine cuisine. They usually dined at Horcher's. Soon, Göring began receiving cash from Thyssen to meet his personal needs. According to Göring, Thyssen gave him 50,000 marks on three separate occasions. But he also kept the money Thyssen gave him to use on party projects. Once, Thyssen gave Göring 50,000 marks for a newspaper which the sometime chief of staff of the SA and subsequent party economic expert Otto Wagener wanted to buy for the NSDAP in the Rhineland. When Wagener turned up in Göring's Berlin apartment and asked him to hand over the money, Göring turned him down flat. He said that he had already used the money for his own public relations activities.

Naturally, Hitler learned about Göring's financial manipulations and Thyssen's gifts to him. During Thyssen's next visit to Munich, Hitler steered the conversation toward his own "precarious" financial situation, one that was truly unworthy of a prominent party leader. He indicated that he lived in a humbly furnished room where he couldn't receive visitors. He had large debts with the bank, not to mention with the Finance Office. And he had to pay his secretary, his driver and his bodyguard out of his own pocket because he didn't want the party to have to pay for such expenses. These expenditures outstripped his income so that he was forced to go deeper and deeper into debt. Unfortunately, he had neither the time nor the business acumen of a Hermann Göring to look for lucrative income sources. He was devoting all of his time to Germany and the NSDAP.

Thyssen was deeply moved. Why had Hitler not mentioned this to him earlier? It was certainly honorable that he didn't wish to be a burden to the party. Thyssen immediately offered to pay Hitler's bank debts and to make all necessary funds available to him so that he could get himself a nice home in a fashionable part of town. He would also provide the proper accessories for a prominent politician. He would even take care of the expenses for the salaries of his personal staff.

Hitler played coy. The offer made by Mr. Thyssen, he said, was immensely magnanimous. There must, however, be no implication that he, Hitler, would be obliged politically in return. If the newspapers were to report that he was "in the pay of big industrialists," it could have a disastrous effect. Thyssen reassured him the money would come from his private kitty in a discreet manner.

Nothing would show up in the books. As far as he, himself, was concerned, Mr. Hitler need not worry. He believed in him. "For me, you are the man who will reunite Germany and make it strong and put an end to the Communist threat. I would never dream of giving you any instructions on your way to that goal because I have the honor of helping you to achieve economic independence." With tears in his eyes, Hitler shook the hand of his magnanimous patron.

Even before Hitler started looking for a new apartment, he bought a new Mercedes, the 100-horsepower 15/70 Compressor, on March 23. Fritz Thyssen was also tapped to finance the start of an illustrated weekly magazine. Heinrich Hoffmann had been trying for months to get Hitler's approval. Together with publishing house manager Amann, Hoffmann and Esser, Hitler founded the *Illustriete Beobachter,* a picture magazine that would particularly help Hoffmann—who alone was responsible for picture procurement—attain growing prosperity. Hermann Esser became the editor-in-chief while Adolf Hitler was the publisher. This magazine was more attractive than the boring *Volkischer Beobachter* and was soon operating at a profit. Amann was now happy because he was able to show his enemy Rosenberg how a financially successful newspaper should be run. Hitler—who each week wrote a leading editorial under the heading "Politics of the Week" and drew a high star fee of 300 marks—made fun of Rosenberg: "All he gives us is deep philosophical treatises, written by professors and dealing mostly with Central Asia." Amann couldn't stand the pseudo-intellectual Balt, who sat for hours on end in the Odeon Café near the Feldherrnhalle Memorial, reading and writing. "There he squats again, that crumb, and makes his poems! He had better put out a good newspaper!"

When sales of *Mein Kampf* shot up to 54,086 in 1930, Max Amann was finally won over to Hitler's side because he was now for the first time earning a real income from the publishing house. Without complaint, he turned the 46,000 marks in royalties over to his Führer.

In 1932, Hitler's income from *Mein Kampf* had been

65,000 marks. During the first year of his chancellorship, it soared to over one million. He'd become a millionaire. He was soon to become a multimillionaire.

# Chapter Ten

# Ladies in Waiting

One of the first women Hitler took a liking to was Erna Hanfstengl, Putzi Hanfstaengl's sister. She was a tall, good-looking, popular lady of Munich society. Erna behaved in a rather cruel, somewhat mocking manner. Many considered her to be arrogant—a type that attracted Hitler. Hitler and Erna were frequently seen together in fine restaurants. It was expected that they would soon become engaged. But then the malicious tongues began to wag, hinting that Erna was of Jewish extraction because her American grandmother's maiden name was Heine. As the rumors grew even more distasteful, Hitler fanned the flames by printing a notice in the *Volkischer Beobachter*: "Rumors are being circulated regarding Adolf Hitler's engagement to a Jewish lady. These rumors are lies. Adolf Hitler is not engaged. Besides the lady in question, Miss Hanfstaengl, is not of Jewish extraction." After this exceedingly tactful statement, the entire city was free to think as it chose. Erna, at any rate, deprived the party leader of her favors, quickly marrying one of Hitler's rivals, a surgeon named Sauerbruch.

Beginning in 1927, the party's friends had been getting accustomed to seeing Hitler in the constant company of a pretty, dark-haired girl. She was no heavenly beauty. Actually, she was rather coarse, with brownish skin and Slavic cheekbones that didn't hide her peasant ancestry. She was 19 years younger than the party leader. Her name was Angelika and her nickname was Geli; she was the daughter of Hitler's half-sister, Angela Raubal, who was keeping house for him on Obersalzberg.

Geli came to Munich from Berchtesgaden in 1927; she had been living in Munich with her mother since the end of 1925. She had musical talent and a passable voice. Hitler wanted to have her trained as a singer in Munich at his own expense. He could already see her in the role of Elsa or Isolde in Europe's opera houses, some day perhaps even in Bayreuth.

At first, Hitler put his niece up in the Klein Boarding House at the English Garden where Rudolf Hess had also been living after the war. Then he got her a room at 43 Thiersch Street, in the house next to his own apartment. Hitler was with Geli every day. One could see them in the Hick Café, in the Stephanie Café, in the Carlton Tea Room, in the Osteria or in the Prinzregenten Café, near the Brown House where Hitler was supervising the remodeling job.

Everybody knew that the relations between the uncle and niece went beyond mere kinship. There were even whispers that Hitler intended to marry Geli. A marriage of this sort would not have been unusual for the family—Hitler's father had also married his niece.

Hitler showered the girl with presents. He bought her furs and jewels and tried to anticipate her every wish. There was only one wish he could not fulfill: the wish of any young girl to have a little independence, the wish to be able now and then to spend some time with people her own age. He stifled her with his jealousy, watching her every step. Of course, Geli in her naive ways enjoyed being by the side of her famous uncle, the politician who was known all over the city, but she often felt confined. Although outwardly Hitler emphasized that he was not her lover but "only" her uncle, he drove away every young man who tried to start a harmless flirtation with her.

When Hitler moved into his new luxury apartment at 26 Prinzregenten Square at the end of 1929, Geli was given a room there. Her freedom of movement was now even more restricted than before. Hitler gave Anni Winter, the housekeeper, the job of chaperon and watchdog. He knew only too well that his niece was a fun-loving girl and that being watched by an older man often got on her nerves. The first explosion took place one day when Hitler found the watchmaker Emil Maurice—one of his former bodyguards and a close confidant from the early days of the party—in Geli's room. They had only had a friendly chat and smoked cigarettes, something that Hitler did not like anyway. Screaming, he called Maurice a "scoundrel" and "skirt chaser". He hit him with his riding crop and threatened to shoot him "like a mad dog" at the next opportunity. Maurice was able to save himself from the blows of Hitler's riding crop only by fleeing. It took Rudolf Hess and Gregor Strasser together to keep Maurice from challenging Hitler to a duel "for slandering his honor." On Hess' advice, Hitler condescended to come up with a lame apology, but the apartment of Prinzregenten Square was off-limits for Maurice from that moment on.

After Maurice's flight, Mrs. Winter heard a loud altercation between Hitler and Geli, one that ended in crying spells by both of the disputants. If an intimate love relationship had not existed between uncle and niece, then it did from that day on.

It was neither a happy nor a normal relationship. Not only were Hitler's frequent and groundless outbursts of jealousy torture for Geli but his bizarre sexual practices shocked and repulsed the young and somewhat innocent girl.

Just prior to his death, Dr. Otto Strasser, who had broken with Hitler in 1931 and who became one of his most bitter opponents, spoke with the author of this book, casting some light on the relationship between Geli and Hitler:

"I liked that girl very much and I could feel how much she suffered because of Hitler's jealousy. She was a fun-loving young thing who enjoyed the Mardi Gras excitement in Munich but was never able to persuade Hitler to accompany her to any of the many wild balls. Finally, during the 1931 Mardi Gras, Hitler allowed me to take Geli to a ball. Shortly before I was to leave to pick her up, my brother Gregor told me that Hitler had just phoned and taken his permission back. I went to Prinzregenten Square just the same. Geli seemed to have won out. Looking into her eyes, I could tell that she had been crying. Hitler stood stony-faced at the door as we left the house to get into the waiting cab. We had a very nice and happy evening. Geli seemed to enjoy having for once escaped Hitler's supervision. On the way back from Schwabing to Prinzregenten Square, we took a walk through the English Garden. Near the Chinese Tower, Geli sat down on a bench and began to cry bitterly. Finally she told me that Hitler loved her but that she couldn't stand it any more. His jealousy was not the worst of it. He demanded things of her that were simply repulsive. She never suspected that people would do such things. When I asked her to explain it, she told me things that I knew only from my readings of Krafft-Ebing's *Psychopathia Sexualis* during my college days."

The author asked Dr. Strasser for details but he refused to give them, "not out of consideration for Hitler but for the sake of Geli's memory." All he would say was, "He was a sadist and a masochist, both in one person."

As we know from research in sexual pathology, sadism and masochism are but two different forms of the same personality disorder and are frequently found to alternate in the same person. There are numerous instances of Hitler's sadistic tendencies. After the attempt on his life on July 20, 1944, for example, he ordered that the execution of the conspirators be filmed in every detail. He watched the film many times in his headquarters. He also ordered the executioner—whom he had specially flown to his headquarters—to perform the rites in a particularly cruel fashion. As the conspirators were being hanged, they died not as was customary—when their necks were broken—but instead were pulled up on the rope and strangled slowly. As they were hanging in the sling, their trousers were pulled down so that Hitler could observe their genitals.

During World War II, the American OSS in the United States questioned a number of people who had developed a close acquaintance with Hitler. The agents also spoke

to the Hollywood producer A. Zeissler, who, during the
early Thirties, had worked for UFA (Universe Film
Company) in Berlin. Although Zeissler's report must be
taken with a grain of salt, it does cast some light on certain sexual practices of the Führer. Shortly after he
seized power in Berlin, Hitler loved to surround himself
with good-looking actresses. Among that group were Anny Ondra, the wife of the boxer Max Schmeling, and Jenny Jugo, a star in many American films. Zeissler also told
the agents about the actress Renate Mueller, with whom
he was working at that time and with whom he was also
friends.

"Renate Mueller at that time was one of Hitler's favor-
ites. She certainly would not have been disinclined to
enter into a sexual relationship with the Führer. She told
me that medieval torture techniques was one of his
favorite topics of discussion. One morning she came to
the film studio visibly upset and said that she didn't want
to get together with Hitler any more. The night before,
she had gladly accepted his invitation to come to his private apartment in the Reich Chancellery, expecting an
evening of love-making. When she got there, they both
got undressed. But instead of jumping into bed with Renate Mueller, Hitler threw himself on the floor before
the actress and begged her to beat him and stomp on
him. Horrified, she refused. He continued to insist, im-
ploring her to do him this favor. She said that he then
humiliated himself before her with the worst self-
accusations and groaned that he was her slave and was
unworthy of being in the same room with her. In the
process, he became very excited. She finally gave in, step-
ping on him, beating him with his riding crop and, upon
his request, heaping obscene insults on him. Hitler, she
reported, became increasingly excited and finally started
to masturbate. Shortly after his orgasm, he suggested in a
calm voice that the two of them get dressed again. After
that, they drank a glass of wine and talked about nothing
noteworthy. Hitler finally got up, kissed her hand,
thanked her for a pleasant evening and rang for the
servant to escort her out. I am convinced that Renate
Mueller was completely honest with me and that she did

not make this story up."

Of course, one could consider Renate Mueller's experience—she committed suicide a few years later—to be the product of a hysterical imagination. The fact is, however, that a whole series of people who knew Hitler intimately, including Putzi Hanfstaengl, repeatedly pointed out that Hitler's sexual inclinations were abnormal. Hanfstaengl went so far as to maintain that Hitler was not at all capable of normal sexual intercourse. But this is contradicted by various diary entries made by Eva Braun and by the fact that Eva once asked Hitler's personal physician, Dr. Morell, to give the Führer a tonic because the latter's sexual potency had declined due to too much hard work.

The unhappy love affair between Hitler and Geli Raubal dragged on throughout the summer of 1931. Hitler traveled frequently. Geli was living as if she were in prison, with Mrs. Anni Winter as her well-meaning warden. Whenever she went out, she was accompanied by one of the wives of Hitler's paladins, Mrs. Hoffmann, Mrs. Hess or Mrs. Amann.

The catastrophe happened on September 18, 1931. Hitler wanted to take his car on a trip to Hamburg via Nuernberg and Weimar. His driver, Julius Schreck, was waiting outside in the Mercedes Compressor. Geli summoned all of her courage and told Hitler that she wanted to go to Vienna to continue her singing lessons. She had learned from reliable sources that Hitler had a young blonde girlfriend who worked in Heinrich Hoffmann's studio. (In October 1929, Hitler had met 17-year-old Eva Braun in Hoffmann's studio; she had been dismissed from the Convent School, and she wanted to learn the photography trade from Hoffmann. Since then, Hitler frequently met the girl, much to the displeasure of her parents.) She, Geli, no longer wished to stand in the way of that relationship.

Hitler flew into a rage. A bitter argument ensued. Hitler finally calmed down. He said that he was pressed for time. They would be able to discuss everything calmly after his return from Hamburg. Geli withdrew to her room after he had left. She didn't want to be disturbed, not even for lunch. About three hours later, Mrs. Winter

heard a shot. She ran to Geli's door and shook it. The
door was locked. She called Geli's name but got no reply.
Mrs. Winter was desperate. Should she get the police and
trigger a scandal? In her quandary, she recalled that Hitler had a private secretary who had his office in the
Brown House on Brienner Street. She phoned Rudolf
Hess. He asked her not to do anything for the time being.
He promised to come right away. Shortly afterwards, he
ran into Gregor Strasser. Together, they broke down the
door of Geli's room. The 23-year-old girl was lying dead
in a pool of blood. She had shot herself in the heart with
Hitler's revolver.

Hess managed to reach Hitler in Nuernberg. He reported to him what had happened. Hitler raced back to Munich while Hess and Strasser tried to figure out what to
do with the body. Strasser strongly urged that the police
be informed, but Hess was against the idea. He was a-
fraid of a scandal. Strasser prevailed, insisting that any
further cover-up of the matter would trigger an even bigger scandal. The police doctor ruled the death suicide by
shooting. Mrs. Winter's statement was taken down. There
was no further investigation. As Hitler arrived in Munich, Geli's body had already been removed. Hitler collapsed from nervous shock.

A whole series of theories and legends have since developed around Geli's death. There is one theory that
says Geli shot herself because she was in love with her
Jewish voice coach. Another says she killed herself because she was jealous of Eva Braun. The most adventur-
ous one maintains that Hitler shot Geli before his
departure because he had made her pregnant and he
didn't want to marry her. Mrs. Winter, Hess and Gregor
Strasser provided Hitler with the alibi he needed to re-
fute this latter theory.

No farewell letter was ever found. It was said that if
there had been such a letter Hess and Strasser would
have removed it because it would have been too incriminating for Hitler. The precise circumstances will never
come to light. Gregor Strasser was shot and killed in the
Berlin Gestapo (Secret State Police) prison on June 30,
1934, and Rudolf Hess, who lived until 1987, never said a

word. Strasser was convinced that his brother died because he knew too much about Geli Raubal's death. The murder theory, however, is on very shaky ground. According to the police investigation, other tenants in the building testified that they heard a shot long after Hitler had departed on his journey. Geli almost certainly committed suicide. She knew where Hitler kept his second pistol and was easily able to get her hands on it after his departure.

After her death, Hitler withdrew to the country home of print shop owner Adolf Mueller on Lake Tegern for several days. Because he kept talking about wanting to kill himself, Hess and his driver Schreck were constantly with him and did not let him out of their sight.

Hitler decided to go on living. He received some consolation from Hamburg where the voters of the Hanseatic city gave him 43 seats in the City Council, a place where the Nazis until then had been poorly represented. Coupled with this good political news, the 19-year-old photo lab technician and photo sales girl Eva Braun brought him out of his despair. Although she would remain loyal to Hitler until the end of his life—and even die with him—she herself would twice attempt suicide because of him.

After her death, Hitler started a Geli Raubal cult. Geli's room in the Munich apartment on Prinzregenten Square was closed off and no one other than Hitler and Mrs. Winter was allowed to enter it. Whenever Hitler was in Munich, he often locked himself in her room for hours on end. He didn't attend Geli's funeral in Vienna because he was physically and psychologically unable to do so, though on the first anniversary of her death, he drove to Vienna to visit the grave. In his book *Vom Kaiserhof zur Reichskanzlei (From the Kaiserhof Hotel to the Reich Chancellery)*, Goebbels made the following remark about this trip: "The Führer went to Vienna for a private visit."

After he took power in 1933, Hitler commissioned the sculptor Josef Thorak to create a bust of Geli, which he kept in his office at the New Reich Chancellery. Adolf Ziegler—whose naturalistic nude paintings Hitler liked, though he also mocked Ziegler as a "master of German

pubic hair"—painted a portrait of her that was later giv-
en a special place in the Berghof and always decorated
with flowers.

On May 2, 1938, Adolf Hitler wrote out his last will
and testament, provided the following, under Point 4:
"The furniture in the room of my Munich apartment
where my niece Geli Raubal lived is to be given to my
sister Angela." Points 3b and 3c in the same will specified
that his sister Angela and his younger sister Paula were
to get 1,000 marks each per month—"in other words,
12,000 marks annually." A certain "Miss Eva Braun, Munich" turned up under Point 3a, to be likewise given 1,000
marks per month—in other words, 12,000 marks annually.
Before 1933, however, Hitler as of yet did not have
that kind of money to bequeath or give away. Eva had
not started making any excessive demands upon his
purse. After she met Hitler, she did not give up her job
in Hoffmann's studio on Augusten Street in Munich. She
was the second-oldest daughter of senior industrial arts
teacher Fritz Braun and had been educated in a Catholic
girls' institute in Simbach on the Inn, opposite Hitler's
birthplace, Braunau. After finishing a business course, she
was hired to work in the photo shop attached to Hoffmann's studio, where she met Hitler. She was of medi-
um-height, had dark blonde hair and blue eyes. She liked
to "highlight" her hair with hydrogen peroxide in order
to appear blonder than she really was. She was certainly
pretty enough, although hers was a doll-like cuteness. Her
older sister Ilse worked as an assistant secretary in the
office of a Jewish physician named Dr. Martin Levi
Marx, while her younger sister Gretl was also hired by
Hoffmann.
Since the end of 1930, Hitler had been seeing Eva, 22
years his junior, with increasing frequency. It is not certain whether Geli Raubal at that time had any grounds
for jealousy. At any rate, Hitler took Eva to the movies,
to dinner in the Osteria Bavaria, to the Opera and invited her to picnics in the city. Later, Heinrich Hoffmann
said: "Neither I nor anybody else detected that Hitler was
intensively interested in Eva. With her, though, it was

completely different. She told her girlfriends that Hitler
was in love with her and that she would certainly
manage to persuade him to marry her."

At that time, Eva had a serious rival in the person of
Hoffmann's daughter, Henriette, who was the same age
(and who later, at the Führer's behest, married Hitler
Youth Leader Baldur von Schirach). Henriette tried very
hard to pull into the lead and bag Hitler for herself, but
she had less success than Eva. It has been said that Henriette (or "Henny") was considered an "easy mark" in Munich university circles. At any rate, the big-breasted, fun-
loving girl was a popular Mardi Gras date.

Hitler at first had no intention of entering into any
kind of relationship with Eva other than a loose love
liaison. There are, in fact, strong indications that Hitler,
after Geli's death, considered marrying Winifred Wagner.
Siegfried Wagner had died in 1930 and Hitler's friendship
with Winifred had remained very close. She was one of
the few women with whom he used the familiar form of
address and her children called him "uncle." In the end,
however, Winifred rejected his marriage proposals because she was repulsed by his unorthodox sexual demands.

At a small party in the autumn of 1930, Hitler met a 29
year-old woman in Berlin whose "beauty and noble appearance" immediately captivated him. Her name was
Magda Quandt. She was the girlfriend of his Berlin Party
Province Leader, Joseph Goebbels. Until the age of 20,
Magda had borne the name of her Jewish stepfather
Friedlander, but in January 1921 she married the industrialist Guenther Quandt, a 38-year-old widower with two
sons. Their son Harald was born in November 1921, but
the marriage soon broke up and she was divorced in
1929. Quandt agreed to pay his ex-wife 50,000 marks for
the purchase of furniture and a monthly allowance of
4,000 marks, so long as she did not remarry. She rented
an elegant seven room apartment in the western part of
Berlin and kept his last name.

During a Nazi meeting in Berlin's Sportpalast, the attractive and elegant Magda Quandt met Joseph Goebbels,

the radical doctor of philosophy and incurable proletarian. Fascinated by him, she joined the party and did part-time work in the provincial party headquarters. Soon she became the provincial party chief's mistress.

It seemed for a while that Magda Quandt would leave Goebbels and go with Hitler but the passionate provincial party chief won out in the end. Goebbels married Magda on December 19, 1931, but Hitler remained a close family friend. Because Magda had lost her 4,000 mark allowance as a result of the marriage, Hitler ordered Goebbels' income to be doubled. The provincial party chief's marriage to Magda turned out to be financially lucrative for Hitler and for the party. Although Goebbels himself was still not very welcome in Berlin's fine circles, his elegant new wife was very much in demand. She was invited to the most exclusive parties, including those given by Crown Princess Caecilie, where she found a whole series of rich patrons for the Nazis.

Magda and Joseph Goebbels tried discreetly to find attractive women for Hitler. After Geli Raubal's death, they introduced him to Gretl Slezak, the 30-year-old daughter of the world-famous opera singer, Leo Slezak. It is impossible to determine how far his relations with "quarter-Jewess" Gretl went, but it is known that Hitler and Gretl Slezak—carefully shielded by Goebbels—were alone together frequently. The bosomy Gretl Slezak was physically the type of woman Hitler preferred. Henriette Hoffmann—who herself was blessed with generous bust measurements—reported how Eva Braun in the beginning used to stuff handkerchiefs into her brassiere in order to be more appealing to Hitler.

In the summer of 1932, Eva Braun felt more and more lonely and increasingly neglected by Hitler. At that time, he was traveling a lot but refused to let Eva accompany him. Whenever he was in Munich, a hasty get-together was arranged in his apartment on Prinzregenten Square followed by dinner with the members of his entourage in the Osteria. On those occasions, Hitler often slipped his mistress an envelope with a 100 mark bill inside, without any greeting or even words of affection. Hitler seemed to

lack any sensitivity about these sorts of things and failed
to realize that Eva was made to feel like a prostitute.

Eva Braun's depression reached its nadir in the summer of 1932. One night in July, she phoned the surgeon
Dr. Plate—one of Heinrich Hoffmann's brothers-in-
law—from her apartment on Wiedenmayer Street (which
Hitler was paying for) and asked him to come
immediately. She had shot herself near the heart with a
6.35 millimeter pistol. Plate had her immediately transported to the private section of his hospital and informed Hoffmann of what happened. Hoffmann called Hitler,
who immediately returned to Munich. The shot Eva fired
was not fatal and the bullet was easily removed. As
Hoffmann later wrote, Hitler immediately wanted to
know if the doctor could keep his mouth shut about the
incident. During a conference he asked Dr. Plate: "Doctor,
tell me the truth! Did Miss Braun inflict a harmless bullet
wound on herself only to make herself look interesting
and attract my attention?" The doctor replied that he was
sure that Eva Braun had really intended to kill herself.
Hitler had even received a suicide note from her, but
destroyed it immediately after having read it.

Hitler said to Hoffmann, "The girl did this out of love
for me. But I didn't give her any reason that might justify the act. Now it is quite clear that I must take care of
her." After thinking for a few moments, he continued,
"The fact that I want to take care of her does not mean
that I am going to marry her. Eva's best quality is that
she is not a political activist. I hate political women. The
girlfriend of a politician must not be smart." Through her
first suicide attempt, Eva Braun was able to get Hitler to
recognize her as his girlfriend.

One day in 1935, while eating in the side room of the
Osteria Bavaria with Hoffmann, Amann, Mrs. Troost and
the Munich Mercedes manager Werlin, Hitler noticed a
young lady, who was obviously English, at a table in the
main room. She embodied the type of big-bosomed Valkyrie who was actually quite rare in her home country.
Hitler was attracted to her. From Hoffmann, who knew
all about such things, Hitler learned that this was Unity

Valkyrie Mitford, one of the six daughters of Lord Redesdale. She was reported to be just as aware politically as her sisters. Diana married the British fascist leader Oswald Mosley and Jessica who, along with her fiance Edmond Romilly, one of Churchill's nephews, embraced the extreme Left.

Unity had moved to Munich in 1934 to study art history. She was an enthusiastic supporter of National Socialism, and the year before had attended the Nuernberg Party Congress. Hitler asked his entourage to invite her to join him. He elegantly kissed her hand and inquired about her art study. Unity replied: "Mr. Hitler, I am not only a university student but also an English fascist."

Hitler talked to her in a very animated manner. Their initial meeting in the Osteria was followed by invitations to the Carlton Tea Room on Brienner Street and attendance at the opera. Unity wrote enthusiastically to Diana, inviting her and her husband Oswald to visit Munich in order to meet Hitler.

The British fascist leader and his wife came to Munich in April 1935 and were received by Hitler for dinner in his apartment on Prinzregenten Square. Diana Mosley recalled that she saw other women of English origin at the next table. They were Winifred Wagner, the Duchess of Brunswick (daughter of Emperor Wilhelm II and granddaughter of Queen Victoria), and her daughter Friederike, who later became Queen of Greece. At that time Friederike was an enthusiastic National Socialist and an active leader in the League of German Girls, the female counterpart of the Hitler Youth. Hitler was less than enthusiastic about Mosley's influence in England.

Unity Mitford was in love with Hitler, but a love affair between her and the dictator probably sprang from the imagination of a *Daily Express* reporter. After 1935, Unity was frequently invited to official events, but Hitler hardly had any further private contact with her. The day war broke out between Germany and England, September 3, 1939, Unity, sitting on a bench in Munich's English Garden, fired a bullet into her head. The wound was not fatal. Hitler immediately saw to it that she received every possible medical assistance and, after her recovery, had her transported to England via neutral Switzerland.

On the other hand, Unity became the direct cause for Eva Braun's second suicide attempt. Eva had been seriously depressed for quite some time mostly due to her jealousy of Unity. On March 11, 1935, she stood in front of the Carlton Tea Room for three hours, where Hitler was dining with movie actress Anny Ondra (later, Mrs. Max Schmeling). Bitterly she watched as Hitler came out and handed Anny a huge bouquet of flowers that had been picked up by one of his SS escorts.

Later, Mrs. Hoffmann rather maliciously and tactlessly informed Eva that Hitler had found a replacement for her. On May 10, 1935, she wrote the following in her diary: "Her name is Valkyrie and that is exactly what she looks like, including her legs. But he loves those dimensions; in other words, if this is so, he will soon have gotten her to become very thin out of chagrin if she does not have the talent for becoming fat on account of grief." On May 28, she wrote the following: "No matter what happens, uncertainty is much worse than a sudden end. Dear God, help me to get to talk to him today because tomorrow might be too late. I decided to take 35 of these things and this time it has to be a 'dead certainty.' If he would only call."

During the night, Eva Braun took 34 powerful sleeping pills. The Jewish physician Dr. Marx—her sister Ilse's employer—saved her life by means of gastric washing.

With this second attempt, Eva seemed to have gotten Hitler finally to decide in favor of her. He continued to reject marriage, to be sure, but she became his official mistress and the woman at the center of his life—if not to the public then at least to the party's staff members.

During the 1935 Party Congress, she sat on the main reviewing stand together with Unity Mitford and Magda Goebbels. She wore a magnificent fur coat, a present from Hitler. When Hitler was secretly informed that Magda Goebbels had made nasty remarks about the Führer's mistress, Hitler became so furious that he denied his old friend access to the Reich Chancellory for several months.

The guests of honor at the Party Congress also

included Hitler's half-sister, Angela Raubal. Like Eva Braun, she stayed in the Deutscher Hof Hotel. Hitler witnessed an ugly quarrel between the two women. Immediately after the Party Congress he and Angela drove back to the Berghof. He immediately asked her to pack her things and leave the house. Hitler gave her a financial compensation of 10,000 marks but no longer wanted her to be around if she couldn't accept and respect Eva Braun. Angela moved to Dresden, where she later married the architect Hamitzsch. A new hostess was brought in from Munich. But the real "lady of the house" now was Eva Braun. She was able to visit the Berghof as often as she liked. She had become the main woman in Hitler's life.

Hitler had a house built for Eva Braun at fashionable 12 Wasserburg Street (today, Delp Street). On March 30, 1936, Eva and her sister Gretl moved in. The house had a living area of about 800 square feet on the first level with an upper floor. The land as such covered 8,000 square feet with a high wall around the perimeter. The house was rather modest but tastefully furnished in modern style.

The neighborhood housed well-known personalities, including aircraft builder Messerschmidt, architect Giesler, publisher Amann and photographer Hoffmann. Eva Braun was given a personal bodyguard, who lived in a small hut in the garden. As a housewarming present, Hitler gave his girlfriend a Mercedes with a full-time driver. The car was kept in the Mercedes Garage on Dachauer Street and was always available to her. Manager Werlin personally supervised the maintenance of Eva's car.

# Chapter Eleven

# The Reich Chancellor

Statistics show that Germany had 5.7 million unemployed on December 31, 1931. Party membership had risen to 807,000. The year 1932 was the decisive year of Hitler's career.

New elections for the office of Reich president had been scheduled for March. When the Social Democrats announced that they were going to vote for Hindenburg, the Nazis stopped supporting the senile field marshal. Hitler announced his own candidacy but soon discovered that he wasn't qualified because when he had given up his Austrian citizenship, he had never acquired German citizenship. A way was soon devised for him to do this. In Brunswick, a coalition government had a Nazi as its interior minister. On February 4, the minister appointed Adolf Hitler as an "assistant professor" at the Technical College. He was to deliver 12 lectures per semester on "Organic Social Science and Politics." This appointment, however, backfired when the college president wouldn't go along. Hitler, he said, lacked the "minimum academic requirements."

The interior minister figured out another way. On February 26, 1932, Hitler was appointed counsellor of government with the Brunswick Embassy in Berlin. In that capacity, he was officially sanctioned "to promote and represent Brunswick interests with the German central government." Hitler, the brand-new counsellor of government, entered the embassy only once and that was to take his oath to the constitution as a new citizen and official. After that, he was given indefinite leave "to pursue political activities." This is how Adolf Hitler became a German. Now he had both active and passive voting rights.

His initial try for the position of head of state failed. During the first round of elections, Hindenburg got 49.6 percent of the votes while Hitler came in second with 30.1 percent; the Communist Thaelmann obtained 13.2 percent and Stahlhelm Leader Duesterberg wound up with 6.8 percent.

During the second round, Hindenburg received 53 percent of the votes while Hitler got 13,400,000 votes, or 36.8 percent. The *Times* published an interview with Hitler: "I have no personal ambition to become the Reich president. I ran against Hindenburg for the sole reason that the system, which we want to smash, exploited his prestige and popularity."

On July 31, 1932, the NSDAP won a landslide election victory. It was now the strongest delegation in the German legislature, with 230 deputies. Hitler was certain that he'd be appointed chancellor. Hindenburg, however, hadn't the slightest intention of doing that. He let Hitler know that he might possibly be considered for the position of vice chancellor. Hitler was insulted. He ordered the SA to be mobilized around Berlin and put it on alert. He threatened to have all Marxists in the city "slaughtered." Papen decreed a state of emergency. War Minister Schleicher told Hitler that the German Army would meet any uprising with force. During a hastily called conference, 85-year-old President Hindenburg did not even offer Hitler a chair to sit in; he let him stand for the full eight minutes and, beating time with his cane, bawled him out like a schoolboy. Hindenburg called him a "faithless fellow" for going back on his pre-election promise to support a cabinet put together by Papen. The press devoured the humiliating spectacle.

Hitler's aura as leader now had some ugly stains. It looked as if the NSDAP was beginning to fall apart. Old party members turned their backs on him. Nobody could understand his "all-or-nothing" policy. Why did he reject a coalition? Why did he refuse to enable the party to join the administration? Even the SA men began to desert him, switching to the Communists or to Otto Strasser's social-revolutionary Black Front. Party members began to call Hitler the "eternal oppositionist."

The party treasury was running dry. The party's debts came to 90 million marks, although privately Hitler had no worries whatsoever about his income. The 1931 royalties for *Mein Kampf* alone were 40,780 marks, with 51,000 copies sold. Amann also credited him with 15,000 marks for his articles in the *Voelkischer Beobachter* and in the *Illustrierte Beobachter*. Regardless of his own situation, the party was in bad shape. The business sector had stopped giving donations. Checks began to bounce. Creditors sent the process servers to the Brown House. Even the otherwise endlessly patient print shop owner Otto Mueller sent an ultimatum: Either the overdue debts were paid or the *Voelkischer Beobachter* would no longer be printed. The SA, with its 400,000 troops, cost 1.2 million marks a week. The SA men were sent out into the street to beg, shaking their little collection boxes.

On November 6, another merciless election was held, because Hitler had toppled the Papen cabinet. Germany had seven million unemployed.

On the top floor of the Kaiserhof Hotel on Wilhelm Street where he kept a suite, Hitler waited for the election results with his most trusted officials. The outcome was shattering. They received two million less votes and 34 less seats in the Parliament than they had the previous summer. The communists made the biggest gains. The mood was one of desperation. The myth of Hitler's invincibility had been shattered. The party could not weather another election with empty cash registers.

Four weeks later, the State Diet elections in Thuringia brought a further decline of 40 percent. The voters no longer seemed to believe in Hitler. The workers preferred to vote for the KPD (Communist Party of Germany), while the nationalist-minded citizens went for Hugenberg's German National People's Party. Doubts were now raised among Hitler's closest associates as to whether they might have overestimated the Führer.

The energetic Gregor Strasser plunged into politics

without any consideration for Hitler's wishes. His brother Otto had dropped out of the NSDAP a year and a half earlier, founded the social-revolutionary Black Front and had become one of Hitler's bitterest opponents. Gregor negotiated with Schleicher, the new Reich chancellor. Schleicher wanted Strasser to be his vice chancellor and kept three important ministerial positions open for the former National Socialist. Schleicher wanted to forge an alliance between the military establishment and the Left. Strasser, who represented the "socialist" wing of the Nazis, was satisfied. He strongly advised Hitler to accept Schleicher's offer and to let the party join the administration.

Hitler ranted and raved, unleashing a flood of insults on Strasser. "You have stabbed me in the back! You don't want me to become chancellor! You want to push me out of the party leadership and put me on the sidelines!"

Strasser didn't know how to deal with Hitler's incomprehensible paranoia. After all, it was Hitler who'd told him to talk to Schleicher in the first place.

Strasser left the Kaiserhof Hotel, wrote a damning letter to Hitler and resigned all of his party offices.

The letter was a bombshell. Hitler was crushed. Strasser's resignation could mean the end of the party. Hitler sent people out to look for Strasser. He wanted to work out an arrangement with the party's most powerful and popular man. Hitler learned to his great joy that his opponent had given up the political fight once and for all. He had gone to Meran, in Italy, for "wine-therapy."

Hitler quickly reorganized Strasser's empire. All provincial party chiefs had to sign an oath of condemnation against Strasser and a declaration of loyalty to Hitler. The insignificant portion of Strasser's organization was given to the bibulous chemist Robert Ley, who had a dog-like devotion to Hitler. Rudolf Hess, Hitler's private secretary until then, became head of the political Central Commission. Hitler had gotten rid of his next-to-last rival in Gregor Strasser. A year and a half later, his last rival would be eliminated.

After the powerful "left" wing of the party had fled, Hitler reached an agreement with Franz von Papen in the home of the Rhenish Baron von Schroeder. Papen wanted to oust his old friend General von Schleicher, with Hitler's help. Papen said cynically, "We will hire Mr. Hitler for our Reich chancellor." The ride on the tiger had just begun.

Four weeks later, President Paul von Hindenburg appointed the artist, painter, author and ex-PFC Adolf Hitler—who'd been a German citizen for all of a year—to the position of Reich chancellor.

As darkness fell in Berlin on January 30, 1933, the city saw a spectacle that should have been a warning to Messrs. Papen and Hugenberg, who had earlier "put Mr. Hitler on the payroll."

From 7:00 p.m. until long past midnight, SA men wearing brown uniforms marched in a huge torchlight procession past the Reich Chancellory to celebrate Hitler's victory. Their footfalls echoed far and wide as they marched through Brandenburg Gate down Wilhelm Street. The bands played old military marches. The torches lit up the cold January night. Adolf Hitler stood at the window of his office in the Reich Chancellory. In the next building, at the window in the Presidential Palace, Hindenburg, the old Field Marshal, looked down upon the marching columns, happily beating time with his cane to the tunes of martial music. The very senile general became the butt of Berlin jokesmiths. Looking at the khaki-colored uniforms of the men in the long SA columns, he thought that he was back in the days of the battle of Tannenberg and said to his State Secretary Meissner: "I didn't know we bagged that many Russian prisoners."

With only six hours notice, Goebbels had organized this mass demonstration, staging it with brilliant and precise choreography.

One of the first decisions Hitler made that night was to remodel the Reich Chancellory. He said that the building was "nothing but a big cigar box." The planning room, which had been good enough for a man of Bismarck's stature, was now fit only for an office chief or a secretary in the Hitler government.

Hitler did not leave the Reich Chancellery until the early morning. He left the building through a rear door and then went to his hotel suite.

On February 7, 1933, a notice was published in the *Volkischer Beobachter* that said Reich Chancellor Adolf Hitler had decided not to accept his annual salary of 29,200 marks and his expense allowance of 18,000 marks. The money was to be given to the kin of SA and SS troops—Schutzstaffel or Protection Squadrons, often referred to as "Elite Guard"—who had been killed in action. The VB (*Volkischer Beobachter*) wrote that Hitler was able to afford this magnanimous gesture because he had an independent income as author and because he considered his public position to be an honorary post.

This so-called renunciation barely scratched Hitler financially because it reduced his tax liability. It also had the tremendous propaganda effect that Hitler intended. His renunciation of salary fed the legend that still exists today, and that is that Hitler—with all of his other faults and monstrosities—was completely selfless concerning his personal finances. Nothing could be further from the truth. First of all, two years later Hitler quietly reversed his "magnanimous renunciation" and again drew both his salary and his expense account. He also successfully avoided paying taxes during his entire unholy reign.

To accomplish this, he gave his aide Julius Schaub the job of working on his tax problem. Schaub was well acquainted with State Secretary Fritz Reinhardt in the Reich Finance Ministry. Reinhardt was an old party member and had earlier been a vocational school teacher of bookkeeping and tax law in Thuringia. Immediately after the Nazis seized power, he was appointed state secretary in the Finance Ministry in order to "politically coordinate" the conservative ministry under Count Schwerin-Krosigk. Soon he became an important figure and was in a position to secure many tax benefits for Hitler and other Nazi leaders.

Hitler immediatley contacted the Eastern Munich Finance Office in whose district he had his home. As a result, Hitler's quarterly payments for 1933 were assessed on the basis of his relatively low income during 1932.

Besides, it was decided that he did not need to pay any income tax on his salary, because he had "donated it away."

In 1933, his annual income rose to 1,232,335 marks. The tax bill for that amount was to have been 297,005 marks. But Reinhardt secured another benefit. Hitler wanted half of his gross income—616,167 marks—to be declared a business-related expense. Here is what Reinhardt wrote to Hitler: "In view of your unusually high expenditures as Führer of the German nation, I agree with your proposal."

That still left a rather high tax bill to be paid for 1933. The amount was due in December 1934. At the end of October, Hitler received a reminder notice. Munich's tax inspector Vogl tried to reach aide Schaub by telephone on November 7, 8 and 9, but without success.

The tax authorities were in a delicate position. For 1933 and the advance payment for 1934, Hitler owed 405,494 marks in taxes. A penalty ruling was drafted but not sent out. The officials waited for instructions from higher up.

Those instructions came soon. Munich's Finance Office President Dr. Ludwig Mirre went to Berlin to discuss Hitler's delicate tax problem with State Secretary Reinhardt. And, lo and behold, a remarkable solution was found. Since August 2, 1934, Hitler had not only been Reich Chancellor but he was also the Reich President—in other words, he was the head of state. One day after Hindenburg's death, Hitler had simply usurped the latter's position in direct violation of the Constitution. Reinhardt and Mirre agreed that the head of state had to be exempt from any tax whatsoever. The tax liability which had accumulated until that moment was simply cancelled. Dr. Mirre issued instructions to the effect that all of Hitler's tax records were to be removed from the files and put under lock and key. On March 12, 1935, Hitler's existence as German taxpayer was officially terminated when his file card and his address label card were destroyed in the Eastern Munich Finance Office.

After Hitler learned that he no longer had to pay taxes, he ordered that his salary as Chancellor and President be immediately remitted to his account again. All records of his royalties since 1934 were destroyed, but reliable estimates show that at least one million copies of *Mein Kampf* were sold each year after 1934. Based on these sales, Hitler's annual royalties were between 1.5 and 2 million marks. In 1944, there were still royalties a-mounting to 5,525,811 marks in Hitler's account at the Franz Eher Publishing House. In 1943 alone, Hitler had collected 569,212 marks from his royalty account.

These high royalties from *Mein Kampf* accounted for only a fraction of Hitler's private income. It should not be forgotten that since 1933, a very large share of Hitler's living expenses, the cost of his motor pool, his secretarial office and his entourage had been borne by the German taxpayer. Personally, he only had to pay for his private apartment on Munich's Prinzregenten Square and for his "vacation home" in the Berchtesgaden Alps. Hitler also continued to be adept at discovering new, tax-free money sources that yielded a handsome profit for him and for others.

Shortly after seizing power, Hitler met the young architect Albert Speer and immediately commissioned him to remodel the Reich Chancellory and his official apartments there. While this was being done, Hitler moved into the apartment of State Secretary Lammers on the top floor of the Reich Chancellory. His valet Karl Wilhelm Krause described the lifestyle of the brand new Reich Chancellor in some detail.

For breakfast, which he had in bed, Hitler would drink two cups of lukewarm whole milk and eat about ten slic-es of Leibniz biscuits as well as half a bar of semi-bitter chocolate that had been broken up into small pieces. His doctors warned him that this kind of breakfast was poison for him because it only made his chronic constipation worse, but Hitler disregarded their advice. The milk he drank frequently led to such severe flatu-lence that Hitler would writhe in pain rather than, on account of his inhibited petty-bourgeois upbringing, al-low the torturous intestinal winds to escape in their nat-ural way.

It took Hitler exactly 22 minutes to take care of his

facial hair. He usually shaved himself, using one safety razor with the Rotbart (Red Beard) brand blade for the preliminary shave and another blade for the follow-up shave. He also trimmed his moustache and shaved the corners. Hanfstaengl thought that Hitler's moustache looked horrible. He once tried to persuade Hitler to grow a goatee, thinking that it would give his face a more striking appearance, but Hitler rejected the suggestion. "My moustache will some day be in vogue in all of Europe, Hanfstaengl," he said. That of course was true in the ranks of the lower-level Nazis. With the exception of Hermann Esser and chauffeur Julius Schreck, this odd Chaplinesque moustache wasn't seen on anyone above the rank of school teacher.

The brand of soap he used was called Steckenpferd-Lilienmilch (Hobby Horse and Lily Milk). Peri was his shaving cream. For skin lotion, he used Pfeilring (Arrow Ring) while his hair lotion was called Dralles Birkenwasser (Dralle's Birch Water). When he took a bath, he liked to put pine needle tablets in the water.

During the early days, he would almost daily go to the Kaiserhof Hotel with two or three companions for tea at around 4:30 p.m. He sat down at the corner table reserved for him, greeted the other patrons in the crowded restaurant, and enjoyed cake and whipped cream to the strains of a Hungarian gypsy band.

Security was lax, to say the least. Not a single police or SS uniform was ever to be seen around Hitler. There was no rope separating the Reich Chancellor from the other coffeehouse patrons. Handbags and attaché cases were not searched. Seats at neighboring tables were available from the head waiter (for a hefty tip, of course). And Hitler was not bothered when Jews sat near him and curiously glanced over at him. He gave the appearance of being a private individual and acted modestly and in a good bourgeois fashion. He never went to the Kaiserhof Hotel in Nazi uniform and ordered his escorts to comply.

According to his valet Krause, Hitler in 1934 had one pair of tails, one tux, one cutaway, one afternoon dress suit, one brown, one blue and one light-colored everyday suit. He also had five uniform blouses, including two tailored to accommodate a belt, three pairs of long trousers and two riding breeches. Hitler's everyday suits were so worn that even a medium level civil servant would hardly have put them on to go to the office.

The wife of Ludwig Troost, his Munich architect, Magda Goebbels and Eva Braun urged him to pay more attention to his wardrobe. But the ladies failed to persuade Hitler to move on to more fashionable clothing styles. He preferred double-breasted jackets made by second-rate Munich tailors. He bought his overcoats in the Berlin ready-made clothing store of Herpich, right off the rack. He continued to wear his trenchcoat, although he had discarded his riding crop at the end of 1934, because it gave him an entirely too revolutionist and brutal image.

He bought his soft velour hats at Seidl's in Munich, while he got his uniform caps in Berlin. Eva Braun thought that his caps were attrocious, maintaining that they made him look like a letter carrier or railroad stationmaster. Her attempts to give the caps style failed, because Hitler's eyes had been very sensitive since he was gassed in World War I and he insisted on wearing very big visors that almost covered the eyes.

With his everyday suit, Hitler always wore black low-cut patent leather shoes. He wore thin silk socks even in his shaft boots. In deep winter, he continued to wear only undershorts, refusing to put on a T-shirt. His dress shirt and collar were always separate. Eva Braun was never able to persuade him to switch to the sport shirts with the collar sewed on in the normal fashion. He wore suspenders, no belt and in place of pajamas he preferred a long linen nightshirt.

His diet was no less strange. Ever since Geli Raubal's death, he had completely foresworn the consumption of meat. Liver dumplings were an exception and his sister Angela Raubal did an outstanding job on them at Obersalzberg. He contemptuously referred to meat broth as "cadaver tea," and he often made fun of his meat-eating entourage. He even disdained fish. When one of his staff members ordered crayfish, he told—with tactless relish—a phony tale about a family who had put its dead grandmother in the brook to attract the crayfish.

He ordered special bread to be baked for him without sourdough and ordered a low-alcohol beer for his own private use. It is not true that he was a teetotaler. He liked to drink a glass of Henkell champagne from the cellars of his Foreign Minister Ribbentrop (who was married to a Henkell). For his frequent colds, he put brandy in his tea and to help his digestion, he regularly took bitters made by the Underberg Firm.

As Krause reported, Hitler, before going to sleep, regularly took two strong sleeping pills, using such medications as Evipan, Phanodorm, or Tempodorm, which were dispensed by prescription only. He disregarded warnings from doctors that these medications were addictive.

In the evenings, the Reich Chancellery was frequently the meeting place for the so-called chauffeur gang. It consisted of Hitler's long-standing driver Schaub, aides Brueckner and Sepp Dietrich, the secretaries and, when they were in Berlin, Heinrich Hoffmann and Max Amann. Hitler loved the company of people who were as devoted to him as they were intellectually inferior. A motion picture projector was always set up and two full-length films were shown. Hitler discussed the selection of movies with Goebbels, preferring harmless society, love and entertainment films. He especially enjoyed musicals that displayed lots of bare legs. Hitler was an enthusiastic fan of Heinz Ruehmann, Henny Porten, Lil Dagover, Olga Tschechowa, and Jenny Jugo. He liked to watch the grand Hollywood spectaculars but didn't care much for humorous films featuring Buster Keaton or Charlie Chaplin. Goebbels, on the other hand was crazy about Chaplin and even once made an unsuccessful attempt to get him to visit Germany.

Hitler displayed similarly plain tastes in the field of literature. He fundamentally disdained fine literature. For relaxation, he read Edgar Wallace and Karl May, and was especially fond of the latter. He really worshiped the latter. "That is the best reading for our German youth," he said. In his libraries in Berlin, Munich and Berchtesgaden, he had all of the works of the prolific writer from

Radebeul—Hitler read all of them.

During his first years as Chancellor, Hitler was very skillful in delegating the monumental volume of office work. He told Albert Speer: "During the first few weeks, they submitted every little detail to me for a decision. Everyday, I found stacks of files on my desk and no matter how hard I worked, they never got smaller until I stopped this nonsense by taking radical action. If I had continued to operate in this way, I would never have achieved any positive results because this schedule left me no time for thinking. When I refused to look at the files, I was told that this would delay important decisions. But that was precisely what enabled me to think about important things. In this way I determined developments and I was no longer run by civil servants."

Hitler knew how to delegate as much as possible to his aides in order to spend as little time as possible on government and party business. Since Hindenburg's death, there had been four business offices that worked exclusively for him: the Reich Chancellery under State Secretary Lammers; the Chancellery of the Führer, under Phillip Bouhler; the Party Business Office, under Rudolf Hess and his ambitious assistant Martin Bormann; and the Presidential Office, under State Secretary Otto Meissner. All of these business offices competed vigorously with each other and quarreled over questions of competence, which Hitler enjoyed because, from his study of Macchiavelli, he understood the power of the divide-and-conquer principle. Hitler loved to spend his time at construction sites, in the studios of architects and artists, in cafés and restaurants and to conduct conversations that were mostly monologues. This tendency grew more pronounced after he had rid himself of Ernst Röhm, his last dangerous adversary, and after he had stripped the SA of its power on June 30, 1934, drowning an alleged coup d'état by the SA in blood.

The German Parliament no longer had any check on him. On March 24, 1933, the German legislature committed suicide when deputies of all parties—with the exception of the SPD, gave Hitler's administration full dictatorial powers for four years. The next Parliament was elected on November 12, 1933, on the basis of the NSDAP unity slate. All political parties, other than the Nazis, were outlawed.

Parliament had deteriorated to a mere rubber-stamp assembly. It had become the parliamentary loin cloth of his dictatorship. Similarly, plebiscites were used to rubber-stamp Germany's leaving the League of Nations, breaking the Lacarno treaties and incorporating Austria into Germany. These elections took place after the fact with "overwhelming majorities" of more than 98 percent. The hand-picked deputies extended the Enabling Law for Hitler in 1937 in a farcical voting process. The F uhrer had become a legal dictator, lawfully confirmed by the "representatives of the people."

In addition, Hitler had dissolved the legislatures of the German states. He was now able to do as he pleased without any checks.

But Hitler didn't feel comfortable in Berlin during the first year of his dictatorship. Whenever he had the opportunity, at least every two to three weeks, he would drive to Munich and then to Obersalzberg. His first stop in Munich was always a visit to the studio of Professor Ludwig Troost, an architect friend, who lived on Theresien Street, near the Technical College. Hitler had met Troost in the drawing room of the Bruckmann family. He was a tall, slim Westphalian with a smooth-shaved skull. When Hitler met him, he was 52 years old. In his youth, he had belonged to a group of architects who, like Peter Behrens, Bruno Paul and Walter Gropius, advocated an almost spartan traditionalism with some modern elements included as a counterreaction to the richly ornamented Art Nouveau. Before 1933 and Hitler's rise to power, Troost had never advanced to the leading group in German architecture.

Although Hitler was more inclined toward an overblown Neo- Baroque, he appreciated Troost's sparse neoclassicist architecture. Troost had given him many ideas during the remodeling of the Barlow Palace on Brienner Street into the Brown House. In 1933, Hitler commissioned him to erect the so-called Führer Building on Koenig Square which in Munich, just a few steps from the Brown House, was to be his office building. In addition, Troost drew the blueprints for the German House of Art on Prinzregenten Street.

Mrs. Troost, who was an interior decorator, worked closely with her husband. She designed the combination of color samples and wallpaper for the Führer Building. As Albert Speer said, "hers were much too reticent to suit Hitler's taste, which was aimed at producing a maximum effect." Nevertheless, he told her he liked it. The good middle-class atmosphere of rich company attracted Hitler and its decent luxury muted his darker instincts. Mrs. Troost, had also designed the interior decor of the Europa ocean liner and Hitler was most enthusiastic about this luxurious, so-called steamer style.

After Troost's death in 1934, Hermann Giesler was given the job of directing Munich's city planning, but Speer became Hitler's real court architect.

Only after seeing Troost and visiting the Munich construction sites did Hitler retire to his private apartment to prepare for dinner at the Osteria Bavaria. The Schelling Saloon, in the next block, accommodated the lower ranking members of his entourage.

The Osteria Bavaria (today Osteria Italiana) was a small artists' restaurant on Schelling Street. It served mostly Italian cuisine and was relatively unknown until Hitler picked it as his favorite hangout during the late twenties. Hitler's entourage usually included publisher Max Amann, Rudolf Hess' still very unobtrusive assistant Martin Bormann, Putzi Hanfstangl, Speer and now and then a painter or sculptor. Occasionally—but very rarely—Eva Braun was also invited to join the group for lunch.

The restaurant consisted of a small main room with an open passageway leading to a small side room where a table was permanently reserved for Hitler. When his arrival was announced, the patrons had to leave the side room and move to the main room. Two SS men would then appear and rope the open passageway off. Then came Hitler and his entourage. The patrons in the main room were able to see the dictator. An attempt on his life with a pistol would not have been difficult.

The guests at Hitler's table almost always included Heinrich Hoffmann who, when in a slightly inebriated state, played the role of court jester and delighted Hitler with his jokes and imitations of prominent party leaders, eliciting loud laughter from the Führer. Hitler was not known for his sense of humor, being unable to laugh at himself. He did, however, enjoy having fun at the expense of others, especially at their misfortune. When Hoffmann imitated the stammering Robert Ley, the gravely-puritanical Hess, or Goebbels with his oily voice—always, of course, in their absence—Hitler doubled over with laughter.

Hitler usually ordered a plain dish—spaghetti or ravioli with tomato sauce, Fachinger (a Bavarian mineral water), followed by palacsintas (dessert crepes) or Kaiserschmarren. He had no objections when the members of his entourage consumed meat or alcohol.

When a Czech weekly came out with an article entitled "Hitler's Pompadour," the dictator had a fit. The article also included a photograph showing Eva Braun at Obersalzberg. To his great astonishment, Hitler discovered that the photo had been taken by his friend Heinrich Hoffmann who, in his harmless avarice, had simply sold it to the Prague periodical. Oddly enough, Hoffmann did not fall into disgrace. Hitler merely forbade him to publish photos of Eva Braun in any German newspaper. Hitler did not want the German people to find out that he had a steady girlfriend, but he also did not want to anger Hoffmann too much. Hoffmann knew too much about Hitler. But Hitler still needed him. Heinrich Hoffmann was one of his best business partners.

# Chapter Twelve

# The Photographer
# With The Golden Touch

There were two men in Hitler's entourage who became multmillionaires because of him and who, in turn, allowed him to earn millions of dollars as part of their secret symbiotic partnership. Hitler was avaricious and powerful. He loved wealth, but he didn't have the inborn business acumen to earn it without the help of others. His partners were protected by—and operated in the shadow of—his power. In addition to their own avarice, they had an unscrupulous business sense which was an advantage for themselves and their Führer.

One of these two men was Max Amann, who was also Hitler's publisher—we will come back to Amann and study the empire he built for himself. The other man was Heinrich Hoffmann, whose official title, awarded to him by Hitler, was "Reich Photo Reporter." He did not hold any position of power within the State or within the Party. His title merely helped him become rich and to make his Führer rich in the process.

Heinrich Hoffmann was born in 1885, the son of a Munich photographer. He learned the photographer's trade in his father's shop and then was trained as a photojournalist on London's Fleet Street. He was a good photographer, winning medals in several international competitions. Shortly before World War I, he settled in Munich as a photographer. During the war, he was a war correspondent and also flew as an observer in reconnaissance aircraft. After the end of the war, he established a studio on Schelling Street in Munich with a shop attached to it where he sold cameras, photographic plates and film to professionals and amateurs.

Hoffmann was 37 years old when he met Adolf Hitler in 1922. He was an internationally respected photo-journalist with a prosperous business. His studio was located diagonally across the street from the editorial offices of the *Volkischer Beobachter*.

At that time, Hitler was extremely camera-shy. There are no photographs of him from this period. Snooping newspaper photographers were not infrequently beaten up by his SA escorts and the photographic plates or film were exposed, rendering them useless.

One day, Hoffmann received a telegram from the Hearst Press in the United States, offering him 1,000 dollars for an exclusive photograph of the rising Munich party leader, a fee that sounded like a fortune in that time of economic deprivation.

For hours on end, Hoffmann surveyed the opposite side of the street from his studio window. When Hitler finally left the editorial offices and was about to get into his rattletrap Selve—together with his driver Haug and his bodyguard Ulrich Graf—Hoffmann rushed out into the street to take his picture. Haug and Graf yanked the camera from his hands and beat him up. Hitler stood by with a bemused grin while Hoffmann ranted about his rights as a reporter and Hitler's role as a public figure.

A few days later, Hoffmann came upon a photograph he'd taken on August 1, 1914, the day of the Bavarian mobilization, showing the vast crowd of people of Odeon Square. The face of the 25-year-old painter Hitler was clearly recognizable in the midst of the crowd. Hoffmann enlarged the segment of the photo, went to the editorial offices of the *Volkischer Beobachter*—this time without his camera—and gave it to Hitler as a present. Their friendship began on that day. Hitler invited Hoffmann to dine with him at the Osteria. A business agreement was signed and sealed: In the future, Hoffmann would be the only person who had the right to photograph Hitler.

Hitler authorized only Hoffman's photographs for publication, receiving 10 percent of the sales proceeds himself. This agreement turned into a gold mine for Hoffmann and made Hitler a pretty penny, too. After 1923, the newspapers and magazines in Germany and around the world were eager to get photographs of Hitler. Because Hoffmann had the corner on the market, he was able to dictate the price.

Hoffmann soon turned his studio over to the party as a business office and moved into larger, more elegant premises on Augusten Street. His studio/citadel there was the talk of the town. Hitler was often his guest, soaking up the Bohemian atmosphere that made him feel like "just another artist among artists."

Hoffmann was soon able to afford a mansion in the ritzy Bogenhausen Section of Munich. After the death of his first wife, he married the daughter of Royal Opera singer Groepke who was said to have lesbian tendencies. Hoffmann's was always an open house and Hitler felt comfortable there. Even after he had become Germany's most powerful man, the Führer visited Hoffmann whenever he came to Munich. Here is what Albert Speer wrote in his memoirs: "When the weather was good, coffee was served in a small garden surrounded by the gardens of other mansions, although it was no bigger than about 200 square meters. In the warm sunshine, the Führer would occasionally take off his jacket and stretch out on the grass in his shirtsleeves. He really felt at home at Hoffmann's place; once he asked for a volume by Ludwig Thoma, selected a passage, and recited it."

Hoffmann became one of the few individuals around Hitler who was allowed to "act up" and get away with it. The Führer overlooked many of Hoffmann's quirks, including his drinking problem, his liberal views on modern art, his friendships with "dubious" fringe groups on the Munich scene and even his contacts with Jews. Once, Hoffmann introduced a Jewish school chum, the son of a rabbi, to a somewhat embarrassed Hitler. Later Hitler said, "Well, Hoffmann, next time we might as well have our coffee in the synagogue."

Hoffmann also served as his friend's middleman in matters more delicate than finance. Emil Maurice—the former comrade-in-arms who'd fallen out of grace because of his alleged affair with Hitler's niece—had managed to get his hands on a folder containing pornographic drawings Hitler had made of Geli Raubal. Hitler got Hoffmann to buy the incriminating artwork from Maurice for the handsome sum of 10,000 marks, which enabled his ex-friend to open a watchmaker's shop in Munich. Hoffmann was only too happy to help his friend. During the early days of his affair with Eva Braun, for instance, Hitler often met his mistress under the protection of the Hoffmann family because her father absolutely forbade his daughter's relationship with a lover who was 23 years older than she.

Although there is no hard evidence of this, it was also said that Hoffmann frequently supplied the Führer with compliant girls from Munich's modelling and prostitution scene who could accommodate the Führer's kinky sexual practices. Hoffmann, at any rate, had a more intimate knowledge of Hitler's private life than any other member of his circle. His chummy contact with Hitler paid off handsomely for Hoffmann, in more ways than one. After he had come to power, Hitler awarded him not only the title Reich Photo Reporter but also made him a full professor.

Between 1932 and 1940, Hoffmann published more than 30 magnificent photography books, some of which were published in editions of more than 100,000 copies. The volume entitled *Hitler in Polen (Hitler in Poland)* sold over 200,000 copies. Some of the other titles from Hoffmann's photography series were *Hitler abseits vom Alltag (Hitler at Ease), Hitler befreit das Sudentenland (Hitler Liberates the Sudentenland), Hitler in Italien (Hitler in Italy), Hitler in seinen Bergen (Hitler in His Mountains)* and *Jugend um Hitler] (Youth and Hitler)*. All Reich party congresses were amply documented by Hoffmann and the subsequent photography books were sold at a handsome profit. They commanded a price of 10-13 marks, which was quite respectable for that time. The Franz Eher Publishing House put out only a few of these books, because Hoffmann didn't want to share the profits with Amann. Hitler gave his photographer permission to establish his own company under the name Publishing House for

Contemporary History. The Führer was perfectly happy with this arrangement because it increased his cut of the profits, too—his job was, after all, to approve the final selection of photographs. Pictures of him and Eva Braun were strictly taboo. If she did show up on a released photgraph, she was an unidentified guest as far as the public was concerned.

Hoffmann even served his Führer as front man for his real estate deals. Heinrich Hoffmann—not Hitler—was listed as the owner of Eva Braun's property on Wasserburg Street. Hitler wanted to maintain the facade of the "poor" Führer even with the officials at the Real Estate Registry Office. He, of course, could have listed Eva Braun as the owner, but that would have conflicted with his ideas about the dependent role of women.

Hitler's combined royalties from *Mein Kampf* and Hoffmann's photography volumes soon enabled him to acquire paintings for his private apartment on Prinzregenten Square and his house on Obersalzberg. Because Hoffmann was himself a passionate art collector, it seemed only natural that he should act as the middleman for these deals and get a cut for himself, too. When Hitler liked a painting or an artist, he didn't look at the price tag, a fact that Hoffmann exploited, knowing he could intercede on behalf of the Führer, who liked to go to galleries or auctions and haggle over prices.

Hitler loved 19th century paintings. He considered that period to be one of humanity's greatest cultural epochs. His appreciation ended with Impressionism, however. He considered Expressionism "degenerate." His favorite painters included Leibl, Hans Thoma, Spitzweg and Eduard Gruetzner, whom he compared to Rembrandt—though Gruetzner mostly painted tipsy monks and wine stewards. Hitler overestimated these technically passable but otherwise mediocre painters. Speer remembered one afternoon in particular at Hoffmann's home when the photographer offered Hitler a Gruetzner for 5,000 marks. According to Speer, the picture was worth at most, 2,000 marks. Hitler said, "What, the price is only 5,000 marks? You know, Hoffmann, this is like taking candy from a baby! Look at the detail! Gruetzner is so vastly underestimated! Rembrandt could not have done a better job!" Naturally, the next painting by Gruetzner cost Hitler much more.

For Hitler's private apartment, Hoffmann procured Lenbach's "Bismarck in Cuirassier Uniform," Franz von Stuck's "The Sin," Anselm Feuerbach's "Park Landscape," many works by Gruetzner and several Spitzwegs. Occasionally, the resourceful art agent would give his best customer a painting as a present, as he did with a painting by Loewith. While Goebbels was visiting on Prinzregenten Square, Hitler proudly pointed the painting out to him. With a nasty sideward glance at Hoffmann, Goebbels commented laconically, "A good painting! No wonder Loewith is one of the most talented Jewish painters." Hitler kept the painting just the same, saying, "People talk a lot. Maybe Loewith wasn't a Jew in the first place." In one of his rare, fleeting attempts at humor, Hitler gave one of his favorite Gruetzner paintings to Robert Ley, the alcoholic creator of the German Labor Front—the one entitled "Boozing Monk."

Hitler felt Hoffmann had such expertise on artistic matters that he dissolved the jury for the annual exhibit in the House of German Art and appointed Hoffmann as the sole selector of artworks—a position that allowed Hoffmann to be sovereign judge of the success or failure of an artist's career. Hitler accepted Hoffmann's choices almost without question. His only beef was with the "Moderns," exclaiming, "I cannot stand sloppily painted pictures where you often don't know which side is up and which is down." Hitler's favorite among the modern painters was Paul Mathias Padua whose "Leda with the Swan," painted with pedantic accuracy, met with his most enthusiastic approval. But as investments, he continued to prefer the painters of the 19th Century.

During the thirties, the enthusiastic pursuit of art—as a means towards successful investment—gripped almost all of the Third Reich's big shots. Göring competed with Hitler as a collector, and then Ribbentrop and Goebbel began sending their agents to the prestigious auctions. Hoffmann went as Hitler's agent. Often, the four Nazi leaders would outbid each other, jacking up the prices of the works way beyond their real value.

Once, Hitler rejected a painting of Bismarck by Lenbach because the price of 30,000 marks seemed too stiff to him. Shortly thereafter, the same painting was put up for auction in the Hans Lange Auction Establishment in Berlin. Göring wanted the painting regardless of its price. When the bidding stopped, the auctioneer's gavel came down for him at 75,000 marks. Göring then gave this same Lenbach to Hitler as a birthday present. Hitler was astonished that he'd gotten this painting, of all things, as a present. When he found out what the price had been he boiled over with rage. On advice from Hoffmann, he issued the following order: In the future, no painting of historical value could change owners without his approval. This so-called Führer Reservation practically guaranteed he'd have first crack at all, paintings that had any historical significance.

Hoffmann was tireless when it came to discovering new sources of money for himself and his Führer. He published a part of Hitler's watercolors in a facsimile folder, several thousand of which were sold at the handsome price of 100 marks apiece. The American magazine *Esquire* acquired the reproduction rights.

Hoffmann himself owned a series of Hitler's watercolors that the Führer had given him as a present. After 1933, watercolors by Hitler commanded fantastic prices. Even during the war, Hoffmann sold one of the paintings for 30,000 marks. Throughout Germany, Hoffmann tried to dig up owners of Hitler watercolors and buy their paintings from them cheap, in order to resell them at a profit of several hundred percent.

The unsuccessful postcard painter of yesteryear could now have become a millionaire from the sale of drawings and watercolors alone. Hoffmann, however, had an even more ingenious idea to fill Hitler's coffers. If Hitler had millions of marks available to purchase paintings, then Hoffmann, as collector and agent, would get his golden cut.

Being a photographer, Hoffmann was familiar with the question of copyrights. He knew an individual has a right to his or her own image. He concluded, therefore, that a postage stamp was also an image of a particular person and was subject to all of the attendant rights. Old Reich President Hindenburg was never paid for his image on German postage stamps, because the idea had never occurred to anyone. The only comment the old buzzard ever made in connection with postage stamps and Hitler was the following bitter remark which was widely reported in 1932, "I will make Hitler postal minister. Then he can lick me on the back side." For Hitler, the little postage stamps with his face on the front—at first, the special stamps and then regular stamps in all denominations—suddenly became a gigantic income source. The fee for the "personality right" was of course in fractions of a percent, but the sheer volume of sales made the thing incredibly lucrative. Both Speer and Hoffmann have said they were present one time when the Reich Postal Minister Wilhelm Ohnesorge handed Hitler a check for 50 million marks in payment for the private use of this personality rights.

After his postal income source had been secured, Hitler's art purchases became even more frantic. Now, for example, he acquired Moritz von Schwind's "Cinderella," "Leda with the Swan," by Leonardo da Vinci, a self-portrait by Rembrandt, the "Honey Thief" by Lucas Cranach the Elder, "Dancing Children" by Watteau, a "Madonna with Child" by Rubens from the collection of the German Crown Prince and the painting "Building Up Silesia" by Adolf Menzel. He even bought paintings by artists he didn't like, such as Franz Marc, Lovis Corinth, Liebermann, Gauguin, van Gogh and Picasso, in order to exchange them in the international art trade for Dürers and Rembrandts.

Presumably because of his own profligate profiteering, Hitler didn't seem to object whenever others in his entourage shamelessly enriched themselves in an unlawful fashion. The following incident is characteristic of the practices: Reich Economy Minister Walter Funk, who was also the president of the Reichsbank, had a vice president named Brinkmann who attracted attention because of his bizarre behavior and was finally declared mentally ill. He once invited the messenger boys and

cleaning women of the Reichsbank to a dinner in the big
banquet room of the Bristol Hotel in Berlin and played
the violin to entertain the guests. He also discharged all
officials at the Reichsbank over the age of 50, giving
them "double retirement." Brinkmann—who was authorized to sign for any amount of money—reached the absolute limit when he handed a check for 3 million marks
to Hermann Göring, the man in charge of the Four-Year
Plan. Göring cashed the check immediately and had the
amount deposited in his personal account. Funk had
Brinkmann declared insane, but Göring refused to give
the money back. Funk turned to Hitler for help, but the
Führer only laughed at Göring's "neat trick" and refused
to intervene. He said Funk should have recognized
earlier that his deputy wasn't right in the head. Year
after year, the unlucky bank president tried unsuccessfully to get Göring to give the money back.

One of the few people to defy Hitler, the avid
collector, was Karl Valentin. This Munich eccentric owned a vast collection of postcards of all kinds, plus a valuable collection of pictures illustrating the Munich of yest-
erday, some stemming from the earliest days of photography. Hitler was interested in the collection and commissioned Heinrich Hoffmann to conduct the negotiations. Valentin demanded 100,000 marks for his treasure
trove because he needed the money to produce a film.
Hitler offered him 30,000 marks in cash plus a monthly
lifetime annuity of 1,000 marks. Valentin's collection was
unique but even 30,000 marks plus annuity seemed too
high a price. Still, Hitler stubbornly insisted on getting
his hands on the Valentin collection. After all, money
was no object any longer. When Hoffmann brought
Hitler's offer to Valentin, the latter grumbled cantanker-
ously: "Just say 'Hello' to the Herr Führer, and if he
doesn't give me those 100,000 marks all at once, he can
do you-know-what with his money!"

# Chapter Thirteen

# Family Ties

Adolf Hitler perceived the term "family ties" in an ambiguous light. He was the exact opposite of Napoleon, who, with the sense of family so typical of a Corsican, ruthlessly channeled money, titles of nobility, lucrative sinecures and entire kingdoms to his numerous kin. For Hitler, his very origin from his clan—in which incest and illegitimacy were the order of the day—was nothing but a big pain in the neck. He was the product of a liaison between uncle and niece, his father and his elder half-brother had been born out of wedlock, and only later were made "legitimate." He was constantly haunted by the fear that he might be determined to be of Jewish extraction. In *Mein Kampf* he devoted very little space to his origin and kin. His sisters and half-sisters were not mentioned at all.

Hitler never wanted his family relations described in detail. He was the product of inbreeding—his mother's paternal grandfather and his maternal great-grandfather were the same person.

Because Hitler was well informed about the extent of inbreeding in his family, he tried to avoid the topic even though he was fascinated by it. He wrote this about the Jewish question: "As a result of a thousand years of inbreeding, the Jew preserved his race and its peculiar nature more effectively than many of the peoples among which he lived." Anthropologically speaking, this statement is utter nonsense. Oriental Jews differ from Jews whose ancestors lived in Northern Europe for centuries, just as much as the particular host nations differ from each other.

Hitler was also afraid of producing a child that might be abnormal due to the inbreeding in his background. This fear was his constant companion during his liaison with his niece Geli Raubal.

His greatest fear in this regard was the possibility that his relatives might exploit his position for personal gain. This would not have bothered him if his image as a pure idealist working only for his fatherland weren't so iron-clad. Any blemish in his background would be magnified around the world.

After his half sister Angela had left Berghof and married the Dresden architect Hamitzsch, his youngest sister Paula came to Berchtesgaden to keep house for him. But the two siblings did not get along. Paula did not always treat her brother with the respect he had come to expect from his his underlings. She had a big mouth and on several occasions called him "crazy," telling him that he might some day "end up on the gallows." Hitler sent her back to Vienna and gave her a modest annuity—on the condition that she change her name! She had a partnership in a small arts and crafts shop in Vienna under the name of Paula Wolf and was happy that only a few of her closest friends knew that she was related to the Führer. In his testament of 1938, Hitler gave her a lifetime annuity of 1,000 marks per month. He provided for his sister Angela with the same settlement. He was on rather good terms with her on Leo (Geli's brother) until 1931, but it cooled off after Geli's suicide. Leo blamed his uncle for the death of his beloved sister and refused to see him anymore. "I will never exchange another word with Uncle Adolf for the rest of my life," he told his mother, a promise he kept.

Hitler did not entirely forget his nephew Leo. When the latter, as a lieutenant of Engineers, wound up in Russian captivity before the siege of Stalingrad, Hitler suggested to Stalin via neutral channels that he be exchanged for Stalin's son Jakob, who had been captured in the autumn of 1941. The Soviet dictator rejected the offer.

During World War I, Hitler maintained close contact

with his many aunts, uncles, cousins, nieces and nephews in Spital, in the Waldviertel section of Lower Austria and always spent his home leave there. This contact ceased after he went into politics. Hitler did not pursue this contact because he was afraid that these relationships would deteriorate to the kind of "pernicious sense of family" for which he reproached Napoleon. Nevertheless, his testament of 1938 surprisingly contained the following clause under Point 2i): "For my relatives in Spital, Lower Austria, the onetime sum of 30,000 marks. My sister Paula in Vienna will determine the distribution of this amount."

Actually, he did not have too much grief with Paula, the Raubals and the Spital kin. The real trouble came from an entirely different side of his family. Hitler's half-brother Alois left the parental home in 1896 at the age of 14 after the altercations with his father had become unbearable for him. Alois, Sr., made it a habit to thrash his eldest son frequently and accused him of being lazy and obstreperous. Alois first became a waiter-trainee in Vienna. He wound up in jail twice for minor theft. In 1907 he was in Paris, working as a waiter. Two years later, he went to Dublin, where he married an Irish girl named Bridget Dowling. A son born to the couple in 1911 was baptized William Patrick Hitler.

Bridget lost her British citizenship as a result of her marriage and became an Austrian. She had some difficulties on that account during World War I. But, by then her husband Alois had walked out on the family, and Bridget and her son lived in London. The outbreak of war gave the unstable Alois an opportunity to neglect his family obligations in faraway England. He neglected them to such an extent that he entered into a second marriage in Hamburg without mentioning the earlier one. His second wife bore a son, whom they named Heinz Hitler. The whole sordid affair came to a head after the war when Bridget found out that her spouse was in court in Hamburg on charges of bigamy. In his letters, Alois desperately asked his first wife to help him. He promised that if the verdict turned out favorable for him, he would be able to provide adequate financial care for her and their son William Patrick. Bridget wrote to the court that she had no hard feelings against her husband. The court imposed a fine on Alois, rather than a prison term. Alois promised, but never sent any money to England to support his family. He tried to excuse his failure by saying that the German foreign-exchange laws would not permit him to send money. Only once did he remit the meager sum of 20 pounds to Bridget via the embassy.

When Adolf Hitler became an international celebrity at the end of the Twenties, Bridget and William Patrick Hitler began to think about whether they ought not to make use of this kinship connection to obtain support payments. They accepted an offer from the Hearst newspapers for an in-depth interview with the Nazi leader's sister-in-law and nephew. When Hitler learned about this interview from Putzi Hanfstängl, because of his press contacts, he was outraged. Hitler sent his nephew a ticket and ordered him to come to Munich. In Alois' and Angela's presence—with Alois acting as interpreter—he bitterly reproached William Patrick for publicizing family secrets that would severely damage his political career. "And to think that I have always been so careful to keep my personal affairs hidden from the press," he exclaimed. "The people must not know who I am. They must not know where I come from or what family I sprang from. Even in my book I did not allow myself to say a single word about those things, not a single word, and now somebody quite by accident discovers my nephew. So they make investigations and they send their snoops on the trail of our past."

After William Patrick promised not to give an interview, Hitler calmed down. He even gave his nephew 100 marks and invited to him to Obersalzberg, where William Patrick met his cousins Leo and Geli Raubal.

To prevent his English nephew from asking any more favors, Hitler maintained that he was not related to him. He said that Alois Hitler had been a foundling whom his father had adopted. But William Patrick would have none of this: He was ecstatic about "being related to the great politician." His father was indignant when he heard this story. He supplied his son with clear evidence that he had indeed been born out of wedlock under the name of Alois Matzelsberger but, after marrying his mother, Alois, Sr., did not adopt him but rather made him legitimate—and that was a big difference. When William Patrick confronted his uncle with this piece of news, the latter Hitler backed off begrudingly.

After Hitler had become Reich Chancellor, William Patrick wrote him a letter. He stated that he was having trouble finding a decent job in England because of his name. Hitler invited his nephew to come to Berlin, but the boy's hopes for a brilliant career under the wing of his famous uncle came to naught. Hitler treated him very coolly and indicated to him that he would not grant him any special privileges. He got his nephew—whose German in the meantime had become passable—a modest position with the Berlin Opel auto agency. William Patrick couldn't live on his income, because he supported his mother in England; his father, Alois, was still behind on meeting his alimony payment. Alois Hitler opened a small beer hall in Berlin, that he traded, in 1937, for a café in the elegant western section of Berlin. His guests included many party members, as well as SA and SS leaders. Hitler forbade his brother to use the name "Hitler" in connection with his establishment in a prominent place. Adolf avoided any private contact with Alois. He, in fact, had better relations with Alois' other son, Heinz, than he had with William Patrick. He found a place for Heinz Hitler in one of the elite boarding schools of the Third Reich, the National Political Educational Institutions. He also invited the youngster to Obersalzberg and on his 14th birthday gave him the collected works of Karl May. But the uncle did not approve of Heinz's wish to become an officer. In the Army his name alone would provide occasions for "fawning favoritism." Heinz became a sergeant and was killed in action during the Polish Campaign.

Heinz didn't cause Hitler any trouble with any excessive demands. On the other hand, there were constant difficulties with William Patrick. The young was not satisfied with the subordinate position which his uncle had gotten for him. He consequently tried to establish

contact with Hitler and was always shooed away by
Hitler's aides Schaub and Brueckner—at times quite
rudely. Whenever he managed to get through to his
uncle, the Führer would slip him a 100 mark bill with the
admonition to be more frugal, but he also saw to it that
he received a raise.

William Patrick left Germany in 1938 and returned to
England. He had found it impossible to share in his famous uncle's wealth. In their last conversation, Hitler
told him brusquely "It is impossible for me to grant you
special privileges."

During that same year, Hitler made a provision in his
last will which is astonishing in the light of his quarrels
with brother Alois and the latter's relatives. In paragraph
3 of his last will, he bequeathed a onetime sum of 60,000
marks to his half brother. Alois never learned about his
brother's "magnanimous" gesture because that testament
was not found until 1953 and then no longer had any legal significance.

In his book *Hitler's Jugend (Hitler's Youth)*, Franz Jetzinger maintained that William Patrick, in an article published in the French newspaper *Paris Soir* on August 5,
1939, stated that his uncle was the grandson of a Graz
Jew by the name of Frankenreither. This is how he extracted his revenge on his uncle.

But there is no word of truth in this, as Werner Maser
had already established. The article mentions neither the
names Frankenreither, nor Frankenberger, and not even
Hitler's grandmother Maria Anna Schicklgruber is mentioned. The piece almost exclusively involves the German
dictator's tight purse strings. William Patrick himself
wrote that he constantly asked Hitler for money and
could not understand why he was told that nobody must
ever profit because he was related to him. Hitler—his
uncle told him—could not help everybody who bore his
name by accident. "It would have been enough," wrote
Patrick, "to give some little sign to fill the pockets of his
closest kin. But he did not make the slightest gesture."
Shortly before the war's outbreak, Hitler learned that his
sister-in-law Bridget Hitler was planning to write a book
about him and the family—with the justification that she

and her son had to earn their livelihood, especially since they could not expect any money from Germany and because her own husband never met his financial obligations.

Hitler then said that he must bring his sister-in-law under control before she could cause damage. Through the German embassy, he informed her in a friendly tone that, because of foreign exchange-law regulations, he was unable to award her an annuity so long as she was living in England. But in Germany, he would see to it that a house and an appropriate pension were waiting for her if she were to decide to move there. But Bridget preferred to stay in her little house in the Highgate section of London. Soon thereafter, she emigrated to the United States, where her son William Patrick was on a lecture tour. Advertised as "nephew of Adolf Hitler," he spoke to full auditoriums and in this way finally earned money because of his uncle's name. His lectures were entitled: "Why I Hate My Uncle." He also wrote an article with the same title for *Look* magazine.

When the United States entered the war in 1941, William Patrick Hitler volunteered immediately but was not accepted. He was still suspect because of his kinship to the Führer. To prove his loyalty, he gave OSS agents a lengthy interview on September 10, 1943. He told many truths, half-truths and untruths about the Hitler family and his relations to his uncle.

In April of 1944 William Patrick Hitler was at last allowed to join the U.S. Navy. On May 12, he was stationed in Algiers, Louisiana. His commanding officer's name was Hess—an interesting name, considering the circumstances.

After the end of the war, William Patrick Hitler was honorably discharged from the Navy. He then worked as a male nurse in a urological clinic. He decided to change his name, no longer wanting to have anything to do with his past and his uncle. He bluntly rejected an interview with historian John Toland. If William Patrick Hitler is still alive, he would be in his late seventies.

Alois Hitler survived the end of the war and at first changed his name to Eberle. The British occupation authorities arrested him because he was carrying forged papers, but he was released again a short time later. The military authorities determined that Alois had never been a Nazi.

He reopened his restaurant in Berlin for a short time but now changed his name to "Hiller"—legally this time. For awhile he was active in the right-wing Socialist Reich Party of Colonel (Brigadier General) Remer. He died on May 20, 1956. His Angela had died in Dresden on October 30, 1949.

Apart from the modest bequests which multimillionaire Hitler had provided for some of his relatives in his 1938 testament, his clan did not get any advantages out of him. One sister was married to a man from Dresden and the other one was shunted to an arts and crafts shop in Vienna. Alois lived in constant fear that his mighty brother might deprive him of his beer joint license if he did not behave. Hitler's niece and mistress committed suicide. One nephew was killed in action as a Army sergeant in Poland, and the other thought that he could make a few dollars with "Fiction and Truth" about his uncle. Truly, these were not "Bonapartist" destinies.

Adolf Hitler, the brother and uncle, on the other hand, had been busy since the middle of the Thirties, becoming not only the mightiest, but also the richest man of Europe.

# Chapter Fourteen

# King Midas

When Wachenfeld, Hitler's vacation home on Ober-salzberg, was being remodeled, Hitler complained to Albert Speer: "Everything is so expensive. I have completely used up the income from my book even though Amann got me an advance of several hundred thousand marks. He's offered me a million marks for my second book. But I am not going to release it yet."

Despite his whining, Hitler had no need to complain. By then, his earnings from *Mein Kampf* had risen to almost two million marks per year—tax-free. The purchasing power of money at that time made his income worth seven times what it would be normally. In addition, a new volume of his speeches was marketed each year, and he received royalties from that publication. *Mein Kampf* had become an instant and seemingly permanent German bestseller ever since the country's marriage license bureaus started donating a copy of the book to every newlywed couple (at the expense of the particular local community, of course).

The thing that makes Hitler's lament about the high cost of remodelling his mountain home such an outstandingly bad lie is the fact that he didn't spend a penny of his own money on the project.

On June 30, 1934—what became known as the "Bloody Friday of the SA"—Hitler wiped out the last remnants of social-revolutionary thinking within the party and "consolidated" Germany once and for all under the umbrella of capitalism. From that day on, German business and industry accepted him as "a gift from God." There were no longer any strikes. The labor unions   had been smashed. Independent wage negotiations had been abolished. Once again, the entrepreneur was "master of his own home." This was indeed a golden age for every employer.

German capitalists decided it was high time to prove their gratitude to the Führer with cold hard cash. The scion who appointed himself spokesman for the business sector was a man who, before the Nazis came to power, had done very little for the party and whose wife to the end of her days had a horror of receiving "that man"—as she called Hitler—in her home because she was afraid he might enter the guest quarters that had once been inhabited by the All-Highest himself, His Majesty the Emperor. This spokesman went by the name of Bohlen und Halbach. His wife was Bertha Krupp, Germany's richest heiress.

At Krupp's suggestion, the Reich Association of German Industry and the Union of German Employer Associations decided to give Hitler a magnanimous present. The syndicate lords founded the Adolf Hitler Endowment of German Industry, to which every employer was required to contribute quarterly and the proceeds of which went to a private fund that was freely available to the Führer. The money, in fact, went straight to Hitler, bypassing the party treasurer altogether. Hitler was in no way obligated to account for the use of the money, and the employers could deduct the donations from their taxes. Based on reliable estimates, this bogus endowment received almost 100 million marks a year, all of which was available to the Führer, "privately and personally."

In response to Krupp's initial inquiry, Hitler immediately indicated that he was ready to accept the generous donations to his fund. He would use them primarily "to promote culture" and "to mitigate the plight of meritorious comrades-in-arms whose troubles were no fault of their own." With unmitigated gall, he told the syndicate lords that under no circumstances would he enrich himself with the money. He was an artist by nature, he implied, and artists were not interested in big money. To avoid their being misused, he wouldn't allow the donations to be managed by his aides or by his own personal business office. He said he'd find a suitable person to manage the money the way he wanted it to be managed.

He now had to find someone who had a reputation for being straight and incorruptible—someone who would not "swindle" the Führer. The most suitable man for the job would have been Reich Treasurer Franz Xaver Schwarz, but Hitler had no intention of giving the party treasurer any insight into the amount and the use of these large donations. He'd already taken one job away from Schwarz—handling the business of the Eher Publishing House, giving Amann sole power there in order to hide his royalty agreements and fees from the Reich treasurer's office. Amann didn't seem like the right man for these millions in donations either. Hitler appreciated his publisher's business efficiency but he knew all too well how Amann loved to line his own pockets.

Many "old fighters" from within the Party ranks were considered for the job, but most had already proven themselves failures at middle-class responsibilities, which is why they'd joined the Party in the first place. They were unable to handle money and many had fallen into debt. Rudolf Hess would have been ideal for this assignment. He had served Hitler as personal secretary for many years, and when it came to finances, he was almost pedantically correct—too correct for Hitler's taste. Hitler also realized that the staggering amounts that were now flowing into the Adolf Hitler Endowment went far beyond the puritanical comprehension of Hess, the Führer's deputy. Hess, however, did have a busy, energetic and hard-working staff director who had experience as a bookkeeper and money manager and who, moreover, was totally devoted to Hitler. That man was Martin Bormann.

Bormann was a trained agronomist. As a young man, he'd spent a few years in prison for his participation in a death-squad-style murder carried out by extreme right-wing Nationalists. At the end of the twenties, he joined the NSDAP and married the daughter of a party judge, Dr. Walter Buch. Bormann was a heavyset man with a notorious sexual appetite both inside and outside his marriage. He was also a tireless worker who rarely slept more than four hours a night. With superiors, he was fawning, but he was rude and brutal toward subordinates. Early in the thirties, he'd distinguished himself by establishing the "NSDAP Aid Fund," a kind of mandatory insurance for party members that yielded a good profit for the party treasury. In 1933, he was assigned to the staff of the Führer's deputy, Rudolf Hess, and given the official title of "staff director" of Munich's Brown House.

The assignment to manage Hitler's donation fund was in keeping with Bormann's ambitions. It meant that he was constantly near Hitler and soon became more familiar with the Führer's private needs than anyone else on his staff, including his immediate supervisor, Hess. Bormann also managed the revenues from the postage stamp scam, handsomely rewarding the photographer Hoffmann and depositing the rest in Hitler's private account.

Nobody ever investigated what happened to the hundreds of millions of marks that passed through Bormann's hands. According to estimates, more than one billion marks passed through the private donation account that was managed by Bormann. By present day standards— and given the purchasing power of that era— Hitler was thus a billionaire several times over.

Bormann managed to sniff out additional money sources for his Führer. Many of his "folk comrades"— especially old women—made donations to the Führer in their wills. The wills' executors would inform the party headquarters in the province where the deceased lived and they would, in turn, forward the amounts to the party's treasurer. Bormann put an end to this practice. In 1935, he wrote a letter to all of the party's provincial directorates, instructing them "in the name of the Führer's deputy" to route inheritances and donations directly to him.

Hitler's secret slush fund was a constant source of concern for treasurer Schwarz. Because he was required to pay the salaries of all full-time party officials, Schwarz normally had veto power over any new hiring not covered by budget allocations. Suddenly, however, he found out that Bormann himself was hiring people and, over

Schwarz's head, paying them out of Hitler's bottomless money well. Schwarz once complained to Speer: "I haven't the slightest idea where Bormann gets all that money. I sent my auditors to his office but he simply kicked them out. He said he was managing money that was exclusively intended for the Führer. The money was none of the party's business."

Hitler didn't anxiously hoard this money or allow it to lie around uninvested. The Adolf Hitler Endowment fund was after all a wellspring that never gave out; it was not a one shot deal. Back when he lived in the Men's Home on Vienna's Meldemann Street, Hitler swore that he would one day be a rich man without any financial worries. He had now attained his goal, enjoying the status with almost naive pleasure. He was able to hand money out left and right undisturbed by bothersome tax collectors, auditors, or cautious, slow-moving bookkeepers like Schwarz. He knew that as long as German industry was making money, his private money sources would be inexhaustible. Thus, he'd see to it that German industry was never better off than under his rule—by launching, for one thing, gigantic armament projects. He also knew that compared to the billions he enabled Friedrich Flick, Gustav Krupp von Bohlen, Albert Voegler and consorts to earn, the Adolf Hitler Endowment, broken down to each individual industrialist, was a modest contribution, one he was entitled to as the "savior of German industry from Bolshevism."

After the war, in Spandau Prison, Baldur von Schirach reminisced: "Whenever Hitler wanted money for *anything,* Bormann paid, regardless of whether it was for a house for a meritorious party member or a gift for Eva Braun." Painters, like Padua and Ziegler, and sculptors, like Thorak, were rewarded just as generously as prominent civil servants and party big shots. Controlling the purse strings enabled Hitler to determine the living standard of his paladins and to reward them with money or gifts, like an absolute monarch, or punish them by withholding funds. Having inexhaustible funds provided an almost erotic stimulation for Hitler.

In the hierarchy of big shots, Bormann now became a

prominent figure. Officially, he had only been a middle-level functionary until 1938, when he was given the title Reich Director. Once word got out that he held the key to Hitler's private cash register, he was courted on all sides, especially by people in debt.

Hitler derived indescribable delight from playing the patron of the fine arts. Each year, Winifred Wagner received several hundred thousand marks from him as a contribution for the Wagner festival in Bayreuth. Hitler even financed a research team for her, one consisting of historians and genealogists whose job was to prove that Richard Wagner was not the son of a Jew, as had been assumed in many quarters. Theater managers took in contributions for gala presentations of *Die Fledermaus* or *The Merry Widow.* Hitler loved these operettas almost more than the heroic music of his demigod from Bayreuth.

No matter what his Führer wished, Bormann did not hesitate to write the necessary check. In 1935, Hitler, accompanied by Speer, visited the Augsburg City Theater along with local Provincial Party boss Wahl. Wahl believed it would have to be remodeled. "Wahl," said Hitler, as Speer recalled, "we are going to remodel it and make it much more beautiful. I will take care of the cost personally." The costs came to several million marks and Bormann paid without objection.

After 1936, Hitler rarely bought his painting and art objects from his book royalties. He simply dipped into the well of the Endowment. Bormann knew nothing whatsoever about art. It was immaterial to him whether Hitler bought a turgid Makart, a Piloty, a Marees or an idyllic Spitzweg. Likewise it was of no consequence to him whether the "art expert" Hoffmann lined his own pockets by inflating the prices. He always wrote the check for the amount Hoffmann demanded.

In November, Hitler bought the apartment on Prinzregenten Square, immediately paying the remaining mortgage of 175,000 marks. He also purchased the entire ground floor and quartered his escort detail there.

Whenever Hitler was in Munich, 14 RSD (Reich Security Service) officers were required to secure the street from Friedensengel all the way to 16 Prinzregenten Square. Other RSD men were ordered to clear the sidewalks whenever Hitler's car pulled up so that he could enter the house unhindered. Hitler demanded that this be done "gently and politely." SS Lieutenant Colonel Rattenhuber, the commanding officer of the Life Guard, expected almost clairvoyant talents of his men: "I demand that every member of the RSD, when it is necessary for him to take action, be able immediately to determine whether the person involved is an enemy of the state who must be kept away from the Führer at all costs or whether he is just a harmless fellow citizen who wants to cheer the Führer and, because of his spontaneous enthusiasm, seeks to get close to him."

Because the roof could be reached from the roofs of the neighboring buildings, an RSD man was constantly standing guard on top. Rods and grilles were built into the chimneys to prevent explosives from being dropped in. A guard room was located on the ground floor so that no one could enter or leave without being noticed. Anyone who was not living in the house and wanted to enter had to show his identity papers and had to prove that he was being expected by one of the tenants. When Hitler was in the building, the residents were asked as politely as possible to receive visitors only in urgent cases. The building residents themselves were not allowed to use keys but had to ring the bell and were let in by the guards.

When Hitler in 1928 puchased Wachenfeld House on Obersalzberg, he had his sister-in-law Angela Raubal registered for the time being as the owner for tax reasons. It was a rather unobtrusive vacation home in the Southern Bavarian style, with the typical wooden balcony in front of the first floor and a shingle roof weighted down with stones. This is how it was presented to the German poeple: "the little house of the people's chancellor", after the Nazis had come to power.

On beautiful summer days, the folk comrades would make a pilgrimage to the "Holy Mountain of the Germans," as Munich Provincial Party Leader Wagner loved to call Obersalzberg. Whenever Hitler was at home, he liked to walk in the meadow in front of the gate, greeting people jovially, chatting with pretty girls, patting children's cheeks and allowing his subjects to move past him in long columns. In 1933 and 1934, these were still harmless and seemingly idyllic scenes.

But starting in 1935, Bormann, using the millions from the Hitler Endowment Fund, began to transform Obersalzberg into a huge construction site. The citizens of Berchtesgaden today still consider Bormann a defiler of nature because he ruthlessly destroyed one of the most beautiful landscapes in Southern Bavaria. The real destroyer of the landscape, however, was Adolf Hitler. Bormann was merely acting on his orders.

The first thing Bormann did was buy land—after all, there was more than enough money available. He was finally able to put together a compound of 10 square kilometers, a piece of property that extended from the 1,900-meter tall Mt. Kehlstein down to the valley, 600 meters below. Bormann was not chintzy when it came to buying the land. Quite a few of the mountain farmers were happy to get rid of their highland properties because the soil was very poor there. Using the good money Bormann was tossing around, a farmer was able to build a new life for himself in a more hospitable area and on better soil. Anyone who didn't wish to yield voluntarily—like those who wanted to hold onto the land of their ancestors—was threatened with forced expropriation. Most capitulated, including the vacation home owners from the cities.

The stubborn ones fared very badly. A farmer named Heinz Jager refused to sell. Bormann snapped at him, "Either you take my offer or I am going to kick you off your farm!"

Jager stuck to his guns. A couple of days later, a car stopped in front of his house. Six SS man got out, forced Jager into the car, and took him to Berghof where Hitler and Bormann were waiting for him. For the first and only time in his life, Jager had a conversation with the Führer. Hitler greeted him politely, extended his hand, and asked him in a friendly tone to sit down. "Why do you not want to sell your farm to me?" he asked gently.

Jager explained that his ancestors had farmed the property. This was his home. He loved the area and wanted to live here in the future and farm the land.

Hitler nodded, silently and slowly. He seemed to understand. Then he looked Jager straight in the eye and said slowly: "I am hereby asking you to sell your farm—for the love of Germany!"

Jager refused. Even love of Germany could not change his mind. He simply said, "No."

"Never before in my life," Jager recalled later, "have I met a man who could change so totally within a fraction of a second. The veins on his temples swelled up and his moustache twitched. If looks could kill! He turned to Bormann and said curtly: 'Do what you must!' Then he stood up abruptly and left the room without dignifying me with a glance."

Jager was taken to the Dachau Concentration Camp directly from Berghof without being allowed to say goodbye to his family. He remained there until 1938. His farm in the meantime, had been forcibly expropriated. His wife had to support the family with the ridiculously low compensation Bormann gave her. After his release from the prison camp, Jager returned to Obersalzberg, as a worker in a construction gang.

The owner of the Zum Tuerken Hotel, located directly above Hitler's Berghof, did not want to sell either. He was shipped to Dachau, where he died of a lung ailment. His land was also forcibly expropriated. Later, the RSD was billeted in the expropriated hotel.

There were other examples of similar unlimited thuggery. In 1938, Hitler told Bormann he regretted that there was one little farm below Berghof that ruined his magnificent panorama of the surrounding area. After he made this remark, he went to Munich for the day. When he returned, the tiny cottage was gone. The place where it stood was now covered with sod. Cows were picturesquely grazing there. Bormann had acquired the piece of land sometime before with the guarantee that the old couple who lived there could stay for the rest of their lives. Following Hitler's ill-humored remark, Bormann went straight to the old folks, pulled out his checkbook, and got a truck to move their property out. The old couple was gone within two hours. A column of workers with bulldozers was already waiting.

Two years earlier, Bormann had displayed similar organizational talent. Hitler had complained that he always had to stand in the bright light of the sun whenever visitors paraded past the house. This was very painful for his eyes, which were very sensititve due to his gassing in the World War. When Hitler returned from a trip several days later, he was able to stand in the shadow of a linden tree with dense foliage and a thick trunk. Bormann had discovered the tree miles away, had ordered it to be dug up, moved over and replanted.

During the summer of that same year, the new building on Berghof—what used to be Wachenfeld House—was finished. With grotesque understatement, Hitler called the project a "remodeling job," but little was left of the original, simple and stylish home. The new building covered an area four times larger than the old one; it had two upper stories, a huge sundeck and a total of 30 rooms. On the ground floor, directly behind the entrance hall, were the drawing room and the conference room, complete with a huge window that could be raised and lowered. On the first floor, Hitler had his living, sleeping, and work rooms; opposite was a suite for Eva Braun. No expense was spared. The columns in the gigantic living room—with its cathedral ceiling—were made of Carrara marble, all of the windows were mounted in lead, and the ovens were covered with specially designed tiles. The furniture, in the "steamer style" preferred by Hitler, was, like everything else in Berghof, contrary to the myth of the "unpretentious Führer."

Hitler himself had drawn up the design sketches. The Munich architecture Professor Roderich Fick was called in as the builder.

In his memoirs, Albert Speer writes, "The retractable window in the drawing room, which was famous because of its huge dimensions, was Hitler's pride and joy. It offered a view of Untersberg, Berchtesgaden and Salzburg. Below the window, Hitler placed the garage for his cars; when the wind blew the wrong way, the drawing room was filled with the pungent stench of gasoline. It was the kind of floor-plan that would have been rejected in any seminar at a technical college."

The storerooms, the garage and bowling alley were in the basement.

Pauline Kohler, who worked as housemaid on Berghof, described the dining area: "The dining room was about 30 by 10 meters in size. The dining table, made of solid oak, stood in the middle. The lamps were hidden. Gentle twilight came from invisible, covered light sources. Four copper etchings by Albrecht Dürer hung on the walls. The floor was covered with a huge Persian carpet."

Pauline, the parlor maid, soon figured out that the Führer lived in a style that was anything but modest. "For the routine meals, the china was made of gorgeous Dresden porcelain but when we had important guests, they ate off plates made of solid sterling."

Each guest room had a separate marble bathroom. A portrait of the landlord hung over every guest bed. On each night table lay a copy of *Mein Kampf.* And for the gentlemen, the drawer in the night table contained discreetly bibliophile editions of pornographic photographs or drawings.

As soon as Hitler's house was ready, Martin Bormann became a scourge of the natural environment. Albert Speer wrote, "With no regard for unblemished nature, Bormann ran a network of roads through the magnificent landscape. Forest trails became asphalt promenades. Barracks housing thousands of construction workers clung to the mountain slopes, trucks with building materials were running on the roads, at night various construction sites were brightly lit because work was being done in double shifts. Occasionally, detonations could be heard thundering through the valley."

Bormann ordered a 14-kilometer fence to be built around the outer perimeter and another one to enclose the "inner perimeter." The parade of visitors in days past was now gone. Simple folk no longer had access. The dictator had come to fear assassination attempts. "Pressing the flesh" had become too risky for him.

Tirelessly, Bormann continued to build with the money

that flowed into the donation fund. He didn't ovelook his own needs, either. For himself and his large family, he selected a rambling, two-story house that was once a home for children. It was located not far from Berghof and was so highly elevated that Bormann was able to survey all of the construction sites from there. Bormann paid for his own house from Hitler's personal slush fund.

A permanent branch of the party business office was soon established on Obersalzberg. Apartments were built for the employees. An entire barracks compound was erected for the guard personnel of the SS Life Guard Regiment. A huge garage was built to house the motor pool and new roads were constantly being added. Hitler wanted a comfortable mountain hotel for his guests. The old Platterhof, where he had spent many weekends during the early twenties with his companions Dietrich Eckart, Hermann Esser and Putzi Hanfstaengl, was torn down and a pompous new building was erected in its place. (Today it is a ski hotel for the United States Army.) The construction on the Platterhof had been underway for awhile when Hitler noticed during an inspection that there was no bar. The architect had either forgotten it or assumed that Hitler, who frowned on the use of alcohol, did not want intoxicating beverages to be dispensed to his guests. Hitler did, in fact, want a bar attached to the hotel, which necessitated wrecking half the new structure. Obersalzberg was in a veritable orgy of money spending. Nobody audited anything, no bookkeeper ever checked any bills or documents. Hitler himself once said, "Obersalzberg is a real goldmine. The only thing is that Bormann is not getting any gold out of it, but he is throwing a lot into it."

Another time, Hitler expressed regret over the continuing noise and confusion and said, "When everything is finished, I will look for a quiet valley and build myself a little wooden cabin there, just like the first one." Nothing, however, ever seemed to get finished. The construction sites were never closed. On the day the Americans occupied the area, construction gangs were still busy digging out new basement foundations and restoring Hitler's house, which had been heavily damaged by bombs. When the war first broke out, Bormann moved most of his operation below ground level and ordered a far-flung shelter system to be built.

A fifteen minute stroll from Berghof, Bormann erected the Mooslaender Teehaus for his Führer, a pavilion to which Hitler frequently made his little pilgrimage after lunch with his table companions. The walk there was also meant to aid in digestion.

Bormann even transformed his Führer into a South Bavarian mountain farmer. The Obersalzberg Estate became one of the most expensive and senseless of his myriad projects. The soil on Obersalzberg is poor and rocky and the climate is rough. The time available for planting and growing is short. Bormann kept 80 cows and 100 hogs in the stables but since the soil's yield was so scant, it was necessary to purchase vast quantities of fodder for the livestock. The estate was a model of, if nothing else, hygiene. The pigpens were tiled, the sows and piglets were given "a shower" daily with a water hose.

Hitler was amused by Bormann's eagerness to turn him into a gentleman farmer. He once asked to look at the accounts. After a few moments of ruminative silence, he laughed out loud, remarking, as his valet Heinz Linge recalled, "Magnificent! This is not as expensive as I thought. A liter of milk is costing me only 5 marks!"

Vegetables and flowers were also raised on the estate, but exclusively in hot-houses. This was so that there would be flowers in the vases at Berghof daily while the Führer's table offered fresh vegetables in the summer and the winter. A mushroom-raising effort was a failure. Beekeeping was more successful, though quite expensive. The bees—hundreds of swarms—had to be kept alive with sugar fodder during the long and cold mountain winters. An expert beekeeper was hired whom, Hitler liked to address as "Mr. Reich Beemaster" in order to mock Göring, who held the title of Reich Master Hunter. Bormann ordered a house built for the beekeeper and his family. In addition to his own home, Albert Speer was given a fully furnished architecture studio at Berghof.

Ever since 1936 when Eva Braun became the unofficial

lady-of-the-house, she was courted by Bormann. He often treated the other members of the household rudely and curtly. Bormann was able to afford this kind of attitude because he was the keeper of the keys to King Midas' treasury. On the other hand, he knew that Eva Braun would not become a threat to him because she was forbidden to become embroiled in politics. With his characteristic tactlessness, Hitler once, in her presence, announced to his guests that an intelligent man could use only a dumb woman so that she would not be able to influence his decisions. Eva seemed to meet these requirements. She was almost exclusively interested in lightweight movies and film stars, fashions, jovial conviviality, skiing and dancing. Hitler, in his own way, seemed to be very fond of her but felt that her movement in high society was limited. Whenever old party comrades came to visit, she was allowed to be present. But the moment Riech ministers, military leaders, or foreign guests came to dinner, she was exiled to her room. This rule applied even to visits by Göring and his wife, the actress Emmy Sonnemann, both of whom heavily emphasized social etiquette and felt that Hitler's mistress was socially far below them.

Eva Braun could not stand Bormann, despising him for his constant affairs with secretaries and housemaids. She, however, was financially dependent on him. Hitler retained one of his indelicate traits of occasionally slipping his girlfriend an envelope filled with money, but he didn't seem to realize what her cosmetics and her wardrobe cost her. Whenever he bought jewelry for Eva's birthday or Christmas presents, he would go to the shop of an old Munich party comrade and pick out a cheap bracelet or a petty-bourgeois necklace. Most of the time he gave her small semiprecious stones, at best worth a couple of hundred marks.

Bormann soon found out that Eva was hankering for something more appropriate. He would take her to the more elite Munich jewelers and allow her to make her selections without looking at the price tags. When she needed cash to buy herself a chic dress or a pair of shoes, she turned to Bormann, who immediately pulled out his checkbook. In the beginning, she had treated her lover's treasurer coldly but as soon as she realized that access to Hitler's money came through him, she changed her attitude.

Bormann's biggest project on Obersalzberg devoured the huge sum of 30 million marks—today equivalent to an even 200 million. It was the teahouse called Adlerhorst on 1,830-meter high Mt. Kehlstein. The ambitious project was completed in September 1938, right in the middle of the Sudeten crisis, and was inaugurated on September 16.

There was a steep, winding road that led past perpendicular rock walls and over high viaducts to an elevation of 1,700 meters above sea level. Once there, two copper and bronze doors opened directly into the mountain. Through a wide, brightly lit tunnel, the road continued another 130 meters into the rock. An elevator made of shiny brass carried the visitor 130 meters higher, directly into the vestibule of the teahouse. At the center of this structure was a circular fireplace and hall with a magnificent panoramic view from huge windows. In addition, a large kitchen, a dining room and a work room, bathrooms, a large sun deck, and rooms for the guard personnel were included on the premises.

Hitler was ecstatic about his teahouse and showed it off to a whole series of guests, including the well-known British journalist Ward Price. German newspapers were forbidden to print any report about the teahouse. Hitler wanted to maintain the fiction that the "people's chancellor" continued to live modestly in his slightly enlarged "little vacation cabin" in his beloved mountains. He didn't know how his plain folk comrades would cope with the knowledge of his luxurious Kehlstein teahouse. Amazed guests at Adlerhorst included, among others, Munich Provincial Party Chief Adolf Wagner, the Prince of Hesse who was married to Princess Mafalda, (daughter of the King of Italy) general Keitel and von Brauchitsch, French ambassador Francois-Poncet and Lady Unity Mitford, Eva Braun's onetime rival. Also, in response to Hitler's wish, the Goebbels couple celebrated their official reconciliation at Adlerhorst following Joseph's affair with Czech movie actress Lida Baarowa.

After one year, Hitler discontinued visits to Kehlstein almost completely. The 30-million mark toy had lost its novelty.

Even before the Kehlstein house was ready, Bormann, in the spring of 1938, accompanied his Führer to Austria which had just "come home again." Early in the afternoon, riding in a field-gray, three-axle, all-terrain vehicle, they crossed the border to Braunau, Hitler's birthplace. It took them four hours to cover the 120 kilometers of highway from Braunau to Linz because of the cheering crowds. In that city, which he had left as a young man and which he considered his hometown, Hitler delivered his first speech on Austrian soil.

In anticipation of this journey, Bormann received a series of assignments that required great discretion. Hitler wanted to be sure that nothing was revealed about his youth, his relatives and his years in Vienna that would contradict his own story in *Mein Kampf*. Files held by the local authorities were inspected, confiscated, and sometimes "bought." Eyewitnesses had to be discovered and if they couldn't be silenced then they had to be eliminated. One example was Reinhold Hanisch, who had lived in the Men's Home with Hitler and who had sold his watercolors. Hanisch had been dumb enough to threaten "disclosure." On Bormann's orders Gestapo Secret Police arrested him. A few days later he hanged himself in his cell to avoid further torture.

Hitler then gave Bormann his "shopping list" for the acquisition of real estate. The house in which Hitler was born in Braunau, the rather modest Zum Pommer Inn, was purchased for 150,000 marks in May 1938. Also acquired was the house that Hitler's father had purchased in 1899 in Leonding, on the southern periphery of Linz and then resold.

Hitler had returned to Linz, the city where he once dreamed of a carefree life with his school chum Gustl Kubizek. Linz, the city that had humiliated him with a lottery ticket. Here in Linz, Hitler now wanted to build the biggest monument to himself that his millions could buy. He would make Linz the new "pearl of the Danube."

It would be "his" city, and his alone. The best team of architects in the Third Reich was assigned to do the planning—Albert Speer, Hermann Giesler and Roderich Fick.

Hitler's pet project was the Führer Museum. It would be an art gallery that would overshadow the world's greatest museums, such as the Louvre in Paris, the Prado in Madrid, the National Gallery in London, the Museum of Modern Art in New York and the Hermitage in Leningrad. "His" museum, with the treasures he acquired as its richest patron, was magnanimously given to his hometown of Linz.

# Chapter Fifteen

# Special Project Linz

Hitler's vision of Linz's future was the vision of a mega-
lomaniac. He would transform the sleepy little provincial
town into the cultural Mecca for a "Europe of the New
Order." Linz would put the hated Vienna in its place.
Hitler wanted it to be a revolutionary model for modern
city planning, replete with ponderous buildings and wide
boulevards. In order to accomplish this, its population
would first have to be quadrupled.

At the center of the new metropolis would be the
Führer Museum, a huge complex of buildings, that at its
own center would be a gallery as big as a soccer field.
The other buildings would house a weapons museum, a
library with rare books and manuscripts, a tapestry
museum with precious Gobelins and carpets, a gallery for
sculpture, another one for furniture and interior design,
and finally a numismatic department.

The real centerpiece would be Hitler's picture gallery.
Only the very finest paintings from all over Europe
would be assembled here. In his humble hometown—
which had in his youth belittled him so unmercifully—he
would build a monument to himself that would make
him the greatest art collector and art connoisseur of all
times.

Hitler realized that the pedestrian tastes of his friend
and art agent Heinrich Hoffmann wouldn't be good
enough for this ambitious assignment. He needed a whole
team of experts, collectors and scholars who knew how
to use proper methodology for a project of this scope.

Following a visit to Italy in 1938—where he visited the
Uffizi Galleries in Florence and other noteworthy Italian
centers of art—Hitler summoned the well-known Berlin
art dealer Karl Haberstock. At that time, Haberstock was
60 years old and had been an NSDAP member since
1933. He had already sold Hitler a number of paintings.
The first one was "Venus and Amor" by Paris Bordone, a
16th Century Italian artist. Hitler had paid Haberstock
65,000 marks for the painting. For his Obersalzberg
home, Haberstock had also sold Hitler Van Dyck's "Jupi-
ter and Antiope," Canaletto's "Santa Maria della Salute,"
and Rubens' "St. Peter in the Boat." The Führer did not
pay him less than 24,000 marks each for any of these
paintings.

In the ensuing years, Haberstock would cut many other
lucrative deals with Hitler. For the planned Führer Museum, he sold him Watteau's "La Danse" at the hefty price
of 900,000 marks and Boecklin's "Italian Villa" for
675,000 marks. During the war, Haberstock was given
special papers that enabled him to move freely through
occupied territories in search of art treasures for the ob-
sessive Hitler.

In his conversation with Haberstock in Berlin in 1938,
Hitler openly talked about the enormous Linz project,
knowing he could count on the art dealers' discretion.
The project was otherwise top secret. Hitler asked Haberstock who he considered German's most outstanding art
expert. Without hesitation, Haberstock replied, "Dr. Hans
Posse in Dresden. Until a short time ago, he was the
director of the world-famous art collection housed there.
Unfortunately, he had some trouble with Provincial Party Chief Mutschmann and was fired." Haberstock was a
friend of Posse's. He knew that if Hitler hired Posse as
his expert, he'd soon get some big business coming his
way.

Hitler respected Haberstock's opinion and immediately
went to Dresden. There he bawled out the nonplussed
provincial party boss, asking him how he could dare fire
an expert of Dr. Posse's caliber. He ordered that Posse be
reinstated and given an official apology.

Dr. Hans Posse, the son of a Dresden archivist, had

been appointed director of the State Art Collection in 1913, when he was a young art historian. Under his direction, the museum gained a distinguished international reputation. Posse, in his own words, was "completely uninterested in politics." He never joined the NSDAP.

Hitler had a number of discussions with Posse, gradually initiating him into the Linz Project. He was fascinated by the breadth of knowledge of his new expert. Posse was blunt with Hitler, openly telling him that his previous art purchases, with Hoffmann as middleman, were fairly mediocre. Hoffmann might be an outstanding photographer but selecting the best paintings and art objects for a gallery of the magnitude Hitler had in mind was undoubtedly too much for him.

Hitler made his decision in the summer of 1939. On June 26, he issued the following order: "I hereby instruct Dr. Hans Posse, Director of the State Art Collections in Dresden, to establish the new art museum in Linz. All State and Party offices are hereby asked to support Dr. Posse in the accomplishment of his mission." At the same time, a secret commission was founded with the title Special Assignment Linz. Posse became its chairman as "the Führer's Special Assistant."

The "team" had now been put together. Other experts were appointed for the various museum branches under Posse's direction. These included Dr. Friedrich Wolffhardt for rare books and manuscripts and Dr. Fritz Dworschak for numismatics. The "clearinghouse" was set up in the Führer Building on Munich's Koenig Square, and the nearby air raid shelter was used as a storage facility. Architect and party official Heinz Reger became the chief of the collecting process; it was his job to inventory and catalog the collection, which he did with such meticulousness that the Allies were able after the war to determine the exact origin of every piece of art.

Posse's aide, Dr. Rudolf Oertel, also became a member of the Special Mission. Two Vienna art historians, Dr. Kajetan Muehlmann, and, as arms expert, Dr. Leopold Ruprecht, were taken on board a little later.

Vienna became the first field of plunder for the members of the Special Commission. The assets and art treasures of rich Jews were confiscated outright—for example, the collection of Baron Louis von Rothschild, the last Austrian scion of this famed banking family. He and other wealthy Jews were allowed to emigrate but they had to leave most of their assets and art works behind as payment for the so-called Reich Getaway Tax. Their art treasures were then officially placed "under the protection of the Reich." Hitler wanted to give the operation at least a thin veneer of legality in order not to look like a common thief and plunderer in the eyes of the world.

The art work that was taken into custody via the Reich Getaway Tax would then be auctioned off "quite legally," with Hitler getting preferrential purchasing rights. From the property of Vienna's Jewish community, Posse selected 122 paintings for the Linz Project, including a Holbein and a Lucas Cranach, three Dutch painters of the 16th Century, eleven Flemings (which included three Van Dycks), 40 old Dutch masters (which included Rembrandt's portrait of Anthonia Coopal), two Frans Hals, two Tintorettos, two Fragonards, two Bouchers and many other valuable works.

Posse only selected the very finest, and Hitler was able to get these confiscated treasures at ridiculously low prices. For example, he paid 12,000 marks for the priceless antique gold coin collection of the Jew Alexander Hauser.

Posse also looked into the open Vienna market. For Rembrandt's portrait of Henrickje Stoffel, Hitler paid the enormous sum of 900,000 marks and he forked over 65,000 marks for an overrated Makart portrait of Cleopatra. He acquired 75 works of art in Vienna in this way, most of them paintings.

The city of Vienna was also pressured into compliance with the Führer's compulsions. In the Austrian gallery, Posse saw Rubens' "Ganymede." He wanted it for the Linz Museum and a "deal" was arranged. The city was forced to swap the masterpiece for one of Hitler's porcelain collections that he no longer wanted. The magnificent Rubens was given the catalog No. 1887 and locked up in the dark air raid shelter of the Führer Building. Art loving "folk comrades" were expected to be good enough to wait until the Führer Museum in Linz was completed. Then the dictator would most graciously deign to show them his treasures.

Among fanatical art collectors, there are pathological fetishists who desire a certain painting or object exclusively for a kind of masturbatory thrill. The pictures are then hung in the locked rooms of their mansions. Only they and an occasional privileged guest may look at them. Hermann Göring was an unscrupulous collector and plunderer who, as Hitler's rival, appropriated for himself some of the world's most beautiful works of art. But Göring, as the warped Nazi incarnation of the sensuous Renaissance man, at least hung or displayed his booty and rejoiced in looking at it. Full of pompous pride, he exhibited his acquisitions to his guests. Hitler, on the other hand, hoarded things without deriving any aesthetic enjoyment from them. Packed in wooden crates, he locked Europe's most beautiful paintings in dark basement rooms and later, in a deep salt mine. This is where he revealed the stingy and paltry side of his character. The man who loved to fancy himself a great friend of the arts really got no joy out of the works he plundered, only out of possessing them.

The Czernin case is a prime example of how the unscrupulous Hitler used his power to force collectors to sell to him. Count Czernin, who lived in Vienna and was the scion of one of Austria's most venerated families, owned the painting "Painter in His Studio" by the great master Jan Vermeer. There are only 30 certified genuine Vermeers in the world. The world's wealthiest art collectors had been outbidding each other for years to get their hands on this painting, but Czernin would not give it up. The American multimillionaire Andrew Mellon had offered 6 million dollars—but to no avail.

Hitler wanted to have that painting. He could not confiscate it because Czernin wasn't a Jew. Hitler tried to ascertain whether Czernin owed any back taxes, in which case the painting could be taken as security and then auctioned off. But Czernin always paid his taxes on time.

Next, Dr. Dworschak tried to "persuade" Czernin. When the Count continued to refuse, Hitler's emissary threatened him with Gestapo torture and imprisonment in a concentration camp. They could always trump up a justification for arresting the Count, and then the painting would simply be confiscated as the property of an "enemy of the state." In 1940, Czernin gave in. Hitler got the picture for 1,400,000 marks and also agreed to pay the sales tax amounting to 250,000 marks—a fraction of what Mellon had offered.

The Vermeer was given the Catalog No. 1096 and soon disappeared into the dark air raid shelter and then into the Alt-Aussee salt mine. The picture didn't see the light of day again until 1945. It was returned to Vienna.

When Czechoslovakia was invaded and conquered in 1939, becoming a "Reich Protectorate," Posse went to Prague as Hitler's art scout. From the famous Lobkowitz Collection he acquired Pieter Breughel's "The Hay Harvest." From the Hohenfurt Monastery came the 14th century altar centerpiece of the unknown "Master of Hohenfurth", to be placed in the Führer Building.

Although Hitler acquired precious little for the Linz Collection from Poland, Göring and Himmler more than made up for him there with their shameless plundering. From the collections of Counts Lubomirski and Czartoryski, Göring selected 30 Dürer drawings and gave them to his Führer as presents.

Following the occupation of France, Holland and Belgium in the spring and summer of 1940, Hitler was much closer to realizing his megalomaniacal dreams about Linz. But he moved cautiously, so as not to vex the Vichy Government too much. The collections of Jews were, of course, confiscated or, in Nazi jargon, were placed "under protective custody." There was never any talk of "expropriation." On July 15, 1940, the following order was addressed to France's Jews: "Moveable works of art whose value exceeds the amount of 100,000 francs must be reported in writing by their owners or custodians by August 15. They must not be removed from their locations." Drastic penalties were threatened for failure to obey this directive.

Very few of the works of art that were part of big Jewish collections like Rothschild, Levy de Benzion,

Kahn or the Seligmann brothers had made it to safety before the Nazi invasion. The Maginot Line had always been considered militarily unbreachable. Certainly, no one expected the Nazis to breach it. Some treasures found "asylum" in the neutral Paris embassies of Spain and Argentina and survived the war undamaged. The rest, however, were up for grabs.

Hitler took very little for Linz from the confiscated Jewish properties. The lions's share went to Göring, who had the "Rosenberg Action Staff"—the biggest organization of plunderers in modern history—working for him. Hitler still wanted to maintain a semblance of legality and "buy" paintings and other art objects. Because of this, Göring often came to have more valuable items than even Hitler had. But from the property of the Rothchilds, Hitler stole 40 paintings, including one Rembrandt, two Goyas, Vermeer's "the Astronomer," one Frans Hals, two Watteaus, three Bouchers and two Fragonards.

An unlimited account was opened for Dr. Posse in Holland. Immediately after the occupation, Nazi big shots and art dealers had invaded Holland to outbid each other at the auctions. Prices skyrocketed. As his bidder and buyer, Posse used 30-year-old art historian Dr. Erhard Goepel and the Jewish art dealer Vitale Bloch, with whom he made an agreement. Posse would protect Bloch against anti-Jewish laws if he gave him first-hand knowledge about where valuable art works could be found, either among collectors, art dealers or at auctions. In December 1940, Posse was able to send the first shipment of purchases to Munich. These included paintings by Breughel, Rubens, Canaletto, Rembrandt, Steen and Ruisdael. The next load arrived in Munich eight months later. Except for ten paintings that belonged to the confiscated Franz-Lugt Collection in the Hague, all of the paintings had been acquired on the art market more or less legally.

Posse spent considerable sums in Holland. He bought the collection of Franz Koenigs (Dürer, Rembrandt) for 1.5 million guilders. The collection of Otto Lanz (Italian paintings, Renaissance furniture) went to Hitler for 2,350,000 Swiss francs. By the end of 1940, Hitler had already spent more than 15 million guilders on the Dutch art market.

As the war neared its end, Hitler had hoarded close to 10,000 paintings and art objects at a value of at least 1 billion marks. This does not include Gobelin tapestries, antique arms and furniture. Packaged in crates, stored in dark cellars and mine shafts, Hitler owned the greatest personal art collection in history.

Some art dealers were able to make fortunes as a result of Hitler's collection mania. There was an entire network of art dealers, sub-dealers, agents and scouts who worked mostly for Hitler's Linz Project and made money hand over fist. They liked working for Hitler because money was no object. It seemed to come from an inexhaustible source. For two Rembrandts, which had belonged to the French collector Etienne Nicolas, Hitler paid 3 million marks plus a commission of 90,000 marks to the Paris art dealer and collaborator Roger Dequoy.

The most important auction establishments were Hans Lange in Berlin, Weinmueller in Munich, the Dorotheum in Vienna and the Hotel Drouot in Paris. Hitler also made purchases in neutral foreign countries; for example, he got two Spitzwegs from an art dealer in Lucerne, along with one Buerkel, one Boecklin and one Uhde. All of these paintings were more in line with Hitler's personal taste than the elitist tastes of his expert Posse.

Of course, Dr. Posse and, after his death in 1943, his successor Dr. Voss theoretically had authority to make advance selections for Linz. There were two art dealers, however, who worked more directly with Hitler. They were Maria Dietrich in Munich and Karl Haberstock in Berlin. They had their own network of agents who were bidding at auctions all over Europe. Commissions were never recorded separately. The two dealers simply added to the final price whatever they considered to be fair and appropriate. There were never any objections.

Hitler's old friend Heinrich Hoffmann also continued his lucrative practice as a middleman. He handled 155 purchases for the art depository in the Führer Building, getting a generous cut of the purchase price. On January 31, 1941, he bought three pictures for 29,000 marks and immediately sold them to Hitler for 35,000 marks. Hoffmann also loved to buy confiscated paintings from the fund for himself, privately. A landscape by Willem van de Velde from the confiscated collection of Alfons Jaffe cost him only 2,000 marks, a ridiculously low sum.

The Munich art dealer Maria Dietrich earned big money; she operated the Almas Gallery at 9 Otto Street and had close business and private contracts with Hoffmann. Her daughter Mimi (a half-Jewess) was one of Eva Braun's girlfriends. Maria had divorced her husband, the Turkish Jew Ali Almas-Diamant, in 1937. Through Hoffmann, she became Hitler's favorite art dealer, even more favored than Karl Haberstock.

In 1937, her annual income was 47,000 marks but in 1938 it had already risen to 483,000 marks and by 1941 the figure was 570,000 marks. According to present-day standards, Maria Dietrich was a millionairess.

Hitler paid her prices without objection. Almost a hundred agents and sub-agents were working for her all over Europe. For a painting by Boucher, which she'd acquired for 140,000 marks, she demanded and got 180,000 marks from Hitler.

Other Nazi big shots like Robert Ley also liked to buy from Mrs. Dietrich. She even managed to palm off four landscapes by the Venetian painter Guardi on the wine-loving Labor Front boss—after Dr. Posse had identified and rejected the paintings as forgeries.

The other big art dealer was Karl Haberstock. He managed to pull off the amazing stunt of acquiring—during the war—a Van Dyck, a Rubens and a Canaletto for Hitler in England. Haberstock had an account with the Swiss Bank on London's Regent Street through which the deal was handled. The paintings reached Hitler via neutral Switzerland. Haberstock also did a lot of business with art dealer Fischer in Lucerne. Through him he acquired one Paris Bordone and one Tintoretto which he sold to Hitler at a big profit. For a Basaiti, which he had purchased for 67,000 marks, he got 90,000 marks. For a 18,000 mark Ruisdael, Hitler paid him 33,000 marks. On a (genuine) Guardi, he made a profit of more than 100 percent.

But his star began to wane after his friend Posse died in 1943. Posse's successor, Voss, blackened Haberstock's reputation with Hitler, apprising the Führer of his excessively high commissions.

By 1943, the air raid shelter under the Munich Führer Building had become too small for the hoarded treasures. It was necessary to find additional storage quarters. The most important new ones became Thuerntal Castle, near Kremsmuenster and King Ludwig's fairy tale castle of Neuschwanstein at Fuessen, which housed the haul of the "Rosenberg Action Staff."

As the number of air raids on Reich territory increased in 1944, Hitler ordered most of the art treasures to be stored in the tunnels of the Alt-Aussee salt mine east of Salzburg. Most works from the Führer Building were moved to the salt mine by October 1944. Only 723 paintings were in the Führer Building as the first American spearheads reached the outskirts of Munich on April 29, 1945.

None of the art works ever got to Linz. Only the wreckage of a megalomaniacal dream is left of Hitler's gigantic art palace in Linz, his personal monument. The tyrant ended up in the same place where he had hidden Europe's most beautiful works of art: in an air raid shelter, deep beneath the earth.

# Epilogue

During the early morning hours of April 29, 1945, while American troops were occupying Munich, the "Capital of the Movement", Hitler dictated and signed his private testament in the shelter under the Berlin Reich Chancellery. Just after he wed Eva Braun in the bunker, he wrote: "Because I believed during the years of the struggle that I could not take the responsibility of entering into matrimony, I have now decided, before terminating my life on this earth, to take as my wife the girl who, after long years of loyal friendship, out of her own free will, came to this almost completely encircled city to share her fate with mine. It is her wish to die as my wife. Death will give us back that which my work in the service of my people robbed us both."

"All my possessions—to the extent that they are of any value at all—belong to the Party. If the latter should no longer exist, they belong to the State and if the State should also be wiped out, then no further decision is required of me."

"I never acquired my paintings—in the collections I purchased down through the years—for private purposes but always for the development of a gallery in my hometown of Linz on the Danube. It is my most heartfelt wish that this legacy be fulfilled. I appoint my most loyal party comrade Martin Bormann as the executor of my last will and testament. He is authorized to make all decisions in a final and legally valid manner. He is permitted to turn over to my siblings everything that has any value as personal memorabilia or anything that is needed to preserve a modest middleclass existence, especially, above all, to my wife's mother and my loyal male and female collaborators—and he knows exactly who they are—headed by my longtime male and female secretaries, Mrs. Winter and others who supported me with their work for many years."

"I and my wife have chosen death to avoid the disgrace of retreat or capitulation. It is our desire to be cremated immediately at the place where I did most of my daily work in the course of 12 years of service to my people."

The "service" he had rendered to the people could be seen directly outside—in the smoking rubble of Berlin.

Hitler's executor, Martin Bormann, was not able to execute anything. In all probability, he died in an attempt to break through the Russian encirclement of the Reich Chancellery, with a copy of the Führer's testament in his pocket. The fortune which had been accumulated by Hitler vanished. His assets, which he had bequeathed to the Nazi Party, were confiscated, along with his art treasures, which were discovered relatively intact in the Führer Building and in the Alt-Aussee salt mines. The artworks and other property that could not be returned to their rightful owners, were placed in the custody of the U.S. occupation authorities until 1951. Since then, all assets have been administered by the Free State of Bavaria.

The vast compound on Obersalzberg is also under the trusteeship of the Free State of Bavaria. Everything there has been leveled to the ground. Of Hitler's Berghof, only the outlines of the foundation walls can be seen in the ground. The teahouse on Mt. Kehlstein still exists and has become a tourist attraction. The farm compound has been leased by the Bavarian government. The Platterhof has become an American vacation hotel.

Approximately seven million marks in royalties for *Mein Kampf*, which had accrued for Hitler in the publishing house account of the Eher Publishing House, were confiscated as Nazi assets. The Free State of Bavaria claims copyrights to Hitler's writings and speeches, though this has been challenged by Hitler's heirs and their testament executor, Professor Werner Maser, a historian. The copyright dispute has not yet been resolved. Only the Stuttgart Institute for Contemporary History recognizes the copyright claims of the heirs. When a limited edition of Hitler's "Second Book" was published in 1961, the heirs received the sum of 3,000 marks.

Who are the heirs? Who might someday be able to claim the remnants of Hitler's private assets?

To be able to bequeath anything, the testator must first be declared dead. Hitler died on April 30, 1945, shortly before 3:30 a.m., at the age of 56, together with his 33-year-old wife Eva. He was officially declared dead only 11 years later, on October 25, 1956. On January 11, 1957, Dean and City Pastor Johann Ludwig made the following entry in the old Braunau baptismal register in which one of his predecessors long ago had recorded Adolf Hitler's birth: "By decision of the Berchtesgaden Lower Court, dated October 25, 1956, II 48/52, declared dead in the name of the State. Braunau City Rectory, January 11, 1957. Johann Ludwig."

On February 17, 1960, the Munich Lower Court, under File No. 2994/48, issued an inheritance certificate for Paula Hitler "concerning the hereditary succession of Adolf Hitler, after Reich Chancellor Adolf Hitler, who died in Berlin on April 30, 1945, on the basis of a testament, following elimination of the fiduciary heir, the NSDAP." She was to inherit two-thirds of the property. One-sixth, each, was to go to the half-siblings Alois Hitler and Angela Hamitzsch, the widow Raubal (nee Hitler). They both, however, were already dead. Paula Hitler died on June 1, 1960, without having come into her inheritance. On October 25, 1960, the Berchtesgaden Lower Court, under File No. VI, 108/60, ruled as follows: "Heirs of Paula Hitler who died in Schoenau on June 1, 1960, are the sibling children Elfriede Hochegger (nee Raubal) and Leo Raubal, at one-half each."

These are heirs who have not inherited anything. It is doubtful whether they ever will inherit anything.

Hitler set the precedent for the expropriation of his own property. For the first time in the history of civilization, he brutally expropriated every last penny of many innocent civilians—people who had done nothing but belong to a different religion or to another "race." Looked at from this perspective, his own expropriation would be quite appropriate. The sufferings which he inflicted upon millions of people cannot be compensated for with any amount of money.

To this very day, many people still hold on to the legend that though Hitler was a terrible foe of humanity, one thing can be said in his behalf—while many of his paladins may have been corrupt and greedy, he had never enriched himself.

It is high time to fling this fairy tale on the manure pile of history now and for all time.

## SELECTED SHORT BIOGRAPHIES

Amann, Max (1891-1957). One of Hitler's earliest collaborators. Joined the NSDAP in 1921. At first party business manager, then publications manager of the Franz Eher Publishing House. President of the Reich Press Chamber. Sentenced to two and one-half years in prison on September 8, 1948. Expropriated in 1949. Died in poverty in Munich in 1957.

Arco, Anton, Count (born in 1897). Reserve second lieutenant, university student. In 1919, shot Bavarian Prime Minister Kurt Eisner and triggered the events leading to the soviet republic. Sentenced to life imprisonment, pardoned in 1925.

Ballerstedt, Otto (1887-1934). Engineer, leader of the separatist "Bavaria League." Murdered in Dachau concentration camp on July 1, 1934.

Blavatsky, Helena Petrowna, nee von Hahn (1831-1891). Well-known lady esoteric. Founded Theosophical Society in 1875. Her followers credited her with extraordinary gifts as medium.

Bormann, Martin (1900-1945). During the Twenties, active in right-wing political underground groups. Involved in death-squad-style murders. Joined NSDAP in 1927. Became director of Party Business Office and was promoted to Reich director in 1936. Sentenced to death in absentia in Nuernberg on October 1, 1946. In all probability, perished in Berlin early in May 1945.

Borsig, Ernst (since 1909, von) (1869-1933). Industrialist. Early supporter of Hitler. Chairman of Union of German Employer Association, 1923-1932. The family enterprise was merged with Rheinmetall A.G. after his death.

Bouhler, Philipp (1899-1945). Reich Business Manager of the NSDAP in 1925. Director of "Office of the Führer" in 1934. Committed suicide on May 19, 1945.

Braun, Eva (1912-1945). Photolab assistant in Heinrich Hoffmann's studio. Hitler's mistress since 1932. Married Hitler on April 29, 1943 and then committed suicide with him.

Breker, Arno (Born in 1900). Classical-realistic sculptor who was highly regarded by Hitler. After 1945, successfully active as sculptor for the foyers of industrial syndicate buildings.

Bruckmann, Hugo (1863-1941). Publisher. Together with his wife, one of Hitler's earliest financial patrons. Member of Reichstag, 1933-1941.

Brueckner, Wilhelm (1884-1954). SA lieutenant and, until 1940, Hitler's chief aid. Fell into disgrace and joined the armed forces in 1941. Held rank of colonel at war's end.

Buch, Walter (1883-1949). Chairman of Supreme Party Court of NSDAP. Martin Bormann's father-in-law. After the war, sentenced to 5 years in labor camp. Committed suicide in 1949.

Burekel, Heinrich (1802-1869). Romantic landscape painter favored by Hitler.

Chamberlain, Houston Stewart (1855-1927). Author and cultural philosopher. Richard Wagner's son-in-law. Already German citizen before World War I. His book "Die Grundlagen des 20 Jahrhunderts" (The Foundations of the 20th Century) glorified the "Aryan spirit" and had a strong effect on the race theory of the Nazis.

Crowley, Aleister (1875-1947). English esoteric and magician. Founded various lodges and secret leagues. His "Buch der Gesetze" (Book of Laws) (1908), is oriented purely along fascist lines. Hitler was familiar with his theories presumably through the "Thule Society."

Dagover, Lil (1897-1980). Prominent German movie actress, highly regarded by Hitler. Star of important films during the Nazi era.

Deterding, Sir Henry (1866-1939). Since 1907, general manager, Shell Syndicate. Sympathized with Hitler and Nazi party.

Dietrich, Otto (1897-1952). At the end of the Twenties, established important contacts with industrialists. Reich press chief of the party, 1933-1945. Sentenced to seven years in prison in 1949 but was released in 1950.

Drexler, Anton (1884-1941). Toolmaker. Co-founder of "German Worker Party" (DAP), for some time also honorary chairman of NSDAP. Broke with Hitler in 1925 and lost all political influence. Died forgotten in Munich.

Duesterberg, Theodor (1875-1950). Second federal leader of "Stahlhelm." Unsuccessful presidential candidate in 1932. Withdrew from politics thereafter.

Eckart, Dietrich (1868-1923). Hitler's first intellectual mentor. Anti-Semitic author, first editor-in-chief of the "Volkischer Beobachter."

Eisner, Kurt (1867-1919). Journalist, feuilleton editor. Socialist. Became first prime minister of the Free State of Bavaria. His death in 1919 was the prelude to the soviet republic.

Esser, Hermann (1900-1981). One of Hitler's earliest comrades-in-arms. Editor of "Volkischer Beobachter." NSDAP propaganda chief, 1925-1926. Became Bavarian economy minister in 1933, president of the Reich Tourist Traffic Association in 1936, and state secretary in the Reich propaganda Ministry. Sentenced to five years in labor camp in 1950 but was released in 1951. No longer visible on political scene after war.

Feder, Gottfried (1883-1941). Engineer. Co-founder of DAP. During the early days, leading ideologist of NSDAP. Drafted party program. His influence declined during the Third Reich. Honorary professor at the Berlin Technical college in 1934.

Flick, Friedrich (1883-1972). Industrial tycoon. Promoter of the Nazi movement and one of the most prominent entrepreneurs of the Third Reich. Sentenced to seven years in prison in 1949 but was released in 1951. Considered postwar Germany's richest man. Stubbornly refused to pay his former forced laborers any compensation.

Ford, Henry (1863-1947). American industrialist. Founder of Ford Motor Company in Detroit. Radical anti-Semite. Sympathized with Hitler and Nazi movement.

Francois-Poncet, Andre (1887-1978). France's ambassador in Berlin, 1932-1938. French high commissioner in the Federal Republic of Germany in 1949, thereafter ambassador in Bonn until 1955.

Frank, Hans (1900-1946). During the Twenties, attorney of NSDAP; became "Reich law leader" in 1933. During World War II, governor-general of Poland. Notorious because of his ruthlessness against the civilian population. Sentenced to death in Nuernberg in 1946 and executed.

Frick, Wilhelm (1877-1946). From 1904 until 1924, worked in the Munich Police Headquarters and from 1919 directed the political police. Although not yet a party member, he supported Hitler and the Nazi movement in the positions he held. Became Hitler's close political advisor. Dismissed from his post because of his support of the Hitler coup d'etat in 1924. Interior minister of Thuringia in 1930. Reich interior minister in 1933. Reich protector of Bohemia and Moravia in 1943. Sentenced to death in Nuernberg in 1946 and executed.

Fritsch, Theodor (1852-1933). Radical anti-Semitic author and esoteric. His racist writings greatly influenced Hitler and the Nazis.

Funk, Walter (1890-1960). Journalist "Berliner Boersenzeitung" (Berlin Stock Exchange Journal). Reich economy minister, 1937-1945; from 1939, also president of the Reichsbank. Sentenced to life imprisonment in Nuernberg in 1946. Released for reasons of health in 1958.

Gansser, Emil (1874-1941). Natural scientist, Siemens manager. NSDAP member from 1921. Introduced Hitler to the National Club in Berlin. Several times procured money in Switzerland.

Goebbels, Joseph (1897-1945). Germany's chief propagandist and cultural dictator. Joined NSDAP in 1924. Initially, Hitler's opponent, supporter from 1926 on. Party provincial chief of Berlin-Brandenburg in 1926. Reich propaganda director of the NSDAP in 1929, Reich propaganda minister in 1933. Controlled German movie industry and the ideological orientation of the press. In 1944, general deputy for total war effort and, in this capacity, practically Hitler's sub-dictator. Committed suicide with his entire family on May 1, 1945.

George, Heinrich (1893-1946). One of the greatest stars of stage and screen during the Weimar era. Later went over to the side of the Nazi rulers. Died in a Soviet internment camp in Sachsenhausen in 1946.

Giesler, Hermann (born in 1898). Architect. Professor in 1938. Hitler helped him and in 1938 appointed him "General Construction Counselor for the Capital of the Movement" in Munich.

Göring, Emmy (1893-1973). Hermann Göring's second wife (1935). Was actress under the name of Emmy Sonnemann. From the time of her marriage to Göring, practically "first lady" of the Third Reich. After the war, sentenced to one year in a labor camp and 5 years performance band. Thirty percent of her private assets were confiscated.

Göring, Hermann (1893-1946). During World War I, fighter pilot and commander of Richthofen Wing. Highly decorated. After the war, test pilot in Sweden where he married wealthy Carin von Kantzow. Joined Hitler in 1922 in Munich. In 1923, fled abroad (Italy, Sweden) for 4 years. Returned in 1923 as representative of Swedish armament firms. Reichstag President in 1931. Prussian interior minister in 1933; founded Gestapo. Prussian prime minister in 1934. In 1935, field marshal-general and commander-in-chief of the Air Force, aviation minister. Special deputy for the Four-Year Plan. Designated Hitler's successor in 1939. Chairman of the Reich Defense Council. Held a series of lucrative positions, include "Reich Master Hunter." Reich Marshal in 1940. Sentenced to death in Nuernberg in 1946. Committed suicide the evening before his execution.

Graf, Ulrich (born 1878, date of death unknown) Charter member of DAP and NSDAP. Hitler's personal bodyguard, 1920-1923. Member of Reichstag, 1936. Honorary SS brigadier general.

Guertner, Franz (1881-1941). Bavarian justice minister, 1922-1932. In 1924, advocated pro-Nazi atmosphere during Hitler's trial in People's Court. Reich justice minister, 1932-1941.

Hanfstaengl, Ernst, nicknamed Putzi (1887-1975). Art historian. Hitler's personal friend from 1922. His contacts opened the doors of Munich society to Hitler. NSDAP foreign press chief, 1931. Alienated from Hitler in 1937. First went to England, and then to the United States. During World War II, became advisor to Roosevelt and the Hearst press. Returned to Germany in 1946 and lived a quiet, withdrawn life in Munich until his death.

Hansen, Theophil (1813-1891). Architect, senior construction counselor in Vienna. Created monumental structures (Stock Exchange, Parliament). Highly regarded by Hitler.

Haushofer, Karl (1869-1946). Bavarian general, professor. Germany's leading geopolitics expert. Interested in mysticism and esoterics. Mentor of Rudolf Hess. Hitler's political advisor during the Twenties. Co-editor of "Mein Kampf." His influence declined during the war. In 1946, committed suicide together with his wife.

Hess, Rudolf (1894-1987). Son of a German wholesale merchant from Alexandria, Egypt. Second lieutenant during World War I. Joined Hitler in 1921. Hitler's private secretary in 1924. Chief of party organization and "deputy of the Führer of the NSDAP" in 1932. Reich minister without portfolio in 1933. On May 10, 1941, flew to England (with or without Hitler's knowledge) to initiate peace negotiations. His mission failed. Declared mentally sick by Hitler. Sentenced to life imprisonment in Nuernberg in 1946. Last prisoner in Spandau until his death, at age 93, in August, 1987.

Himmler, Heinrich (1900-1945). Farmer with degree in agriculture. Joined Hitler in 1922. Police chief of Munich in 1933. Commander of SS and chief of German Police in 1934. Reich interior minister, 1943-1945. Since July 20, 1944, also commander of the replacement army. Relieved of all official functions by Hitler on April 28, 1945. Committed suicide on May 23, 1945, after his capture by British troops.

Hoffmann, Heinrich (1885-1957). Hitler's personal photographer, close confidant, and business partner. His daughter married Reich Youth Leader Baldur von Schirach. In 1947, sentenced to five years in a labor camp as a "Nazi profiteer" but released shortly thereafter. Although almost all of his assets were confiscated, he lived comfortably until his death on his photo files which, with 2.5 million photographs, constitute a unique historical record.

Jung, Carl Gustav (1875-1961). World famous psychologist and psychoanalyst. Created a psychological typology theory and also used mythological and cultural-historical material.

Kandinsky, Wassily (1866-1944). Russian painter and graphic artist. Hitler's contemporary in Schwabing.

Kapp, Karl (1858-1922). Prussian politician. In 1917, founded the "German Fatherland Party" which was against ending the war. In 1920, launched an unsuccessful coup d'etat against the republican government.

Keitel, Wilhelm (1882-1946). Officer. Chief of the Armed Forces High Command, 1938-1945. Promoted to the rank of field marshal-general in 1940. Totally devoted to Hitler, nickname "Lakaitel" ("Lackey"). Sentenced to death in Nuernberg and executed for signing criminal orders (Commissar Order, executions of hostages).

Kirdorf, Emil (1847-1938). Industrial tycoon in Ruhr Region. One of the first prominent German entrepreneurs who joined the Nazis. Obtained financial support for Hitler.Co- founder of Rhenish-Westphalian Coal Syndicate and other large concerns. Kirdorf was considered a ruthless exploiter and foe of the labor unions.

Klee, Paul (1879-1940). Famous German-Swiss painter and graphic artist. Hitler's contemporary in Schwabing.

Kraus, Karl (1874-1936). Viennese dramatist, lyricist, journalist and satirist. Conducted masterful stylistic struggle against language abuse. Gave early warning against incipient Fascism and Nazism.

Kriebel, Hermann (1876-1941). Bavarian first lieutenant. Military leader of "Bavaria Fighting League." Imprisoned for participation in 1923 Hitler coup d'etat. Later, military advisor to Chiang Kai-shek. Consul-general in Shanghai, 1934-1939, thereafter chief of personnel in the Foreign Office.

Krupp von Bohlen und Halbach, Gustav (1870-1950). German arms tycoon. In 1906, on urging of Emperor Wilhelm II, married the heiress of the Krupp Syndicate and took her family name. Initially rather reserved toward Hitler, later developed into a supernazi. Was to be tried in Nuernberg on charges of exploiting forced laborers. Was declared unable to stand trial because of his mental condition (senility) and died on his estate in Bluehnbach, Austria.

Kubizek, August (1889-1971). Hitler's closest boyhood friend. Became conductor at various theaters and music teacher. Met Hitler again in Linz in 1938 but Hitler maintained his distance and used the polite form of address in speaking to him. Hitler did nothing to further his career, instead, warned him to keep quiet about their background.

Lammers, Hans Heinrich (1879-1962). Chief of the Reich Chancellery, 1933-1945. SS lieutenant general. Sentenced to 20 years in prison in 1949; released in 1952.

Lanz von Liebenfels, Joerg (actually: Adolf Josef Lanz) (1874-1954). Former Cistercian monk and con-man (baron, doctor), race-fanatic and author. In 1900 founded a lodge by the name of "Order of the New Temple" and published a magazine, "Ostara", which greatly influenced Hitler during his years in Vienna.

Lehmann, Julius Friedrich (1864-1935). Munich publisher. He and his publishing house supported the Navy and Germany's power politics interests. Party member from 1922 and Hitler's financial supporter.

Ley, Robert (1890-1945). Chemist. Party member from 1924. Founded the German Labor Front and in 1933 smashed the free labor unions. NSDAP Reich organization director in 1932. Tried to control government housing construction. Scheduled to be tried in Nuernberg on charges of organizing slave labor; committed suicide before start of trial.

Loos, Adolf (1870-1933). Architect in Vienna. His work exerted maximum influence on the objective modern style of building. Rejected by Hitler.

Ludendorff, Erich (1865-1937). Colonel-general. During World War I, chief of supply and, together with Hindenburg, practically Germany's military dictator. Figurehead for 1923 Hitler coup d'etat. Alienated from Hitler after coup d'etat. Under the influence of his second wife Mathilde, nee von Kemnitz, he developed into a paranoid anti-Semite, anti-Free Mason and anti-Catholic. Warned Hindenburg against appointing Hitler Reich chancellor.

Makart, Hans (1840-1884). Hitler's favorite painter. Created glittering pictures of historical and allegorical content in abundant burst of colors. His art, embodying a decorative approach, influenced the fashions and interior decor of the period of Promoterism (when many bogus companies were established).

Marc, Franz (1860-1916). One of the most famous modern painters. Hitler's contemporary in Schwabing. Hitler considered his famous painting "Tower of the Blue Horses" degenerate.

May, Karl (1842-1912). Prolific writer of light literature (American Indians, Far East) with heavy racist and fascist undertones. Was Hitler's favorite author of belletristic literature.

Mayr, Karl (1833-1945). Bavarian General Staff officer. Hitler's superior in the Army Intelligence Division, 1919-1920. Later, Hitler's opponent. Murdered in Buchenwald Concentration Camp in 1945.

Meissner, Otto (1880-1953). Chief of the Presidential Office under Hindenburg and Hitler; held rank of minister of state in 1936. He was cleared of all charges in 1945.

Mosley, Sir Oswald (1896-1970). British politician. Until 1924, member of the Labour Party. In 1930 founded the "New Party" which, beginning in 1936, called itself "British Union of Fascists and National Socialists." Courted Hitler who considered him to have very little influence. Interned during World War II for security reasons. Disappeared into obscurity after 1945.

Muehsam Erich (1878-1934). Author. Anarchist and participant in 1918-1919 revolution in Munich. Member of first soviet government; released from fortress imprisonment in 1925. Arrested in 1933. Hanged himself in Oranienburg Concentration Camp in 1934.

Mutschmann, Martin (1879-1948). NSDAP Nazi provincial boss in Saxony, 1925-1945.

Niekish, Ernst (1889-1967). Participant in Munich soviet government. Later as, leader of National Bolsheviks, tried to approach Otto Strasser. Imprisoned for 8 years during the Third Reich. After 1945, member of the SED German Socialist Unity Party which he left on June 17, 1953.

Prussia, August Wilhelm, Prince of (1887-1949). Fourth son of Emperor

Wilhelm II. Joined NSDAP in 1930 and SA in 1933. Front man for Nazis to attract supporters of the monarchy. SA lieutenant general. After the war, sentenced to 2 years in labor camp as an example, did not serve sentence.

Rauschning, Hermann (1887-1961). Joined NSDAP in 1926; was Danzig Senate president, 1933-1934. Increasingly disassociated himself from Hitler and Nazi ideology. Emigrated to Switzerland in 1936 and then to the United States.

Reventlow, Franziska, Countess of (1871-1918). Outstanding figure on the Munich Bohemian scene. Wrote sketches, novels, lively descriptions of Munich life from 1900 until World War I.

Röhm, Ernst (1887-1934). One of Hitler's and the Nazi Party's earliest supporters. As captain in the Reichswehr, he provided a cover for Hitler's conspiratorial activities at the beginning of the Twenties and supplied him with Reichswehr money. Participated in November coup d'etat and was dismissed from Reichswehr. In Bolivia as military advisor, 1928-1930. Recalled by Hitler and made leader of SA in 1931. Arrested in 1934 by Hitler on charges of attempting a coup d'etat. Shot in Munich's Stadelheim prison.

Rosenberg, Alfred (1893-1946). Architect. Baltic emigrant, German citizen from 1922. During the Twenties, semiofficial party philosopher, radical anti-Semite. In 1923, editor-in-chief "Volkischer Beobachter." In 1933, director of the Foreign Policy Office of NSDAP. In 1940, confiscated art treasures in France. In 1941, minister for occupied eastern territories. Sentenced to death and executed in Nuernberg.

Roller, Alfred (1864-1935). Famous stage designer in Vienna, admired by Hitler. Roller worked closely with Gustav Mahler and created the sets for all the premieres of Richard Strauss operas.

Rust, Bernhard (1883-1945). High-school counselor. Joined NSDAP in 1922; became Nazi provincial boss of Hanover. Minister of science, education, and popular development, 1934-1945. Committed suicide on May 8, 1945.

Sauerbruch, Ferdinand (1875-1951). World-famous surgeon. From time to time, enthusiastic supporter of Nazism. During the war, he was the topmost military physician. After 1945, cleared in denazification proceedings.

Schaub, Julius (1898, date of death unknown). Hitler's close companion from 1922. Druggist by profession. At first was driver, then personal aide with the rank of SS lieutenant general. In 1945, destroyed Hitler's secret files.

Schreck, Julius (1891-1936). NSDAP member from 1921, Hitler's favorite driver until his death in a traffic accident in 1936. Occasionally, because of resemblance, acted as Hitler's double.

Schroeder, Kurt Freiherr von (1884-1965). Cologne banker. President of the Cologne Chamber of Industry and Commerce. Arranged the decisive meeting between Papen and Hitler, leading to Schleicher's ouster. Became chairman of the board of many banks and industrial firms and was made honorary SS brigadier general.

Schwarz, Franz Xaver (1875-1947). "Old Fighter" since the earliest days; NSDAP treasurer, 1925; Reich director, 1935. Died in internment camp in 1947.

Semper, Gottfried (1803-1879). Important architect and art theoretician, creator of the Dresden Opera. Highly regarded by Hitler.

Speer, Albert (1905-1981). Joined the party in 1932. Became Hitler's favorite architect in 1933. Was given huge assignment to draw up new urban development plans for Berlin. Reich minister of armament and production, 1942-1945. Tried in Nuernberg on charges of using slave laborers and sentenced to 20 years in prison. Released in 1966.

Strasser, Gregor (1892-1934). Leader of the social revolutionary wing of the NSDAP. Hitler's most dangerous rival inside the party. Resigned all offices in 1932 and thus made Hitler "acceptable" to capitalism. Murdered on Hitler's orders by SS on June 30, 1934.

Strasser, Otto (1897-1974). Gregor's younger brother. Journalist. Initially, independent Social Democrat, then, together with Gregor leader of the "left" wing of the NSDAP and publisher of newspapers outside the Eher Syndicate. Broke with Hitler in 1931 and founded his own party of "revolutionary national socialists." Fled to Prague in 1933 and later, via Switzerland and Portugal, to Canada. Returned to West Germany in 1955 as a private citizen.

Streicher, Julius (1885-1946). One of Hitler's early comrades-in-arms. Provincial party boss of Franconia, owner and publisher of the hate sheet "Der Sturmer (Hotspur)." He was the most rabid and pornographic propagandist of anti-Semitism. In 1940, relieved of all offices but remained publisher of "Der Sturmer." Sentenced to death and executed in Nuernberg in 1946.

Thorak, Josef (1889-1952). Adolf Hitler's favorite sculptor. Specialized in heroic male figures. Created colossal sculptures. Acquitted during denazification.

Thyssen, Fritz (1873-1951). Leading German industrial tycoon who supported Hitler financially for 15 years. Later had falling-out with Hitler and fled to France in 1939. Extradited by the Vichy government in 1941. Survived concentration camp and went to Argentina after the war.

Troost, Paul Ludwig (1878-1934). Hitler's favorite architect whose neoclassicist style for a while became the official building style of the Third Reich. Remodeled the Brown House according to Hitler's designs and designed the House of Art in Munich.

Valentin, Karl (actually Valentin Fey) (1882-1948). Well-known Munich comic, used his camouflaged wit frequently against the regime. Remained relatively unharrassed because he was a close friend of Heinrich Hoffmann.

Voegler, Albert (1877-1945). Leading German industrial tycoon. Chairman of the board of the United Steel Works. One of the first industry bosses who channeled money to Hitler. Committed suicide on April 13, 1945.

von Brauchitsch, Walther (1881-1948). German general, field marshal-general from 1940. Army Commander-in-Chief, 1939-1941. Dismissed by Hitler in 1941. Died on October 18, 1948, in the British Military Hospital at Hamburg.

von Epp, Franz Ritter (1868-1946). Bavarian officer. Colonel in World War I. After the war, organized counter-revolutionary Free Corps and "liberated" Munich from the "Reds." Joined NSDAP in 1928. Reich governor of Bavaria in 1933. Promoted to the rank of general in 1935. Was among Hitler's critics inside the party. Shortly before the end of the war, attempted an uprising against the NSDAP in Bavaria.

von Hasenauer, Karl (1833-1894). Architect in Vienna. Creator of the Vienna Burg Theater. Highly regarded by Hitler.

von Hindenburg und Beneckendorf, Paul (1847-1934). During World War I, supreme military commander and field marshal. German president until his death. In 1933, appointed Hitler Reich chancellor because he did not want to approve a limited military dictatorship by General von Schleicher for "reasons of constitutional law."

von Kahr, Gustav Ritter (1862-1934). Bavarian prime minister, 1920-1921. Monarchist. General state commissioner, 1923-1924. Ruled jointly with General von Lossow and Colonel Seisser. President of the Bavarian Administrative Court, 1924-1930. Was arrested by SS men on June 30, 1934, and slain in the Dachau Moor.

von Lossow, Otto Hermann (1868-1938). Bavarian lieutenant general. Bavarian state commander of the Reichswehr. In 1923, member of the junta (Kahr, Lossow, Seisser). Died a retired general overlooked by Hitler.

von Papen, Franz (1879-1968). Politician, first with Center Party, then an independent. Penultimate Reich chancellor of the Weimar Republic (Cabinet of the Barons). Helped Hitler oust Reich Chancellor Schleicher. Under Hitler, vice chancellor, then ambassador in Vienna, and afterwards in Ankara. Acquitted during Nuernberg trials. Sentenced to eight years in labor camp by German authorities; released in 1949. Afterwards, tried unsuccessfully to justify his role.

von Pfeffer, Franz (1888-date of death unknown). Early member of NSDAP. SA chief of staff, 1928-1931. Later, SA lieutenant general. At war's end, commanded a Volkssturm "Home Guard" division.

von Piloty, Karl (1826-1886). Director of Munich Art Academy. Along with Spitzweg and Gruetzner, was one of Hitler's favorite painters.

von Ribbentrop, Joachim (1893-1946). Obtained title of nobility through adoption. Prosperous as a result of marriage to Anneliese Henkell, daughter of Germany's richest champagne maker. Joined NSDAP in 1932. Ambassador in London, 1936. Foreign minister, 1938-1945. Snetenced to death at Nuernberg in 1946 and executed.

von Scheubner-Richter, Max Erwin (1884-1923). Former tsarist officer. Leading position in Russian emigre organizations. NSDAP member, 1920. Hitler's important money supplier. Killed during 1923 Hitler coup d'etat.

von Schirach, Baldur (1907-1974). Joined the NSDAP as college student. Reich youth leader and chief of the Hitler Youth, 1933-1940. Reich governor of Vienna, 1940-1945. Sentenced to 20 years imprisonment in Nuernberg; released in 1966.

von Schleicher, Kurt (1883-1934). Career officer. General.    Reichswehr minister, June 1932. From December 1932 until the end of January 1933, last chancellor of the Weimar Republic. Tried to stabilize political situation through limited military dictatorship, which Hindenburg rejected. On June 30, 1934, shot and killed in his Berlin apartment by an SS detail.

von Seisser, Hans Ritter (1875-1973). Chief of the Bavarian State Police, 1923. Member of junta under Kahr. Went abroad in 1933.

Wagener, Otto (1888--date of death unknown). SA chief of staff, 1929-1930. Head of the economic policy department of the NSDAP, 1931-1933. Afterwards, relieved of all functions.

Wagner, Adolf (1890-1944). NSDAP member since 1923 (Nazi party provincial chief of Munich and Upper (southern) Bavaria. Bavarian interior minister after 1933.

Wagner, Otto (1841-1918). Viennese architect. Went beyond Art Nouveau and propagated a turn away from the decorative style. Disliked by Hitler.

Wagner, Robert (1895-1946). Reichswehr officer. Participated in Hitler coup d'etat. Party provincial boss of Baden, 1925-1945; Also Reich governorin 1923. In 1940, chief of the civilian administration in Alsace.

Wagner, Siegfried (1869-1930). Son of Richard Wagner, achieved little success as composer. In 1909, took over artistic direction of the Bayreuth Festivals. Married Winifred Williams in 1915. numbering many Jews among his friends, in contrast to his wife, had a cool relationship with Hitler.

Wagner, Winifred (1897-1980). Wife of Wagner's son Siegfried. One of the first female party members. Helped Hitler socially and financially. After the war, she was forbidden to direct the festivals. In her film interview with Syberberg, shortly before her death, she still unreservedly declared her belief in the "positive sides" of Hitler's personality.

Weber, Christian (1883-1945). Servant in the Munich "Blauer Bock" Hotel at the beginning of the Twenties, very early NSDAP member. Bookmaker in Daglfing. NSDAP city council member in Munich, 1926-1934. After 1933, president of the German Hunting Museum and president of the Economic League of German Riding Stable Owners. Killed in 1945 by Bavarian insurrectionist against the Nazis.

Weber, Friedrich (1891-1954). Veterinarian. Leader of Oberland Free Corps in 1923. Sentenced and imprisoned with Hitler. Later broke with Hitler. Military veterinarian during World War II.

Werlin, Jakob (1886-1958). Hitler's Mercedes supplier. Early NSDAP member. During the Twenties, Munich representative of Daimler-Benz, later manager. SS regimental commander. Inspector-general of motor transport in 1942.

Wiedemann, Fritz (1891-1970). Hitler's superior battalion executive officer during World War I. Later joined Nazis and, after 1933, became Hitler's military aide and foreign policy advisor. Alienated in 1939. Became consul-general in San Francisco, later in Tientsin. After the war, farmer in Southern Germany.

Ziegler, Adolf (1892-1959). Hitler's favorite contemporary painter. Pedantic realist "master of German pubic hair." President of the Reich Chamber of the Arts.

# BIBLIOGRAPHY

Abel, Theodore: Why Hitler Came into Power, New York 1938

Angebert, Jean-Michel: The Occult and the Third Reich, New York 1974

Berthold, Will: Die 42 Attentate auf Adolf Hitler, München 1981

Beyer, Hans: Von der Novemberrevolution zur Räterepublik in München, Berlin (Ost) 1957

Brenner, Hildegard: Die Kunstpolitik des Nationalsozialismus, Reinbek 1963

Bronder, Dietrich: Bevor Hitler kam, Hannover 1964

Bullock, Alan: Hitler. Eine Studie über Tyrannei, Düsseldorf 1957

Charlier, J. M.: Eva Hitler geb. Braun, Stuttgart 1979

Czichon, Eberhard: Wer verhalf Hitler zur Macht? Köln 1967

Daim, Wilfried: Der Mann, der Hitler die Ideen gab, München 1958

Deuerlein, Ernst: Der Aufstieg der NSDAP 1919–1933 in Augenzeugenberichten, Düsseldorf 1968

– Hitler – Eine politische Biographie, München 1955

Domarus, Max: Hitler, Reden und Proklamationen 1932–1945, München 1965

Drexler, Anton: Mein politisches Erwachen, München 1919

Eckart, Dietrich: Der Bolschewismus von Moses bis Lenin. Zwiegespräche zwischen Adolf Hitler und mir, München 1925

Eitner, Hans Jürgen: Der Führer. Hitlers Pesönlichkeit und Charakter, München 1981

Engelmann, Bernt: Krupp, München 1978

Fest, Joachim: Hitler. Eine Biographie, Frankfurt, Berlin, Wien 1973

Frank, Hans: Im Angesicht des Galgens, Neuhaus bei Schliersee 1955

Giesler, Hermann: Ein anderer Hitler, Leoni 1978

Görlitz, Walter und Quint, Herbert: Adolf Hitler. Eine Biographie, Stuttgart 1952

Greiner, Josef: Das Ende des Hitler-Mythos, Zürich, Leipzig, Wien 1947

Gun, Nerin E.: Eva Braun-Hitler, Leben und Schicksal, Velbert, Kettwig 1968

Haffner, Sebastian: Anmerkungen zu Hitler, Stuttgart, München 1979

Hagemann, Walter: Publizistik im Dritten Reich, Hamburg 1948

Hale, Oron J.: Presse in der Zwangsjacke, Düsseldorf 1965

– Adolf Hitler – Taxpayer, in: American Hist. Review 1965

Hanfstaengl, Ernst: Zwischen Weißem und Braunem Haus, München 1970

Heiber, Helmut: Adolf Hitler. Eine Biographie, Berlin 1960

Heiden, Konrad: Adolf Hitler. Eine Biographie, Zürich 1936/37

Hindele, Josef: Hitler war kein Zufall, Frankfurt 1962

Hitler, Adolf: Mein Kampf. 2 Bde. in einem Band, München 1938

– Hitlers „Zweites Buch". Ein Dokument aus dem Jahre 1928, Stuttgart 1961

Hitler, Bridget: The Memoirs of Bridget Hitler, Ed. by Michael Unger, Dallas 1979

Hoffmann, Heinrich: Hitler was my Friend, London 1955

Hoffmann, Peter: Hitler's Personal Security, London 1955

Hofmann, Hanns Hubert: Der Hitlerputsch, München 1961

Infield, Glenn B.: Hitler's Secret Life, New York 1979

Jaeger, Charles de: The Linz File. Hitler's Plunder of European Art, Exeter 1981

Jenks, William: Vienna and the Young Hitler, New York 1960

Jetzinger, Franz: Hitlers Jugend. Phantasien, Lügen – und die Wahrheit. Wien 1965

Jochmann, Werner (Hrsg.): Adolf Hitler. Monologe im Führerhauptquartier 1941–1944. Die Aufzeichnungen Heinrich Heims, München 1980

Jones, Sidney J.: Hitlers Weg begann in Wien, Wiesbaden, München 1980

Kallenbach, Hans: Mit Adolf Hitler auf der Festung Landsberg, München 1943

Katz, Ottmar: Prof. Dr. med. Theo Morell. Hitlers Leibarzt, Bayreuth 1982

Kempner, Robert M. W.: Das Dritte Reich im Kreuzverhör, München, Esslingen 1969

Kohler, Pauline: I Was Hitler's Maid, London 1940

Krause, Karl Wilhelm: Zehn Jahre Kammerdiener bei Hitler, Hamburg o. J.

Krebs, Albert: Tendenzen und Gestalten der NSDAP. Erinnerungen an die Frühzeit der Partei, Stuttgart 1948

Kubizek, August: Adolf Hitler, mein Jugendfreund, Graz, Göttingen 1953

Lang, Jochen von: Der Sekretär, Stuttgart 1977

Langer, Walter C.: Das Adolf-Hitler-Psychogramm, München 1973

MacGovern, James: Martin Bormann, London 1968

Maser, Werner: Adolf Hitler. Legende, Mythos, Wirklichkeit, München, Esslingen 1971

McKnight, Gerald: The Strange Loves of Adolf Hitler, London 1978

Olden, Rudolf: Hitler, Amsterdam 1936

Pauwels, Louis und Bergier, Jaques: The Morning of the Magicians, New York 1963

Pool, James und Suzanne: Hitlers Wegbereiter zur Macht, Bern, München 1979

Rauschning, Hermann: Gespräche mit Hitler, Zürich, New York 1940

Roxan, D. und Wanstall, K.: The Jackdaw of Linz, London 1964

Schirach, Baldur von: Ich glaubte an Hitler, Hamburg 1967

Schirach, Henriette von: Anekdoten um Hitler, Berg 1980

Schoenbaum, David: Die braune Revolution, Köln, Berlin 1968

Schwarzwäller, Wulf: Rudolf Heß, Wien, München 1974

Sebottendorf, Rudolf von: Bevor Hitler kam, München 1934

Shirer, William L.: Aufstieg und Fall des Dritten Reiches, Köln, Berlin 1961

Smith, Bradley F.: Adolf Hitler, His Family, Childhood and Youth, Stanford 1967

Speer, Albert: Erinnerungen, Berlin 1969

– Spandauer Tagebuch, Berlin 1977

Strasser, Otto: Mein Kampf, Frankfurt 1969

Suster, Gerald: Hitler, The Occult Messiah, New York 1981

Symonds, John: The Great Beast. The Life and Magic of Aleister Crowley, London 1971

Thyssen, Fritz: I Paid Hitler, New York 1941

Toland, John: Adolf Hitler, New York 1976

Wagener, Otto: Hitler aus nächster Nähe, Frankfurt 1978

Waite, Robert G.L.: The Psychopathic God. Adolf Hitler, New York 1977

Walker, Malvin: Chronological Encyclopaedia of Adolf Hitler and the Third Reich, New York 1978

Winkler, Hans Joachim: Legenden um Hitler, Berlin 1961

Wulf, Josef: Presse und Funk im Dritten Reich, Gütersloh 1963

– Martin Bormann, Hitlers Schatten, Gütersloh 1962

Ziegler, H. S.: Adolf Hitler, aus dem Erleben dargestellt, Göttingen 1964

Zoller, Albert: Hitler privat. Erlebnisbericht seiner Geheimsekretärin, Düsseldorf 1949

# INDEX